Information technology in special libraries

Recent developments in information technology (IT) have brought about particular benefits for the organisation of special libraries. But until now very little has been written which addresses the specific needs of special librarians in this area.

Information Technology in Special Libraries is a book which addresses these needs. The contributors, each experts in their own fields, provide a comprehensive and practical guide to IT in special libraries. The first part of the book looks at areas such as the planning process, areas of application, how to choose software packages and hardware, online searching, and relationships with users. The second part of the book consists of three case studies written by contributors who have been directly responsible for the introduction of IT in their libraries – a medical library, a company library and the library of a management training institution.

This book will be of interest to anyone considering whether, when and how to introduce a computer system into their library.

Margaret Brittin is a library and information consultant. With wide experience of a number of commercial environments and of special and academic libraries, she has written and edited a number of publications relating to business information and fee-based services.

Information technology in special libraries

Edited by
Margaret Brittin

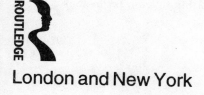

London and New York

First published in 1992
by Routledge
11 New Fetter Lane, London EC4P 4EE

Simultaneously published in the USA and Canada
by Routledge
a division of Routledge, Chapman and Hall, Inc.
29 West 35th Street, New York, NY 10001

Typeset in Palatino by LaserScript, Mitcham, Surrey
Printed and bound in Great Britain by
Biddles Ltd, Guildford and King's Lynn

British Library Cataloguing in Publication Data
A catalogue record for this book is available from the British Library.

Library of Congress Cataloging in Publication Data
Information technology in special libraries / edited by Margaret Brittin.
    p. cm.
Includes bibliographical references and index.
ISBN 0–415–03824–3
    1. Libraries, Special–Automation. 2. Information Technology.
    I. Brittin, Margaret, 1947–
Z675.A2I55 1992
026'.000285–dc20   92–19480
                                                        CIP

Contents

List of figures and tables   vii

1 Introduction and overview   1
Margaret Brittin, Library and Information Consultant

Part I Introducing information technology into the special library   13

2 Installing information technology in special libraries   15
Jacqueline Cropley, Information Consultant

3 Choosing software and hardware   28
Hilary Dyer, Senior Lecturer, Department of Information and Library Studies, Loughborough University

4 Choosing a software package   53
Caroline Moore, Manager, Library Information Technology Centre

5 Online searching   73
Louise Amor, Independent Consultant

6 Relationships with users   98
Fiona Henderson, Head of Information Services, Norwich and Norfolk Chamber of Commerce and Industry

Part II Case studies   107

7 The use of computers in the Information Services Unit at the British Gas Management Centre   109
Russell Gain, Support Services Manager, British Gas Management Centre

8   Developing a computer system for an NHS hospital
       library
       Ian King, Librarian, Bradford Royal Infirmary   122

9   Making IT work in an industrial information service
       John Ellis, GKN Technology Ltd   141

     Index   152

Figures and tables

FIGURES

8.1 Drawing up the data structure   126
8.2 Inmagic data structure   131
8.3 Transmission of requests   132
8.4 Order form   133
8.5 Standard draft memorandum   135

TABLES

3.1 Software selection   35
3.2 Software selection showing comparison between
     two products   43

Chapter 1

Introduction and overview

Margaret Brittin, Library and Information Consultant

The aim of *Information Technology in Special Libraries* is to provide a comprehensive and practical guide to the introduction of information technology (IT) to special libraries. Although much has been written about IT in libraries in recent years, it has mainly been in the context of large public and academic library systems and special librarians, searching for help and guidance, will find that little has been written which addresses their specific needs.

It is hoped that this book will go some way towards filling that gap as it is made up of contributions from writers who have direct experience of IT in special libraries or who are experts in their particular field. Throughout, the aim has been to provide a practical rather than theoretical approach to the subject and it is addressed to those who are having to make real-life decisions as to whether, when and how to introduce IT to their libraries. It is assumed that readers will be thoroughly familiar with normal library and information-service routines and will have at least some familiarity with the general principles of how computer systems work and their uses.

The first part of the book takes the reader through the necessary steps for introducing IT into the special library and examines areas such as:

- the planning process including needs analysis, designing specifications and making a case to management;
- areas of application and how to choose software packages and hardware;
- online searching; and
- relationships with users in terms of services and benefits offered, marketing, promotion and training.

The second part of the book consists of three case studies, written by contributors who have been directly responsible for the introduction of IT in their libraries. The libraries are widely differing in type – a medical library, a company library and the library of a management training institution – and the solutions arrived at for their particular situations were different. However, they all provide valuable insights into how decisions were reached which achieved a balance between ideal solutions and what was practical in the context of their organisation's circumstances and culture; how the systems were implemented; and how services to users were improved.

A book like this could not have been written ten years ago as the application of IT to special libraries was then only in its infancy. The early stages of library IT development did not produce a good match with the needs of special libraries.

Although special libraries were at one time at the forefront of technological development, with the initial introduction of computers their position fell back through no fault of their own. Now there are signs that the pendulum is swinging back.

Older readers and those trained at library schools in the early 70s will remember the exciting techniques being used for information retrieval in special libraries in those days – punched cards, optical coincidence cards and light boxes. Many special libraries were also at the forefront of online searching when it began to appear on the UK scene in the early 70s. Where they fell behind was in the other areas of library work which were candidates for automation – circulation, housekeeping, acquisitions, serials control and catalogues.

These areas of library work began to be automated in the 1970s but for many years activity was centred on large libraries, mainly academic and public. Systems started in the area of circulation control, spread to internal uses such as acquisitions and cataloguing and finally to public areas such as OPAC (online public access catalogues). The characteristics of all these systems were that they were designed to run on mainframe computers and were turnkey systems ideal for handling a large number of transactions (e.g. BLCMP, GEAC, OCLC). There was also an emphasis on the manipulation of MARC (machine readable catalogue format) records. Special libraries at that time are unlikely to have had access to sufficient mainframe computing power and if they did, they would have found that the systems were not designed for the special library market and its particular needs, typified by a comparatively low, erratic number of transactions and an emphasis on non-standard material.

The situation changed dramatically during the 1980s with the arrival of powerful micros and the advent of off-the-shelf software packages designed specifically for library use. The business micros which came on to the market were reasonably priced and within the budget of most special libraries, but with sufficient storage capacity for most special libraries' needs. Many special libraries started off with one micro and have grown from there to develop sophisticated networking within their organisation's system. Parallel to this has been the development of software packages for library use which are suitable for the needs and budgets of smaller libraries, although often not designed specifically for special libraries. Indeed, some would argue that they are still not especially well suited to those particular needs. Whereas the packages were at one time very clearly divided between information retrieval packages and housekeeping packages, these are now converging and there are a number of integrated packages available which cover every aspect of library activity.

So special libraries have caught up in the automation race in the last few years and a lot of interesting work is emerging in this area. Many special librarians have seized the opportunities offered by IT enthusiastically and have used it to good effect to offer new and improved services to users, to increase their profile and to consolidate their position within their own organisation. In many cases this has led to the integration of external and internal sources of information, spearheaded by the library.

TYPES OF SPECIAL LIBRARY

The other reason for the initial slow spread of IT in special libraries lies in the much more fragmented nature of special libraries than the relatively homogeneous public/academic library areas. Fragmented it may be, smaller it is not (contrary to popular opinion). Although the libraries themselves are generally smaller than other types of library in terms of the number of units and the number of staff working in them, they form a significant part of the total library market. According to some calculations, 54 per cent of professional posts in the UK are in special libraries (Turner 1986). Although the Library Association is not an organisation in which special librarians are particularly well represented in terms of numbers, the latest figures (Library Association 1991) show special librarians making up 17 per cent of the membership as opposed to public librarians who make up 29 per cent. But because there are so many types of special library, with widely differing needs and types of user, it is difficult to form a coherent picture of the sector as a whole. This is highlighted by segmenting the major sectors of the special-library market and their characteristics.

Company libraries

This is probably the biggest sector of the market but again with many different types of library within it. The longest established company libraries are those in industries and companies with a long-established R & D function (e.g. chemicals, pharmaceuticals, foods, petrochemicals), and these have traditionally offered employment for information scientists. But the last twenty years has seen growth in the business information sector with many companies setting up libraries and information units dealing specifically with business information. These units can be within the traditional manufacturing sector as above, where they have either been created alongside a scientific and technical oriented library or integrated into an expanded existing unit. However, the recent growth of the service sector has led to a corresponding increase in libraries and information units in this area, particularly in the area of professional and financial services. Nowadays most of the major financial institutions (banks, stock-brokers, accountants) have well-developed library and information units. This is also the case with the larger professional services – lawyers, architects, management consultants, advertising and PR agencies.

Health service libraries

Again there are many subsectors within this sector which can range from libraries providing services for patients; libraries based at particular hospitals providing services mainly for medical and related staff; and libraries in Regional Health Authorities. The stock they provide can vary from straightforward recreational material, to complex medical and scientific information, to material relating to health service management and policy issues.

Government department libraries

This is a more homogeneous sector, but again with widely differing subject areas, ranging from detailed technical material relating to the activities of that particular department to more general business and economic information.

Professional bodies' libraries

These can vary from the libraries of learned societies, where the emphasis is on traditional scholarship, to professional bodies representing a highly skilled, professional membership.

Other special libraries

The list of other types of special library is almost as long again. There are many local authority libraries which are not public libraries and could be considered as special libraries, e.g. libraries in local authority departments such as planning, economic development, social services, services provided to councillors and local government officers, and a variety of other special libraries such as libraries in prisons, chambers of commerce, research/ trade associations, trade unions, political parties, quangos, voluntary organisations etc.

NATURE OF SPECIAL LIBRARIES

With such a plethora of types of library it is obviously not going to be easy to draw any universal conclusions. Nevertheless, there are some common characteristics that emerge.

Special libraries are characterised by:

Size

Special libraries will vary in size from one person (or less!) to maybe up to fifty, but there are few special libraries with over twenty staff and most will only have a small number with a significant minority being 'one-person libraries'. So, we can say, as a general rule, that most special libraries are smaller than most public/academic libraries. This means that in the majority of cases there is not the degree of job specialisation to be found in larger libraries, e.g. it is less likely that there are staff whose only responsibility is cataloguing, but more likely to be someone who has an involvement in the whole process through ordering, cataloguing, retrieving, circulation and maybe even shelving. There is less likely to be a staffing hierarchy or career structure.

Incidentally, there is probably a greater likelihood of finding unqualified staff carrying out professional roles in a special library than in other types of library. There is still to some extent the mistaken impression among the (non-librarian) management of these organisations that anyone can run a library, and it is not uncommon for them to think that someone's secretary can easily run the library in his or her spare time or that it is the ideal place for someone who is no longer needed in, or is not suited to, another part of the organisation. These attitudes are slowly changing but it is a mistake to think that they no longer exist. This is not to minimise the excellent work carried out by some non-qualified staff in special libraries who have often found themselves in this kind of work through no choice of their own but have discovered that they do have a real aptitude for it. However, in most cases this is no real substitute for a properly trained and experienced professional who can take a broader view of information work than that offered by working within one organisation and who has a network of professional contacts. Nowhere is this breadth of experience and network of contacts more vital than in the IT area.

Users

Most special libraries have a well-defined group or groups of users whose needs and interests are well known and can be specifically, and to some extent individually, catered for. This holds across the board whether users are consultants in a management consultancy, partners in an accountancy firm, scientists involved in R & D, doctors and nurses in a hospital, civil servants in a government department, members of a professional body or local councillors. In most cases users can be quantified and there is a clear understanding of who are the target groups, who the library is supposed to be serving and what are the priorities.

Obviously, in some cases special libraries will also provide a service to the general public, or try and help the general public, or may offer a free service to members/internal users but a priced service to external users. But in most cases the library's responsibilities towards its various groups of users will be well defined.

Material

Most special libraries will have large stocks of non-standard material, i.e. material other than books or journals. The types of material will vary enormously according to the type of library: internal reports, technical papers, conference proceedings, trade literature, annual reports, minutes of meetings, press cuttings, pamphlets, standards, patents, audio-visual material etc.

Services

Because of their size and their close relationship with known users, special libraries have traditionally placed a great emphasis on the active provision of information services rather than the reactive library housekeeping activities of getting material on shelves and recording loans. In fact in some special libraries the information function is actually separate from the library function although existing in parallel. The types of service traditionally offered by special libraries include current awareness, press cuttings, selective dissemination of information etc.

IT AND SPECIAL LIBRARIES

What kind of issues do these characteristics of special libraries raise in the area of IT?

First of all, the special library considering the introduction of IT may find its size a problem, although this is less likely to be the case today. Many software packages, particularly for information retrieval and cataloguing, are now suitable for use in smaller libraries although this is less likely to be the case for other applications such as circulation and serials control. The special library may find that its number of titles (e.g. serials) is too small to justify the outlay and conversion to automated packages or may find that circulation modules are not suited to its needs where loan periods can be irregular (or at the discretion of the librarian) or the library may not be staffed at all times for the loans to be recorded on the computer. In some cases existing manual systems – if working efficiently – may be preferable.

The small size of special libraries is likely to be more of a problem in the area of staffing. With few specialist roles in special libraries, there is less likely to be an IT expert on the staff. There may of course be computer expertise within the organisation which can be brought in to help but they are likely to be busy people with little knowledge of specific library applications. In most cases library staff will need to develop a greater level of knowledge of IT and its library applications and to get more closely involved in the initial decisions and implementation than the majority of staff in bigger, non-special libraries. This may seem a daunting prospect, particularly if the special library is very small, and the staff can feel very isolated. On the other hand, this close level of involvement should mean that the system chosen should be the right one for both the library's and the users' needs – a situation that is by no means always the case in larger libraries where those taking the decisions can be remote from users of the system, whether they are other staff or library users.

The special library's traditional emphasis on non-book material may also present a problem, although not an insurmountable one. Many of the packages available are based on the premise that most of the library's stock will be books, conforming to the format of standard bibliographical records. However, there are a number of packages now available which do cater specifically for non-book material as well as books, offering differing levels of flexibility.

However, despite the particular problems that special libraries have experienced in relation to IT, there can be few units which will have remained untouched by it in the early 1990s. There are still a number of special libraries (although probably few) which have managed to escape the inexorable advance of IT so far but are now facing up to it – possibly because their organisation is itself tackling the challenge or possibly because a change of staff in the library has brought in new attitudes and expertise. There will be a larger number of special libraries where some limited use of IT is made (most likely online searching) but where decisions now have to be taken as to whether and how to introduce IT into other areas of their operation.

And it is important not to forget that the special-library sector is probably one of the few current growth areas of the information world. They have suffered cutbacks in staff and resources as severe as the other sectors in the economic recession of the early 1990s but there are still a number of new special libraries being set up in a variety of organisations. Newly appointed staff in these units will be faced not only with the task of setting up the unit, but also with the decision as to whether to use computer systems and if so, which systems to use and when.

Whatever the differing circumstances, decisions about the introduction of IT need to be made on the firm basis of fact and logical thought.

It is vital that IT is introduced, not because it is a good thing to do *per se*, but because in every application it can be proved that it will bring tangible benefits to the library and its users. There is no point in introducing IT for IT's sake – a careful consideration of the systems which could be automated needs to be made to assess whether there is a good match between the system itself, the needs of users and the hardware and software available. Most manual systems can be adapted to make them suited to automation but this must only be done if tangible benefits ensue – if a manual system is efficient and suited to the needs of users and the automated version would make it less so, it is far better to stick to the manual system.

BENEFITS OF IT

Having said this, there are a number of benefits to special libraries and their users to be gained from adopting IT, although, as has been stressed above, this will not automatically be the case in all circumstances. These can be summarised as follows:

Increased access to information sources

One of the major benefits that IT offers is in providing access to a far wider range of information sources than is possible from a manual system. The most obvious example of this is online searching, which is not only much quicker than manual searching but also provides access to a huge range of databases and primary and secondary material far larger than any special library could hope to stock. Another example is a computerised catalogue, which offers far more access points than a manual catalogue – author, title, keywords, words in titles etc.

Improvement to existing services

IT can and should offer the chance of introducing significant improvements to existing services and increasing the match between those services and the needs of users. It may be a case of improving the efficiency of procedures. For example: streamlining the ordering system so that items from suppliers can be chased regularly and automatically, streamlining the circulation system so that it is easier and quicker to keep track of loans and send out overdue notices; targeting a current awareness/ abstracting bulletin closer to users' needs; or simply improved output and presentation of results (e.g. a current awareness bulletin being word processed and laser printed rather than typed or 'cut and pasted').

Development of new services

Going beyond this stage, it is probable that the introduction of IT will lead to the development of completely new services and products as well as improvements in existing ones. The flexibility and speed that IT offers means that new services which would be virtually impossible to provide through manual means suddenly become relatively easily achievable. Examples could include the provision of an SDI (selective dissemination of information) service to users or the development of internal databases (e.g. internal reports, expertise within the organisation) which could in turn be integrated with output from external databases.

Higher profile for the library

If the library can be seen to be heavily involved in IT applications within its organisation or even at the forefront of innovations in that area, then its overall status within the organisation is bound to improve and this can lead to increased responsibility and influence for library staff.

The integration of internal and external sources of information, which has been mentioned above as a benefit of IT, can work very much to the special library's advantage. If the library is seen to be involved in this area, there is a greater chance of recognition of the librarian's skills – that skills involved in organising, indexing, exploiting, disseminating formal information sources are just as applicable to the informal and internal information networks which flourish within most organisations. If through the use of IT, the library can spread its influence into all aspects of information within the organisation, then the concept of information resources management – managing the total information resources of the organisation – becomes a reality and a legitimate area of activity for the library.

This last area is in some ways the most sensitive because it touches on the area of organisational politics rather than practicalities and to a certain extent there are conflicts between the two areas.

Whereas we have said earlier that IT should only be introduced if there are clear practical benefits from doing so, the reality is that information professionals can only ignore IT at their peril. If they resist the introduction of IT they risk being marginalised even more than may already be the case and the focus of information resource management may well move elsewhere in the organisation (most probably to the computing department or research function). They are then likely to suffer from downgrading and underresourcing and the whole service could go into a downward spiral from which it is difficult to recover.

Therefore in reality, information professionals in special libraries have little choice as to whether to introduce IT if they wish to advance in their professional lives and the services and status of the library. Information technology is here to stay and anyone in the special library field – or other library fields for that matter – who is interested in career development and progression must grasp the IT nettle. These issues have been highlighted in the recent British Library report *Information UK 2000* (Martyn *et al.* 1991).

The issues therefore lie in most cases not with whether to introduce IT or not but in choices as to which areas are most suitable for automating and decisions as to appropriate hardware or software, gaining management approval, planning and implementation. It is these areas which this book addresses.

REFERENCES

Library Association (1991) *Annual Report*.
Martyn, J., Vickers, P. and Feeney, M. (eds) (1991) *Information UK 2000*, London: Bowker-Saur.
Turner, C. (1986) 'Undergraduate courses in library and information studies', *Library Association Record* 88:(3): 139–40.

Part I

Introducing information technology into the special library

Chapter 2

Installing information technology in special libraries

Jacqueline Cropley, Information Consultant

PLANNING THE INSTALLATION

The installation of IT has become so commonplace that librarians take many of the issues for granted and simply compare the merits of one system against another. It is easy to become distracted by the technical specification and to forget to define the actual aim. Yet now that there is a wide choice of systems covering the broadest range of special-library activities, with extensive facilities for customisation, the best results will only be obtained by careful consideration and planning. Automation has always meant looking at operations afresh and building systems for the future, but it is tempting to concentrate on solving the problems of the past. Installing information technology requires effort and a strong commitment to a direction for the future. Taking time at the planning stage prevents wasteful reworking and premature replacement of systems.

Given that computer equipment and software is comparatively cheap there is a tendency to think that there is little need to plan. The cost is minimal when written off over three to five years. The drive towards placing a computer on everyone's desk means that the purchase of equipment and systems is seen as a minor decision. Provided that the chosen combination fits with the overall systems strategy, approval is virtually automatic. The real costs of information technology are in the expectations and the investment in time and effort. Once a new method of working is established the momentum of development and implementation carries it through. If the direction is wrong at the start it is hard to change. Modern systems are flexible and can be adapted as requirements alter or as mistakes in the original specification are corrected. In the light of this, insufficient attention is paid to the definition of needs in the first place. Unfortunately, although adjustments are possible, they are rarely instantaneous and without consequence. The ability to make changes should be retained for positive development. User patience can become exhausted. Once a computer system is operational it is expected to run smoothly. If a system is inadequately planned the period immediately after it goes live will be fraught with problems. Tinkering at that stage destroys all confidence, just at the point when effort is needed to learn new operating practices.

ANALYSING REQUIREMENTS

The decision to install information technology should follow an assessment of needs and methods. This is as important for a small system as for a large one. The scale of the study will be appropriate to the size of the proposed system, but the process should not be neglected. It is important to consider how the new operating methods affect other areas of business as well as the part for which automation is contemplated. Will there be more or less work overall? It is not unknown for a department's costs to increase dramatically as the result of computerisation elsewhere. The full systems analysis which precedes the introduction of a major project picks up this sort of point. It may be missed if the analysis is only cursory because the system is thought to be too small and cheap to warrant detailed examination. Whether the project is large or small, whether the chosen solution is turnkey or is a shell system needing further development work, look at everything which will be affected. This is the only way to achieve a successful implementation. There are many stories of computerisation projects which do not deliver what is required, of alienated staff, and of machines which are underused because people do not understand why or how they should use them.

Systems analysis examines:

- what tasks are being carried out;
- how they are performed;
- who does them using what;
- why they are done;
- when, how often and for how long;
- how they are measured;

- how the value of the activity is assessed;
- what is the effect;
- who benefits from it;
- what is the cost; and
- what are the alternatives.

In business terms, how does the activity contribute to the goals of the organisation and what is the most cost-effective method for carrying it out, taking all factors into consideration? Given the impetus to automate, often at great speed, it is tempting to answer these questions subjectively. Arriving at an objective assessment means spending time talking to the different categories of people involved – staff and library users – and examining the options. The effort will be recouped later as the project is implemented more efficiently. The opportunity must be taken to challenge embedded methods of thinking and processes whose origins no one can remember. They may be still valid, as longevity can be a sign of robustness, but it is important to express the purpose anew. More often changes in circumstances mean there are better practices.

HUMAN FACTORS

The element least attended to in systems analysis is the 'who'. Human factors are neglected. In a small special library, with perhaps only one or two staff equally involved in decision making, this should not be a great problem. But it is vital that the human element is not overlooked in larger special libraries and this applies to any special library large enough to have a staffing structure and hierarchy where decisions are not taken collectively. Automation projects fail because people are expected to be subservient to machines. The study of previous working practices should not just be a measurement of throughput and work flows. Information technology empowers individuals to be more effective. This may mean achieving more with the same number of people; it may mean performing more of the routine work with machines so that fewer people are needed; occasionally it creates more jobs. It is vital to give as much thought to the people and their requirements as to the technology. Unless there is the intention to replace the existing staff, consideration must be given to their skills, abilities, wishes and concerns. Talking to staff at all levels is essential and they should be kept fully informed of progress. In many cases it is possible to involve everyone in the decision making. This ensures that all factors are taken into account and encourages commitment.

Consideration of human needs goes further than purchasing computer systems which are user-friendly. Few library suppliers claim that their product is anything less – user comment may be radically different. It must be clear to the people who will be working with the new system what the purpose of change is, and how the chosen technology will contribute to this goal. There is more work for each person while the system is being installed – and so the statement of planned benefits should outline improvements which are attractive to the staff in order to encourage them to put in the effort. This may be more interesting work, less of a disliked task, shorter hours at peak times, the chance to carry out previously delayed projects, training for greater responsibility, the development of new skills, or promotion opportunities. Keeping everyone abreast of progress and explaining set-backs helps to retain people's interest in the project.

Now that information technology is familiar, it is easy to forget that some members of staff are not comfortable with increased automation. There are two main fears. The first is that a computer system will be imposed regardless of the effect that it has on people's ways of working and additional demands on their time and abilities. The other is that the system will underperform. There will be considerable effort spent trying to make it run properly, but it will not come up to expectations; or else they will be criticised for allowing the machinery to sit idle in a corner because there is not enough time to get it to work. Many people have direct experience of these situations. Even modern systems go through periods of difficulty. As well as planning for technical problems and building time for delays and modifications into the implementation schedule, it is important to explain to the staff how these will be addressed.

Encouraging people to talk about their misgivings may also bring to light any flaws in the specification for the new technology. If an individual cannot see how his or her function will be carried out in the future something may have been missed out. At the very least there is a problem with communication. Each person should have a clear view of how his or her job is affected. If there are unknowns, for example because it is hard to predict customer response and subsequent demand, then this should be explicit and the assumptions outlined. Otherwise the plan may seem too vague and probably doomed to failure.

TRAINING

Training provision should be based on the requirements of the staff. In a large installation instruction is standardised because of the number of people who have to learn the new procedures. This is rarely the case with a small system. Time can be spent on individual demands. Schedule training for as soon as the staff need it and adjust their work so that they can attend. People need a full overview of the system. Demonstrate how it contributes to the objectives of the group and the organisation. The stages of the project should be listed with the reasons, targets and duration. This enables everyone to monitor progress. Delaying the teaching of proper practices forces people to find their own methods, with the danger of developing inefficient habits. For cost reasons one or two people only may be allowed full training. This is a mistake, but if it is an immutable policy those individuals must pass on their knowledge properly to their colleagues.

MANAGEMENT CONCERNS

If the people whose jobs are directly affected by the installation of information technology have legitimate concerns, the case is even more serious for the management of the organisation with final responsibility for the project. Most senior managers have seen thousands of pounds seep away as automation costs run out of control. Overstated potential benefits which are never realised have caused the decision makers to look at automation with a jaundiced eye. Yet there is general willingness to accommodate sensible ventures. Whatever the scale of the proposal it is vital to lay out a well-presented business case. This sets out what the installation plans to achieve, how it will do this, how the implementation will be effected, the costs and the benefits. The statement should be simple and non-technical, yet show a sound understanding of the practical issues covering the hardware and software, staffing, procedures, resources for start-up, maintenance and operation, and services. Pay particular attention to the projections of cash flow and total expenditure, as these will receive concentrated attention. The reasons for deciding upon the

chosen system should be balanced against a brief outline of
rejected alternatives to show the advantages of the proposal and
to demonstrate that there has been sufficient evaluation.

SCHEDULING TARGETS

Think out the implementation schedule carefully as the success of
the project will stand or fall on the ability to reach stated goals.
Benefits must be quantifiable and measurable. The steps towards
attaining them should be clearly laid out. Otherwise there will be
many expressions of frustration if the system does not come up to
people's expectations, particularly if one or more elements meets
difficulties, however minor. Goals should be realistic and
attainable, since missing them reduces people's commitment and
motivation. A firm compromise must be established between the
practicalities of the automated system, the abilities of the staff to
develop expertise, and the demands of management.

It is important to have an early achievement. This may be
small, but it should not be trivial. One statement of 'Don't tell me
we have gone to all that effort just to get this!' will undo all the
good work to date and condemn future advances to a barrage of
sneers. There should be a new product or service, or a significant
increase in efficiency which can be immediately demonstrated,
even if it is only in pilot form. For example, an information
bulletin as a by-product of an automated catalogue system, or a
rapid compilation of data from an information retrieval system
will provide an indication that the technology works and the
benefits will be delivered. Every computer installation has
something which can be done quickly. Find the example which
matches the organisation's need and enter this on the plan as the
first objective. An early success reassures the staff, the management and the systems operators.

Beyond the first goal identify progress points which bring the
project steadily towards full implementation. A series of prime
objectives and interim stages checks that everything performs
according to expectations. If anything goes seriously wrong, the
effects can be judged against the plan and decisions made
accordingly. Without a definite schedule it is easy to get lost in
the detail. No matter how good the computer system and how
finely tuned it is towards requirements, there will be many things
to attend to. Processing backlogs, entering retrospective data,

learning new information sources or remembering new procedures take so much time and effort that the final aim is often forgotten. When it is eventually recalled the new service will probably be found wanting.

Because of the importance attached to meeting these targets, allowance should be made for things to go wrong and processes set up to rectify them. Proper planning gives the supplier the opportunity to express the real needs for the system, controlling over-optimism. It is tempting to provide a rosy view of information technology in order to obtain approval and to pursue a dream of efficiency and improved services. Setting goals and determining to measure performance against them roots the project in reality and creates a sounder structure for success.

BUDGETING

Costs escalate because of over-optimistic estimates of what can be achieved in a given space of time by a limited number of people. Unless there is significant new computer development on the part of the system vendor, hardware and software costs will be largely fixed. Variable elements should be estimated and spelt out, for example the possibility of upgrades needed to increase system speed at busy times. Maintenance and training costs should not be underestimated, or else they become a source of irritation. Contingency funding to deal with slippage in the programme is needed if targets are to be reached. Labour charges account for a major proportion of the budget, either in terms of extra staff or overtime and expenses for the regular librarians. Meal allowances and taxi fares for late working can bite into the figures unless properly planned. Itemising each cost element and detailing the basis means that a proper evaluation of the project can be made for each stage.

DEVELOPING THE SPECIFICATION

To make sure that all parties are clear about what needs to be achieved, careful attention must be given to the formal specification. This is the document which outlines the tasks to be automated and the requirements for the computer system. An essential for developing a major information technology installation, it is a useful step even when a small project is being considered.

The specification covers each operation and describes the requirements and priorities. Performance indicators lay out standards in order to achieve the desired level of service. The document covers physical aspects such as hardware, disk and memory capacity, and printer compatibility. The human resources and needs should be outlined. Examples are whether or not the system will be run by a computer expert, how much training the users will receive, affecting their competence to deal with complex structures, the time spent at the terminal and needs for large screens, anti-glare and anti-static features and ergonomically sound furniture. Input and output requirements such as diskettes and online data feeds, the need to interface with other software, and specially formatted data should be described. Standards for system reliability and maintenance schedules form a significant part of the operational element. It is important to give thought to future developments as this may affect the choice as to a closed system or one which permits interfaces to other operations at a later date, such as mass storage systems or add-on library management modules.

TECHNICAL ASSISTANCE

Most organisations will have a computer department or someone on the staff with responsibility for and expertise in this area. The computer department will have good experience in laying out the system requirements. Calling on their aid can be invaluable to ensure that the technology parameters are properly mapped out. The computer personnel can be the librarian's best allies, leading to a more knowledgeable evaluation of available computer systems and a structured approach to the process. Successful automation depends upon two aspects, the development of effective working practices and the appropriate selection of technology. By working with the in-house experts, or the organisation's advisers, the librarian can concentrate on the first criterion, leaving detailed technology concerns to the experts.

Special libraries have requirements which are out of the mainstream for their organisation. This can set up a barrier between the library staff and the computer department or information technology advisers. The technical personnel are deemed not to understand the library's need and the librarian is accused of independent action which does not follow automation policy. In-house information technology departments expend most of their effort on the prime activity of the organisation. Automation may concentrate on secretarial and clerical activities, production control, research and development, or financial monitoring and recording. Systems strategies enforce compatibility to allow users to communicate and share records and to provide standard inputs and outputs. Library systems need flexibility and a fast response to change. Information retrieval systems may require high-speed access to a variety of external computer services. Cataloguing and database construction demand substantial storage capacity. The standard hardware and software in use throughout the rest of the organisation may suffice for the library's purposes, but usually modification is necessary. The technical experts may be reluctant to do this if they feel the only beneficiary is a single department, unless there is an integrated information policy in place delivering multiple-access points to the library systems. Fearing the imposition of restraints the librarian is tempted to find his or her proprietary solutions.

It is up to the librarian to explain the requirements to the computer personnel so that they understand the differences from standard configurations and the reasons. They will also be able to find similarities and links where the demands match the overall systems strategy. The solution may be produced in-house, especially if the tradition is to develop customised services internally. The first step is to make the business case well enough to obtain priority to move ahead quickly. With so many proprietary library systems on sale it is more likely that one of these will be selected. The role of the in-house computer department becomes an advisory one, with the supervisory function of maximising compatibility with the rest of the organisation's systems. Checking capacity, speed, upgrade paths, operating issues and maintenance, they leave the librarian free to concentrate on the functions. This helps to avoid the situation where the practical aspects of the applications and the tasks to be carried out are forgotten in the rush to come to grips with the technical issues.

ASSESSING COMMERCIAL SYSTEMS

There is little point in being unrealistic in the production of the specification. Unless the proposed installation is to be designed from scratch be aware of what commercial systems are available when the document is being drawn up. This is where the correct assessment of priorities is important. There are fundamentals which must be achieved to obtain the appropriate level of service. Any system chosen must match these criteria. Beyond that other features form a wish list, containing items at different levels of desirability. Selecting a commercial product usually means a compromise. The specification serves as a checklist to keep the objectives in view and measures how close to the perfect system it is possible to get. There may be functions on offer which were not detailed as requirements. Their absence from the original list is a reminder that they may be a distraction from something more important which is not available.

The specification process has two phases. The original demands are used to select the supplier. The document keeps the emphasis on the objectives and the priorities, rather than working backwards from the vendor's description of capabilities, which can only be indicative. The second stage is a revised study once the supplier and system have been determined. This is an important part of the contract since it sets out exactly what is expected and how the installation will be implemented. It must be properly planned, as it sets the path to be followed throughout the whole project.

TIME MANAGEMENT

It is easy to get distracted because of the increased workload during the system implementation. Losing sight of the library service during a process of change leads to trouble. While the librarian's concentration is on the plans and the complexities of bringing them to fruition, day-to-day issues may be neglected. Ways for dealing with regular tasks must be found and built into the schedule so that matters are not allowed to slip. In larger libraries the service standards which the junior and line staff are expected to maintain must also be kept up by the library management. This is vital for staff morale as well as for smooth operations. Sound time-management practices are essential, as are clear lines of responsibility. The people who are charged with the implementation should have sufficient authority and autonomy to deal with issues as they arise. Though the library manager will want to deal with major concerns, too much intervention can be counter productive. If aspects of the new service do not go according to plan the important factors are to concentrate on the predefined goals and to allow those people who are best able to deal with the problem area to do so in the most practical manner. This prevents minor irritations from acquiring undue importance.

Though automation achieves gains in efficiency and effectiveness in the long term, the periods immediately prior to and just after installation are difficult. Maintaining service levels is essential, yet the staff have to cope with a variety of new tasks. Explaining their jobs, planning, attending briefings and bringing their work to a satisfactory point for automation all require more effort than normal. In a special library where the staff complement is small, thought should be given to the possibility of bringing in temporary staff cover before the system is installed. Relieving people from their other duties helps them to participate properly in the development process. Planning for additional personnel just for data input after the project is running, while common, ignores the earlier demands. If the permanent staff are too busy it is their involvement in the new operation which suffers; they concentrate on the day-to-day matters which require immediate attention and commitment to the new project and momentum are thus lost.

MAINTAINING SERVICE

While the transfer is being made from one method of working to the other, everyone has to put up with imperfect systems. Automation often follows a time when the operations have been severely stretched. The regular process of making adjustments to an existing activity may have been interrupted by a decision to wait for the new technology. The staff complement may have been run down, in prospect of increased efficiency. During implementation there are many inadequacies to be accommodated. Things may go wrong. If there is a period of parallel running, using both the old procedures and the new, the doubled workload means there is no time for detail. The wait seems too long for products and services scheduled for the later stages of the project. Although all this may be as planned, the inability to deliver a high-quality service is an irritation for both staff and customers. This should not be underestimated. It causes demoralisation and demotivation. If standards are not to be lowered permanently, each concern must be addressed. It is important to keep the focus on the planned sequence of achievements to show the purpose and the results to be attained.

EVALUATION

Evaluating the success of the project follows directly from the planning process. Measuring how well each target has been met demands a combination of objective and subjective factors. Opinions should be sought from those working with the new technology and the library users. No matter what the investment of effort and money it is important to listen to comment carefully and to respond in an appropriate manner. Acknowledgement of a concern may be followed by a counsel of patience if the end result will be satisfactory. If there are early signs that a part of the project is not going to work, this should be dealt with as soon as possible, without destroying the whole schedule. Evaluation takes into account the library users, the staff and the management who provided the funding. Each sector has different needs which can be addressed in separate reports. If the project is lengthy, progress briefs keep all eyes focused on the objectives.

The specification agreed with the supplier forms the basis for evaluation of performance against the contract. If a good dialogue has been carried on throughout the project there should be plenty of opportunity for detailed assessment. Discussion of requirements and results compared with expectations helps the vendor to develop and update the product. Improvements can be incorporated into the system during installation if they do not require a great deal of work. Substantial changes take longer and the librarian should plan to include them at a future upgrade point.

IMPLEMENTATION

Installing information technology is a complex process even with the sophisticated hardware and software now available for library systems. Careful and realistic planning helps to carry the project through effectively. Once the stages and the markers are set, attention can be given to the people who are responsible for undertaking the work needed to bring about the transfer. Accommodating the needs of the various interested parties keeps the aims and benefits in sight. It shows where the emphasis should be laid without getting lost in detail. Monitoring progress and reporting back draws the project along and keeps each development under control. If this procedure is followed there is every chance that the installation of information technology is not just an automatic step for its own sake but a means to deliver an improved library service.

Chapter 3

Choosing software and hardware

Hilary Dyer, Senior Lecturer, Department of Information and Library Studies, Loughborough University

Choosing software and hardware entails consideration of the individual functions which are to be automated together with wider issues, such as supplier reliability, hardware, price and so on. This chapter sets out many of the broader issues while chapter 4 examines the features of currently available library software.

Greater consideration has been given to software selection because its choice will, to some degree, dictate the hardware to be purchased and because hardware changes very quickly relative to the speed of publication.

SOFTWARE

Software is a series of instructions to enable the computer (or hardware) to perform certain functions. Programs are usually written for a particular computer or operating system[1] and, since IBM entered the microcomputer market, it has been dominated by MS-DOS. Apple computers, particularly Macintoshes, are becoming increasingly popular, however, due largely to their graphic user-interface. In opposition, 'Windows' environments have been developed on MS-DOS and a range of software is now available. The choice between the operating systems depends upon user preference and software availability.

Some librarians, however, are not in the fortunate position of being able to choose both the hardware and the software. They may be obliged to use the employer's mainframe or organisational policy may restrict them to a particular make of computer. In such cases, obviously, it is necessary to limit the choice of the software to that available on the given hardware, although

Bawden (1988) argues that there may be good reasons for pressing for a stand-alone system. He lists the reasons as:

- a need to use microcomputer hardware to assist in communicating to the outside world, for example for online searching or for other purposes;
- independence from the problems of a shared system, for example unhelpful computing staff, inconsistent response times, and so on;
- new features which are often available in microcomputer software before they make an impact on mini or mainframe software;
- to provide an opportunity to evaluate software which may be more readily available in demonstration disks for microcomputers than is possible with the mainframe version of the same software;
- to serve the interests of a minority of users at less cost and inconvenience than would be involved with mainframe software.

Buying or writing software

Restrictions on software choice imposed by hardware availability or by lack of money, often give rise to the question of whether or not to develop software locally using the organisation's own computing staff or even a computer-literate librarian. Although, at first, this may seem a desirable option it can often create more problems than it solves.

Writing software is a time-consuming task, and staff time, especially that of computing staff, is valuable. Thus the hidden cost of creating software is immense. Another problem is that the priority which can be given to the library program by the computing department is often lower than that of other departments, such as salaries or finance, and so the time taken to write the program may be much longer than desirable. Additionally, the complexity required by library programs is often not appreciated by computing staff and the resulting program may be inadequate for the library's requirements. Even if the software is successful, there may be problems ensuring that the necessary support is available when needed.

If the program is successful, however, the library may be better served by the tailor-made program than an off-the-shelf product, but the cost may well outweigh the benefits accrued by automation.

The alternative is to buy a program 'off the shelf'. Software packages exist to cater for stock control, from acquiring, through cataloguing and issuing, to discarding an item. Similarly, there are packages available for financial management, library planning, information retrieval, communications, and so on. Ready made programs have the advantages that many of them have been tested by other libraries and, because the development cost is spread over a range of customers, are cheaper than the equivalent program produced in-house. Buying a package is not without its problems, however, for while it is true to say that a range of software is available, it is equally true that no one product is likely to perform all the functions which are needed and so a compromise must be sought.

Type of software to purchase

It is first necessary to establish the type of software which may be required. In a special library, a number of functions may need to be performed, not all of which will fall neatly into the category of library housekeeping software. Rather, it is likely that software such as database management systems, text retrieval packages and business software will be equally useful. The four categories of software are described below:

Database management systems (DBMSs)

DBMSs themselves fall into several categories, of which the most common are the file management systems and relational database management software.

File management systems These usually offer only one record format per file. This is known as a flat file format. Records can contain only a limited number of fields, each of which is usually of a fixed length. File management systems have the advantage of being simple to set up and to use, but cannot cater for large records or files and speed of searching is usually slow, especially on larger files.

Relational database management systems In these, files are created as tables of rows and columns. Multiple files can be created, each with a different format. These files can then be linked together in a variety of ways, either at database creation or when searching the files, using the field which is the key to each record. Multiple files can be searched, simultaneously, despite the different formats. The main advantage of relational file structure is that links between information can be retained, without needing to rekey any information. For example, names and addresses of suppliers can be held in one file, which can be used as a mailing list and details of their products can be held in a separate file, using a different structure, but retaining links between the two files to indicate the relationships between the suppliers and the products.

DBMSs are well suited to records which are fixed in length and highly structured, although some systems offer variable field lengths. They also perform well if arithmetic functions are required – and editing, importing and exporting data are also facilitated – but there are problems to using DBMSs in library and information work. The main drawbacks are the (often) fixed length of the records and fields, and the slow, sequential searching of files. DBMSs may also be case intolerant when searching, that is they will only retrieve 'Smith' when entered as 'Smith', not 'SMITH' or 'smith'.

Relational database systems usually also offer a programming language which may be used to develop routines or menu interfaces in addition to the database. A computer-literate librarian may find that a DBMS offers an inexpensive solution to assist in creating a tailor-made product. Indeed, many of the dedicated housekeeping packages for microcomputers are based on DBMSs, the supplier having developed the applications routines and improved retrieval performance. The decision as to whether or not to use them will depend on the amount of local expertise available and the complexity of the task to be automated.

Text retrieval packages

Text retrieval software, as its name implies, allows the storage and retrieval of variable-length text. It does so by means of an inverted file index which contains all the words from the file, together with a reference to their position in the file. The inverted file is searched initially on retrieval, enabling a rapid response. Indexing is usually automatic and it may be possible to select both the fields to be indexed and the method used. Similarly, the field and record structures may be user-defined. Fields and records in text retrieval software are typically variable in length and usually accommodate more than a DBMS record. Complex retrieval commands, with full Boolean logic are common and thesaurus control may also be available. Output formats are usually flexible and can normally be user-defined.

Text retrieval software is well suited for mounting the catalogue or other information databases, but has drawbacks for use elsewhere in the library. Library housekeeping functions are seldom included, and, if they are, the updating of the index can slow the operation to a less than acceptable level. Indeed, many systems allow only batch updating of records and indexes. For the most part, such systems are command-driven although some have developed interfaces which are more appropriate for a novice user, incorporating menus and user-defined features.

Library housekeeping software

Library housekeeping is the term used to describe the acquisition and control of stock. A number of packages exist to assist the librarian of the special library, but many of them assume that operations are the same as in a larger library but on a smaller scale. Little account is taken by some suppliers of the range of tasks which may be performed, such as abstracting single documents, summarising a number of documents on a topic, acquiring 'grey' literature, and making permanent loans of material to some individuals or departments. As the market for special library software increases, the range of suitable software is also likely to increase, but there may still be some librarians who find that the complexity of their information unit is not catered for in the range of products available at the price they can afford.

Business software

A number of packages are sold under the heading of office automation or business software. These include spreadsheets, integrated software (database, spreadsheet and word processor combined) and word processing/text retrieval software. The variety of functions performed in a special library may make the use of such packages beneficial.

Spreadsheet software comprises rows and columns of figures into which text, numbers, or formulae may be entered. The formulae indicate to the program what figures are to be used in the calculation and how they are to be combined. Thus it is possible to set up spreadsheets to perform a range of functions, such as calculating the cost of the online search service, or specific aspects of it, or to assist in the calculation of the budget. Libraries which are self-financing may find such a facility particularly useful. The spreadsheet software may also produce the results of the calculations in the form of histograms or pie charts, printed separately or, if part of an integrated package, incorporated in a word processed document.

Also available are packages for searching 'free text' files, data-base files or downloaded data. Word processed documents are 'free text' files, some of which may be regarded as the information base of an organisation's activities. The software indexes and searches unstructured text and can find any occurrence of words or phrases located across multiple files. 'Wild card' searches and combined searches are all accommodated.

Criteria for choosing software

The criteria for software selection can be divided into three sections. The first is the functional requirements of the software, which concerns the features necessary to perform a particular function. The second is general requirements pertaining to all software and the third aspect is that of user requirements.

Functional criteria

Chapter 4 details the types of function that might reasonably be expected from currently available software. Not all features are available on all systems, however, and a compromise is necessary. In order to ensure the best compromise, a careful analysis of the library's requirements must be made. The initial evaluation of the system, (chapter 2) should have established the reason for automation, e.g. whether saving time or accelerating certain processes was the most important issue. This will help to establish the priorities of the automated program. With these objectives in mind, the next step is to list all the functions required of the computer system, e.g. acquisitions, cataloguing, etc. Within these functions, particular features should then be noted, such as: 'the catalogue must cater for 13,000 books', 'a minimum of 600 loans at any time must be possible', or 'the operator must be able to word process downloaded files in Word Perfect'.

These requirements need to be prioritised, as no system is likely to offer everything. One way of indicating the relative importance of the different functions is to award 'marks' out of ten, using one as the least important. This gives a fine grading of options but, for that reason, can be difficult to apply. A simpler technique is to nominate items as 'mandatory' (i.e. the program *must* offer the facility), 'desirable' (it would be very nice, but is not essential) and 'luxury' (there is no need for it, but if it is available, it could be useful). These criteria and their associated ratings could be listed on a chart, such as the one shown in table 3.1.

General requirements

Files The files used as the basis of an information retrieval or library housekeeping system should be evaluated from the point of view of the record structure they support and the number of records which can be held.

The record structure accommodated must be adequate for the task, i.e. sufficient fields of adequate length. In order to assess the required data structure, it is necessary to ascertain what data are to be held, what elements need to be in separate fields and what length each field should be. Field lengths are measured in characters; letters, punctuation and spaces all being counted. The longest example of a field is the most critical.

The number of records which will be needed, anticipating for future growth, is vital to ensure, not only that the software can accommodate the required number, but also that it can operate adequately. With some systems, it may be possible to hold a large number of records, but, above a certain number, performance will deteriorate.

A database takes a long time to create and is the most costly part of the system. It is therefore vital that the software can handle it adequately and, if not, that the data can be readily transported to another package should future needs dictate. This

Table 3.1 Software selection

Function	Rating	Software A	Software B	etc.
Cataloguing				
Stock:				
15,000 monographs	M			
3,000 pictures	M			
250 maps	M			
Bibliographic record:				
MARC input desirable	D			
Abstract of 200 words per item	M			
Subject searching by keywords	M			
Online thesaurus	D			
Subject searching by class number	D			
etc.				
Serials control				
Routing:				
Open loop	M			
Easy deletion of reader from multiple journals	D			
etc.				
Price				
Hardware required				
Hardware price				

may require that bibliographic output from the system is in MARC format, and that other data are in ASCII.

MARC is the name given to a standard machine-readable catalogue format, which enables bibliographic data to be transferred between systems. MARC input may also be desirable to enable the use of pre-existing catalogue records, such as the MARC tapes available from the British Library. The American Standard Code for Information Interchange (ASCII) enables text to be transferred between machines by making it possible for one machine or software package to read text created on another. It does not, however, cater for different file structures, for which a special reformatting program would need to be used.

Records Fields may be fixed or variable length, or even a mix of the two. The desired size of fixed-length fields needs to be estimated prior to setting up the system and they are then, as their name implies, unalterable. As a consequence, if the entry is longer than the field it must be truncated or if it is shorter, the unfilled spaces are stored as blanks in the database, thus consuming disk space unnecessarily. On a microcomputer with limited disk capacity, the length of fixed fields needs to be carefully estimated.

A variable length record, in contrast, enables data of any length (up to a given maximum) to be entered without padding. Because of the maximum limit, however, some preliminary calculation is still required. A variable-length field structure is better suited to text handling than a fixed-length field, but such packages can be expensive.

Indexing Indexing has already been mentioned in the context of text retrieval software. An inverted file index enables rapid retrieval, but is not without disadvantages. One drawback is that the index must be created before searching can take place. This may be done in a number of ways:

- online, i.e. immediately after inputting or amending a record, making it immediately accessible online on all keys, but causing a delay between the input of one record and the next;
- in batch, i.e. all the indexing is carried out as a separate function which may be done overnight;
- in background, on a batch of records, i.e. run separately, but allowing the operator to perform other functions at the same time.

Index creation can be very time consuming. For files of several thousand records it can take several hours to index the contents, the exact time depending on the package and the complexity of the records. Indeed, it is not unknown for the process to take several days in extreme cases. With a single-task system, no other task can be performed at the same time as the index is being created, so this must be taken into account if the computer is to be heavily used.

Another problem is that the index itself may consume considerable disk space. For files of several thousand records, the index may consume as much as 60–200 per cent again of the size of the database, depending on how much of the record is to be indexed. This needs to be taken into account when estimating the required disk capacity.

Various indexing methods are available and some packages offer more than one. The more common options are:

- full field indexing. The whole content of the field is used as an indexing term. This means that the whole text of the field must also be used as a search term, individual elements of the field not being indexed. It is useful for handling names, such as author names, thus attaching the forename and surname to one another. Searching in a text retrieval system usually allows for truncation, so that if only the surname is known, the first name or initials can be truncated;
- free text indexing. Each individual word becomes an index entry;
- tagged indexing. The operator selects words or phrases for indexing. This can be useful to highlight one or two key words from a large field of text, reducing the space consumed by free text indexing, but entails operator effort on input;
- manual indexing. The index terms are entered in a separate field. This, obviously, takes more space in the file, but helps to overcome the problems of natural language indexing, enabling a controlled vocabulary to be used.

Some systems also offer the facility of a serial search, enabling the user to retrieve any text whether or not it has been indexed. This has the advantage of reducing the need for indexing text but, as it is very slow in searching (especially on large files), it should be used with care.

Access and security It is important to prevent unauthorised access to the system, and password protection may be desirable. In many systems, it is possible to password protect access, not only to the whole program, but also to the various functions and subfunctions within it, enabling different levels of user to operate different parts of the system as their password permits. Similarly, parts of records may be protected. If public access is provided, such control may be desirable.

User requirements

In order for the software package to be an effective tool, the user needs to be able to interact with it without frustration, boredom or confusion. This means that the dialogue used by the system should be appropriate to the user's level of skills and knowledge. (The term 'dialogue' is used to mean the instructions that the user issues to the computer and the information that the computer displays for the user.)

Types of user Computer users are not uniform in their experience, skills or expectation. Cole, *et al.* (1985) identify four groups of users of computer systems:

- naive users who have little or no knowledge of the task to be performed or of computer systems;
- casual experts who understand the application thoroughly, but have little or no computer knowledge;
- associative experts who have considerable familiarity with computer systems but little knowledge of the particular application;
- experienced professionals who have skills in both computing and the task for which the computer is used.

Cole and his colleagues point out, however, that these categories are not discrete and that people move between them. A novice user of an OPAC (online public access catalogue), for example may become a casual expert in time or an experienced professional may regress to a casual or an associate expert through lack of practice.

The type of dialogue best suited to each category of user varies with the user, the task performed and the frequency and duration with which the task is performed. A novice user for example needs prompts indicating options available and the implications of making a particular choice. A casual expert requires to be guided through the system, but can comprehend terminology relating specifically to the task. The converse is true of the associative expert who is unlikely to need prompting to hit the RETURN key but may require information on the function being selected. The experienced pro will want power and flexibility above all and could become irritated by the distractions of prompts and help messages.

Thus, in choosing software, the nature of the predominant users must be considered. Complications arise, however, because of the changing nature of users. Users not only change categories over time, they may change according to the task being performed, so that an experienced online searcher becomes a mere associative expert when operating the issue system for example.

One solution may be to acquire software with an adaptable interface. Some software, for example, offers a default menu (a list of options from which choices can be made) but with a 'hidden' command-driven interface for experienced users. In many systems, common commands (e.g. SAVE, EXIT, HELP) are executed by use of the function keys, a list of the uses to which function keys are put usually being displayed at the foot of the screen or on a template which fits on the keyboard.

User characteristics   All people have characteristics which affect the way in which they process information. This, in turn, has implications for the software interface.

Memory   Memory is divided into short- and long-term memory. Short-term memory can be disrupted by the receipt of competitive information, such as an interruption by a colleague or the telephone. Some systems demand the use of short-term memory (or a notepad!). On some issue systems, for example, if a reader number is not known it may be found by searching the reader file, but it must then be input manually in order to issue an item. If interruptions are anticipated as part of a task, it is desirable if minimal use is made of short-term memory.

Mental capacity   A person's mental capacity governs the amount of information which can be received and processed at any one time. Some users may become quickly tired if too much information is presented at once, and clear screen layouts can assist in minimising mental overload. Other users may become quickly bored by having to page through several screens. Therefore, layouts which are appropriate to the task, and which include as much relevant data as possible, in the right order on the minimum number of screens, should be sought.

Perception   Skills in perception will affect the speed with which an individual will be able to identify relevant information on a screen and will therefore affect the performance of the operator. To assist an operator's perception, judicial use of coding, such as highlighting, inverse video, colour or blinking should be used.

Interface design In order to maximise an operator's effectiveness, the interface design should take into account his or her strengths and limitations, some of which are mentioned above. Factors which make for a 'good' interface include: consistency in the position of headings and prompts; consistency in the use of commands and function keys; clear screen layouts; and minimal use of the operator's memory. Additional features include the amount of control the operator has over the system, and the clarity and tone of the help and error messages. Other factors are mentioned in more detail below because of their particular application to library and information software:

- Ease of movement throughout the system. Is it possible, for example, to access the same record in different functions without re-identifying it, e.g. having found a record in the enquiry function, is it possible to transfer it to the circulation function for reservation purposes, or is it necessary to re-key the details of the item to be reserved?
- Data entry or editing. Most systems offer full screen input, where data are entered onto a form on the screen, but the ease of editing, which is an important consideration, varies from system to system.

  It is desirable to be able to overtype, insert, or delete characters, rather than to have to rekey the whole field. Indeed some systems provide full screen editing facilities akin to those offered on word processing systems, with complete cursor control, i.e. the cursor can be moved around the screen, and any field can be changed as necessary. On other systems, editing must be carried out on a field-by-field basis, whereby it is necessary to identify fields which need amending: sometimes it is necessary to re-enter the whole field.

  Some software packages provide various kinds of checks on data as they are entered. This may be to alert the user to the existence of a duplicate record, to an invalid date or code, such as an ISBN, or to the absence of data in any mandatory fields (as required by the system or defined by the user).
- WIMP is an acronym for Windows, Icons, Mice and Pull-down

menus and is used to describe a form of interface which is increasingly common in general-purpose software, especially that running on the Apple Macintosh. Used with a mouse to point to and select from the menus, the WIMP interface is intended for use with naive users, yet it is popular with many experienced users because of the speed which may be developed in its use. Although not adopted in its entirety, some of the features, notably windows, are becoming more common in library and information retrieval software. A window is the term used to describe a section of the screen which temporarily overlays the rest of the screen. It may contain data from a menu, or another file, such as an authority file (e.g. a list of authors). The data in the window may sometimes only be used for reference, saving use of the operator's memory or, in other systems, for selection, i.e. to choose an alternative function from a menu or to select an indexing term from a list (the term then being automatically transferred to the input screen).

- Help. Most systems provide some form of help. It may be context specific, i.e. it relates to the field or function where the user requests help, or it may be general, tutorial help which may be used at any stage to give guidance on how to operate the system or to remind the user of commands. Some systems offer user-definable help screens, which may be useful if the function or the library places unique demands on the operator. Helpful error messages are also important.
- Feedback from the computer to the operator is important. This may simply be to indicate the number of items which have been retrieved on a search or to inform the operator of the reason for any delay. Another form of feedback is to prompt the user as to the course of action currently available to him or her.
- The response time of the software/hardware combination will be dictated by a number of factors, software, hardware and data, and it may not always be easy to determine how a given product will perform. Contact with existing users of the software is likely to be the best source of information on how the package behaves in real life rather than demonstrations. Usually, rapid response times are desirable, but the frequency of performing a particular task and the possibility of doing something else in the intervening period are important ameliorating factors.

Establishing a shortlist

Armed with a list of functional criteria, the next step is to select a shortlist of products. For most special libraries, it is assumed that microcomputer hardware and software will be required, but it may be worth considering mainframe software, with a general application, such as the text retrieval software, Status, if it can be used throughout the organisation. The advantages are that, if a mainframe is already in use, computer staff, rather than library staff will deal with the day-to-day running of the system, ensuring backups, maintenance etc., and the overall cost of the system to the organisation may be less than a stand-alone system. On the other side of the argument, however, must be balanced the need to compromise the library's requirements with those of other users.

Having decided what kind of software is required, it may then be helpful to select from among the range available by consulting one of the increasing number of software directories a list of which can be found on p. 52.

Once the shortlist has been drawn up, it is necessary to obtain more information from the suppliers and to see demonstrations. It is also helpful to visit reference sites to see the products in operation and to assess the views of its users, both at managerial and operational level. Demonstrations show all the best facilities of the software, but can attempt to hide the weaker spots. The list of criteria (table 3.2) can assist the questioning of demonstrators and can be used to provide an at-a-glance comparison of the relative performances of the competing products.

On the example shown, the letters 'Y' (yes) and 'N' (no) have been used to indicate whether or not a feature is present and the categories 'VG' (very good), 'G' (good), 'M' (moderate), 'P' (poor) or 'W' (weak) to indicate how well it performs. Such a chart can help to provide an objective guide to decision-making. In the example shown, software package A scored over B overall because the mandatory requirements were all met, whereas in B two were not.

Other considerations

Once a shortlist has been compiled, use of the checklist may help to decide between them, but other factors that may sway the

Table 3.2 Software selection showing comparison between two products

Function	Rating	Software A	Software B	etc.
Cataloguing				
Stock:				
15,000 monographs	M	Y	Y	
3,000 pictures	M	Y	N	
250 maps	M	Y	N	
Bibliographic record:				
MARC input desirable	D	N	Y	
Abstract of 200 words per item	M	Y	Y	
Subject searching by keywords	M	G	VG	
Online thesaurus	D	N	Y	
Subject searching by class number etc.	D	Y	Y	
Serials control				
Routing:				
Open loop	M	Y	Y	
Easy deletion of reader from multiple journals etc.	D	Y	Y	
Price				
Hardware required				
Hardware price				

balance should be considered. These are: the price; documentation; support; training; supplier reliability; and what other customers think.

Price Obviously, the price needs to be one which the library can afford, but hidden factors may affect the true cost of the software. The cost of the hardware required to run the package may be greater than that of a more expensive package, data input may be slow (for example, there may be no MARC input facility or the interface may be cumbersome) thus consuming staff time, or maintenance and training may add to the cost.

Documentation Sometimes the documentation supplied with a system is poor. In order to be able to operate a system effectively, good instruction is important and this can be provided by the manual. The text needs to be easy to understand, should avoid jargon where possible, and a good index should be included. Examples in the text are useful.

Support Most suppliers offer software support or maintenance for around 10–15 per cent of the software cost per annum. The support on offer may vary according to the supplier, but typically includes telephone assistance, and error correction. (No software is released totally free of bugs, so this facility is very useful.) In addition, some suppliers are willing to visit the site to sort out problems and may offer online support via a modem (if you have one).

Training Training is important, in order to learn the most effective way of operating the system. The supplier should offer some form of training, usually at around £150 per day.

Supplier reliability The microcomputer software marketplace is unstable, especially in the library and information field, and a look at the company accounts to help determine whether the supplier will still be in business to offer the needed support would not go amiss. The length of time the company has been operating can also be an indicator of how likely it is to remain solvent.

What other customers think A full customer list is desirable, but commercial interests may preclude companies supplying full lists. It is important to be sure that the product really does live up to its promise in the working environment and that the company continue to treat customers well after they have paid!

HARDWARE

Having selected the best software for your needs, consideration needs to be given to the hardware requirements. It may be advisable to assess the hardware once a shortlist has been drawn up if the chosen products inhabit different hardware environments. Hardware suitability may make the difference between the success or failure of a system.

Single- or multi-user

The most obvious requirement will be that of whether more than one person can use the system simultaneously. There are two main methods of enabling multiple access, the first is by using a multi-user microcomputer, the second is via a network. Multi-user computers tend to be larger and to offer all the security requirements in terms of controlling access to files, ensuring that two operators do not simultaneously amend a record, for example. The disadvantage of multi-user computers is the initial cost of the system, which has to be expended at one time.

A more common method is to network several computers together, which gives access to shared peripherals, but does not always offer data security. Most software offers its own facilities for securing data over a network, however. It is possible, with a networked system, to start with one or two computers and to increase the number over time.

In view of the complexity of the whole area of multi-user computing, it is advisable to discuss individual requirements with the supplier, or a suitably qualified consultant.

Processor

At the centre of the microcomputer is the central processing unit (CPU) in which the basic processes take place. The speed at which these processes occur is determined by a clock which pulses data through the CPU; the clockspeed is usually quoted in Megahertz (MHz) or millions of times per second (Leggate and Dyer, 1985). The type and speed of processor will affect the speed of operation of the computer. The 486 processor is currently very popular because of its speed, but it should not be thought that a fast processor will necessarily speed operations. A number of other factors must also be considered, such as memory size, disk speed and software performance.

Main memory

The main memory or RAM (Random Access Memory) is used to hold the program currently being run, the data being input to or used by the system, and the operating system. The size of memory available will affect the speed of operation of certain programs and, indeed, whether some programs can be run at all. Speed of operation is affected because, if insufficient memory is available, different sections of the program have to be retrieved from disk as required. If all the program is resident in memory, faster operation results.

When purchasing hardware, it is necessary to ensure that it has sufficient memory to run the chosen software at a reasonable speed. It should be noted that the nominal RAM size may not all be available to the user, part may be consumed by the operating system, compilers or other utilities, the remainder being shared between the program and the data. Thus it is the *available* not the *nominal* RAM which needs to be considered (ibid. 1985).

Sometimes, use is made of ROM (Read Only Memory) to run operating systems or software. This has the advantage of freeing RAM and can also contribute to faster operation. In order to purchase ROM software, it is necessary to buy the processor containing the program and slot it into the hardware (or to get someone else to!).

Disk

It is assumed that most special libraries will need a hard disk computer, i.e. one which has a large-capacity disk fixed into the machine. Typically hard disks start at 20 Mb (Megabyte or 1 million characters), but can be purchased with capacities up to over several hundred Mb.

All microcomputers will have at least one floppy disk drive. Floppy disks used to be 5.25 inches in diameter and encased in cardboard. Standard now are the more robust and larger capacity 3.5 inch disks, which are encased in plastic.

The storage space quoted for disks is sometimes for the disk in its unformatted state. In order to use a disk, however, it needs to be formatted for use with a particular machine. This not only has the effect of making it incompatible with another make of computer, but also reduces the storage capacity of the disk; a point which needs to be considered when calculating the necessary disk capacity.

In order to estimate the required disk size, some calculations must be made. Disk space will be required for the operating system, applications software and data. The supplier should be able to give details of the space required for software, but data requirements need to be calculated by the user. Consideration needs to be given to the files which will be held: databases, word processed text, spreadsheets, mailing lists, etc. Each file will need to be separately calculated. Maximum file size needs to be measured in terms of both present and future needs. If the software to be used utilises fixed-length fields, it is necessary to calculate the maximum length of all the fields (in characters) that will be required and add together the number of characters per field to ascertain the length of a record. The file size will be obtained by multiplying the anticipated number of records by the record size. If variable-length fields are used, the average field length should be used as the basis of the calculations.

It is important not to underestimate file sizes, because it is the initial cost of the disk drive which is expensive, relative to the cost of the disk space. For example, a 40 Mb disk is not twice as expensive as a 20 Mb disk.

The data on the hard disk are vulnerable to software and operator errors, or even accidents caused by static electricity or uneven electrical currents. For this reason, it is vital to devise a method of storing a separate copy of the data. A floppy disk can be used for small files, such as word processed text, but is usually inadequate for larger files, such as a catalogue or database. It is advisable, therefore, to purchase a tape streamer for backup purposes. A tape streamer uses high-capacity magnetic tape and a single tape can store the contents of a 20 Mb hard disk.

It may be desirable to purchase a CD-ROM drive, if CD-ROM facilities are to be used instead of online searching. Standardisation has not yet been reached among CD-ROM producers, but the most commonly used format is the 'High Sierra'. Once again however software – or in this case the database – should dictate the hardware purchased. If multiple databases are to be used, a conflict of interests may occur and some, even using the same format, may require reconfiguring prior to operation.

Visual display unit (VDU)

Criteria to consider when choosing a VDU are the screen size, the character set and the controls. There are a number of other factors which could be taken into account but, in reality, the decision is likely to be made on the basis of the functionality of the hardware.

Screen size

The physical size of the screen, measured diagonally, should be at least 30 cm to ensure comfortable viewing. It should be possible to tilt and swivel the screen to position it to avoid glare and to obtain the most comfortable viewing angle.

Character set

The character set should be clear and unambiguous (look particularly for possible confusion between 0 [zero] and O [the letter O], and 1 [one] and l [the letter 'el'] or I [capital 'eye']).

Controls

Brightness and contrast controls should be available within easy reach of the operator from a sitting position.

Casing

The outer casing of the microcomputer should be in a neutral colour and a non-reflective finish. Ideally, it should be dirt resistant.

Data capture

In order to input data to a system, a variety of instruments are used, most commonly the keyboard, a mouse and a barcode reader.

The keyboard is the one which is most frequently used for inputting text. If it is to be heavily used, it is important that it conforms to certain standards in order to maximise productivity and minimise input errors. Put simply, the keyboard needs to feel comfortable in use, the legends need to be easy to read and resistant in use, the size and position of frequently used keys, such as SHIFT and RETURN need to be such that they cannot easily be mistaken for other keys and that alternatives are not pressed in their stead. Function keys, if used, need to be clearly labelled and separated by colour or position.

Mice are hand-held devices, attached to the VDU by a cable, which when moved around a flat surface cause the cursor to move in an equivalent manner. They are usually employed in conjunction with icons and menus from which selections may be made by pressing a button on the mouse. Although still relatively little used in library software, they are increasing in popularity.

If large amounts of repetitive data are to be entered, such as when issuing items to borrowers, barcodes are often used for input. In selecting a barcode and reader, accuracy and ease of use must be considered. (Some codes do not read easily and require two or three attempts.) Ease of printing the barcode may also be important, and if barcodes are to be printed in-house, this has to be borne in mind when purchasing a printer.

Printers

Printers transfer the data from the computer onto paper. The factors that need to be considered in selecting a printer are: speed, price and quality, but in addition, there could be added: noise and the ability to output foreign language diacritics or barcodes.

The most commonly used kinds of printers for library and information work fall into three categories: dot matrix, jet and page.

Dot matrix printers

Dot matrix printers form the letters by pressing a matrix of dots on the single print head against the paper. The dots are pushed forward or held back to form the shape of a letter or other character. The number of pins making up the head varies, the larger the number, the better being the quality of the printed character. Although 9-pin arrays are standard, 18- and 24-pin models are also commonly available.

Dot matrix printers have the advantage of being able to form diacritics (which helps with foreign language material and graphics, including barcodes). The main disadvantage is that, although near letter quality (NLQ) printing is usually offered as an alternative to draft, unless an 18- or 24-pin head is used and the character set is good the resulting printout is not really acceptable in formal correspondence. Dot matrix printers are usually cheaper and faster than their competitors, however, and may therefore be a useful second printer for draft copies or client use.

Jet printers

A jet of ink is squirted at the paper in the shape of a character from a single print head with the result that the printed output is clear, with good black/white contrast. In addition, because there is no impact involved, i.e. no hammer is hitting against a ribbon, the printer is quieter than either a dot matrix or daisy wheel printer. This may be an important consideration where a printer is frequently used in a reading room. Ink, bubble and colour jet printers are available.

Page printers

Page printers are by far the fastest model of printer on the market, operating by making an image of the page to be output and printing a page at a time. Page printers are usually designed to operate by using laser or LED (light-emitting diode) technology. The quality of the printed output is usually superior to that of an electric typewriter and in some cases, close to commercial printing. Used with a range of fonts and a desktop publishing system, a page printer can achieve high-quality copy suitable for camera-ready input for commercial printers. Thus it can be used to produce publications from the library or information unit: ideal if the unit is a frequent compiler and distributor of high-quality printed material. As might be guessed, however, page printers are also the most expensive. Once purchased, the expense does not stop as toner, like that used in a photocopier, is consumed in large quantities. If a page printer is needed for the library's purposes, it is cost effective to purchase a cheap dot matrix printer for draft copies, the cost of such a cheap printer being only the equivalent of about two bottles of toner.

Accessories

Printers do not operate without certain accessories, such as paper and ribbons.

Paper Most people think of computer paper in terms of the fan-folded, tractor-fed paper. Tractor feeds may well come as standard with a printer, but have the disadvantage that special paper needs to be purchased. It is not possible to use a tractor feed with the organisation's headed notepaper, for example, unless it has been specially printed. The other drawback is that, unless the recipient does not mind having fan-folded paper with perforations at the side, some effort is necessary to rid the paper of these features.

An alternative is to use a sheet feeder, which clips onto the printer and holds a batch of cut sheets (such as headed paper) which it then feeds into the printer one at a time, when needed. Unfortunately, these are not cheap. (Page printers use only cut sheets.) If cut sheets are only rarely required, it is possible to use the grip feed, which usually also comes as standard, and feed the sheets in one at a time by hand, but it must be remembered that staff time also costs money.

Modems

For online searching or to link with the organisation's mainframe, a modem may be needed. Modems enable computers to communicate with other computers via the telephone network by converting the signals from the computer into a code which can be recognised by the telephone network. One of the main features to look for is the speed of transmission and receipt of data, 1200 baud being an acceptable minimum. Integral modems, i.e. ones which are mounted onto a chip which slots into the microcomputer are neat and help to reduce clutter at the workstation.

Compatibility with other equipment

The library or information unit is unlikely to operate in isolation from the rest of the organisation it serves, and there may well be a need to be connected electronically as well. Because compatibility is specific to particular computers, it is necessary to discuss the library's requirements with various suppliers.

NOTE

1 The operating system is, in turn, a series of instructions which enables an operator or program to use a computer. The same operating system may be used on a range of computers, thus enabling a software package to be run on more than one type of machine.

SOFTWARE DIRECTORIES

Dyer, H. and Gunson, A. (1990) *A Directory of Library and Information Retrieval Software for Microcomputers* (4th edn) Aldershot: Gower;

Kimberley, R. (ed.) (1990) *Text Retrieval: A Directory of Software* (3rd edn) IIS and Gower;

Leeves, J. (1989) *Library Systems: A Buyer's Guide* (2nd edn) Aldershot: Gower;

LIBRARY JOURNALS

C & L Applications, published by the Information Partnership, Suite 42, 140 Tabernacle Street, London EC2A 4SD;

The Electronic Library, published by Learned Information Ltd, Woodside, Hinksey Hill, Oxford OX1 5AU;

IT's News, published by the Library Association Information Technology Group, editor: Stephen Hume, London Business School Library, Sussex Place, Regents Park, London, NW1A 4SA;

Library Micromation News, published by the Library Information Technology Centre, South Bank Technopark, 90 London Road, London SE1 6LN;

Program, published by Aslib, The Association for Information Management, 20–24 Old Street, London, EC1V 9AP;

Computers in Libraries, published by Meckler Corporation, 11 Ferry Lane West, Westport, CT 06880, USA;

VINE, published by the Library Information Technology Centre;

COMPUTING JOURNALS

PC Magazine, published by Ziff-Davis Publishing Company, One Park Avenue, New York, NY 10016, USA;

Practical Computing, published by Reed Business Publishing Ltd, Quadrant House, The Quadrant, Sutton, Surrey, SM2 5AS;

Which Computer, published by EMAP, Abbots Court, 34 Farringdon Lane, London EC1R 3AU.

REFERENCES AND BIBLIOGRAPHY

Bawden, D. (1988) 'Specific roles for microcomputer software in an information department', *Aslib Proceedings*, 40 (1): 1–7.

Cole, I., Lansdale, M. and Christie, B. (1985) 'Dialogue design guidelines', in B. Christie (ed.) (1985) *Human factors of information technology in the office*, Chichester: Wiley, 212–241.

'Hello World . . . ' (1989) *PC Magazine* 2 (3): 65–72.

Leggate, P. and Dyer, H. (1985) 'The microcomputer in the library: II. Hardware and operating systems', *The Electronic Library* 3 (4): 260–74.

ACKNOWLEDGEMENTS

This chapter was written after discussion with the Library Information Technology Centre whose input is acknowledged with thanks.

Chapter 4

Choosing a software package

Caroline Moore, Manager, Library Information Technology Centre

There is now a wide market in computer software and systems for library applications. These cover library management or housekeeping routines such as acquisitions, cataloguing and circulation control; the creation of in-house databases for sophisticated information retrieval; and, in a wider context, the setting up of various data sharing and data acquisition systems. This chapter discusses the automation of in-house routines and looks at what software is available and suitable for special library environments and applications.

In the special library, as in any library, the introduction of IT and the technological infrastructure will depend on organisational policy and strategy as well as on the library's local requirements. However, in many cases, cost effectiveness will dictate that the small special library run a dedicated microcomputer system rather than share a larger machine. Therefore, for the most part, the software considered below is for microcomputers, most commonly running under MS-DOS, with multi-user applications handled through a local area network such as Novell. Recently multiuser UNIX-based systems are becoming available. As yet the Apple Macintosh has not featured largely in the library software scene. However, some library housekeeping packages are available and, as the price of these machines continues to fall, more packages can be expected to appear.

When considering automating library activities, and looking for suitable commercially available software, there are three basic options to consider:

- purchase a general purpose database management system and use that as a tool to develop your application;

- use information retrieval software; or
- buy a readymade library housekeeping package.

Each has its uses and role which are discussed in turn below.

DATABASE MANAGEMENT SYSTEMS

DBMSs are general-purpose database packages best suited to applications where the records are fixed in length and highly structured. They permit the user to set up and define his or her own databases and, within each, the structure of the records. The characteristic features of the DBMS have already been discussed in chapter 3 so here it is only necessary to note the type of library applications for which they may be suitable. Because they are general-purpose packages addressing a very large market, they are usually considerably cheaper than the other software developed specifically for libraries. They are most applicable for very small libraries or very small files where simple retrieval and output in the form of sorted listings are required. Examples of applications to which DBMS have successfully been applied are the creation of a file of journal subscriptions and renewal dates so that renewal alerts can be provided; a simple journal holdings list; the creation of journal distribution lists with the DBMS able to cater for the common problem of global change; and, of course, the creation of a simple catalogue. This may be of books, but also of other materials. The DBMS can also be used very successfully to store and organise files of non-bibliographic information such as staff lists, name and address files, organisations or societies. Typical packages popular in libraries are the dBase family from Ashton-Tate (dBase II, III+ etc), DataEase, Superfile and Delta.

However, the general DBMS is less suitable for more complex automation requirements. As a provider of basic tools on which the user can develop a system, the DBMS, admittedly, offers cheapness and the ability to tailor the application exactly, within the limitations of the package being used. Some can also be used as a programming language to develop applications. However, the do-it-yourself approach demands local skills, understanding of the package, and time to undertake the applications development – none of which ought to be underestimated even if skilled and experienced computer staff are being used to develop the application. Library routines demand relatively complicated use of the DBMS, particularly if data has to be transferred between files (for example, pulling in borrower's data or supplier's name and address data). Often the choice is between writing out records from one file to another – cumbersome in a realtime situation – and writing pieces of linking software so that the linkages between files are user transparent and do not require operator intervention. A further complication is that a transaction carried out on one file may require data to be updated elsewhere in the system. The other drawback of DBMS is that retrieval is poor, inverted indexes are rare, and slower string searching techniques may be used. Many of the dedicated housekeeping packages do, in fact, make use of a DBMS, but in these cases the supplier has developed all the applications routines and, in addition, improved the retrieval.

INFORMATION RETRIEVAL SYSTEMS

The second option is to purchase an off-the-shelf information retrieval (IR) system. IR systems (which are also called text retrieval systems) are designed to deal with the particular problems of handling text and are usually the most suitable software for setting up anything other than very basic text databases.

At their simplest, IR packages consist of programs to create, search and maintain text databases. Characteristically they offer:

- user-definable, variable-length fields and records;
- a choice of indexing methods;
- powerful retrieval capabilities including word and phrase searching, truncation, field searching, the use of full Boolean logic, set creation and refinement; and
- flexible, user-designed output formats, for screen, disk and for hard copy.

Additional facilities such as linked thesaurus files, synonym control, SDI features, and, most recently, image handling, are available in some packages.

Most libraries' first concern when considering automation is to computerise their catalogue as the routine of creating, duplicating and filing cards is tedious and labour intensive. A computerised system will make more efficient use of the staff time available and provide a valuable online information source which is more flexible in terms of searching and output than a manual system. Indeed, for the special library where the emphasis is often on sophisticated retrieval of information and generating reading lists or current awareness services, this may be the only activity worth automating. For these types of automation requirement, the IR package is usually a good choice.

Types of IR package

IR packages are suitable for many different types of text-based database and can be used for storing the complete free-format texts of reports, newspapers or legal documentation, as well as more structured consistent-format information, such as bibliographic data describing book and non-book items, company or product information files, inventories, medical records, etc. Packages vary in their ability to handle these different types of textual information: some are suitable for either structured data, e.g. Inmagic, or full text data, e.g. Extract; others, such as Status-PC, can handle both.

A number of reasonably priced packages for indexing and searching free text files have recently become available, examples being Zyindex and Ize. They are intended for general business use, often accepting files in various word processor formats, and are used mainly as a means of locating information contained in letters, memos and other day-to-day business documents. These may be useful in the library as well as in the general office environment for which they are intended.

IR packages, for many years the little known alternative to the DBMS, have recently received a big boost in the development of document imaging processing (DIP) systems: these systems make use of scanners to convert whole pages of information into a machine readable format in a matter of seconds. As the need for expensive keyboarding is beginning to disappear, the IR package is coming into its own as a means of indexing all the newly available machine readable data.

As the IR market has matured, packages with a special focus have emerged. Two examples worth mentioning in the present context are the personal reference managers such as Pro-Cite, Reference Manager and BIB/Search, and the picture library systems such as Phototracer and Lanslide.

There are many IR packages on the market; over seventy microcomputer-based systems are currently included in *Text*

Retrieval: A Directory of Software (Kimberley 1990) with another thirty for larger computers. To compare their features and hence their suitability to a particular application, it is useful to examine different functions under the following series of headings.

Record structure

Data in a computerised database is held in records, where each record is structured in a similar way. Data in a catalogue database, for example, is normally divided between fields in which particular types of information are stored: title, author, publisher, publication date, pagination, abstract, keywords, shelfmark are all examples of fields likely in the catalogue of a special library. Each field is identified by a field label or tag, such as AU for author, TI for title. Users define their own record structure, which involves specifying how many fields are required and naming them, and specifying how those fields are to be indexed. This freedom in specifying a database makes IR packages suitable for many different types of material, from standard monographs to the many different forms of non-book materials.

The structure of the record very often has implications for the search process so it is important to be aware of how the package retrieves information before finally deciding on record structures: some packages will allow subsequent changes to be made but this often means exporting all the data, making the required changes, and re-importing the data.

Catalogue entries can be unpredictable in terms of sizes of fields and records. To use the bibliographic record as an example, some might have short or long title entries, with or without authors, with or without abstracts, with one or many keywords. Systems which can accommodate variable-length fields and records, and allow fields to be repeated as necessary, are therefore best for handling text data. Some packages, usually at the cheaper end of the market, set limits on the number of characters per field and fields per record which may be too restricting for some applications. Because packages differ in the maximum length of any record they will allow and in the maximum number of fields within a record, it is important to decide in advance of looking at software, how much space will be needed for the average and for the longest record, and in what way the information in each record will be divided into fields. A few packages are similar to the DBMS in that they work with fixed-length fields and records, and store blank spaces if the data does not completely fill the fields or if a field is left blank.

These systems can soon fill up the disk space available, unless a compression program is available to compress the data and remove blank spaces.

The database index

The ability to search for a word or phase anywhere in a record is the prime reason for using an IR package. To achieve this flexibility of searching, the majority of packages use inverted index files, that is, alphabetically sorted index terms which have pointers to where they occur in records. The inverted file index looks very much like a back of the book index. An enquiry is matched against the index terms in the index, and the number of 'hits' or items retrieved is displayed on the screen. The advantage of this type of indexing is that it provides quick searching regardless of database size. The disadvantage is that the index must be created before searching can take place and the index itself may take up considerable disk space, as much as 60–200 per cent of the space of the database, depending on the package and on how much of the record is indexed. Index creation can be time consuming, especially as the database grows. With a single microcomputer system, no other work can continue on the computer while the index is being created so this must be taken into account if the machine is to be used for several applications.

Indexing options

Part of the task of setting up the retrieval system involves deciding which fields are to be added to the index and in what form. Most software packages offer some flexibility in type of indexing and all automatically strip common or 'stop' words, such as 'and', 'of', 'the', 'but', etc., from the text, to avoid unnecessary use of disk space. Some packages allow the user to define their own stop word list.

It is usually possible to decide for each field how the contents will be treated. The exact choice of indexing method varies between packages but the more common options are:

- full field indexing – the whole content of the field is entered into the index (ideal for handling whole titles, dates and other numeric fields);
- full text indexing – where each individual word becomes an index entry;
- tagged indexing – where on input, selected words or phrases can be marked so they are indexed, even if they occur in a field designated for no indexing;
- manual indexing – where the required terms are added by the librarian to a special index-term field;
- no indexing – the field is not indexed. Information in such fields is not necessarily irretrievable, but the 'serial search' techniques used to find unindexed character strings are likely to be very slow, especially as the database grows;

Some packages allow a combination of two or more types of indexing on any one field. For instance, it may be desirable to index the title field both as a single entry and as free text to give improved subject access. As with manual systems, the choices made dictate the flexibility of retrieval and some compromise has to be reached between providing too few and too many paths to a record.

Data input and editing

Inputting data is very time consuming and should not be under-estimated when planning an automated system, especially if existing manual records are to be added to the system. It is important therefore to ensure flexibility of input and editing. Different packages offer different methods: examples are full-formatted screen entry or line-by-line field prompts. Ideally editing should be cursor controlled and offer word-processing-like features. Validation of data entry can be useful and the ability to call up authority files provides a valuable means of controlling data consistency.

If data entry facilities in a package are not very flexible or user friendly, it may be possible to use another more specialised text preparation and editing package: Headset, developed for use with Inmagic and now part of Headfast, can also be used with other IR packages; other data preparation packages such as ScreenMaster permit user-defined screens to be developed.

Alternatively, the package may be designed to accept data in some of the more common word processor formats: Assassin, Extract and Personal Librarian are examples.

After records have been created or edited, most packages require a separate updating process, as described above, actually to index and add the records to the database.

Searching

Searching is usually command driven, menu driven, or both; this third option permitting each individual user to select whichever method is appropriate to his or her own level of expertise. The latest developments in retrieval are concentrating on ease of searching, but command-driven systems, which require the user to know the search language, are still common. Once learnt, however, this method usually has the advantage of speed in specifying the search strategy. On processing the search command, the system should respond with the number of records found to contain the chosen search term(s). Most systems assign set numbers to the different searches and allow the searcher to reuse sets in subsequent search commands. Word, phrases or sets can often be combined together using Boolean logic operands: AND, OR, NOT. Some packages (e.g. Inmagic) require that the field(s) to be searched are specified in the search statement. For some types of search, like an author search, this is quite acceptable, but for a subject enquiry where a global search of the whole record may be needed, it can be rather cumbersome. Other packages (e.g. Assassin-PC) can only search across the whole record. Most flexibility is offered by those packages that cater for both whole record- and field-specific searching. Facilities such as truncation (usually right hand, but more rarely left hand as well), wild card and range searching are made available in different ways. Where the database is to contain a fair amount of full text information, proximity searching is important so that words can be retrieved in context. In general the more expensive packages have more search facilities.

With a 'menu-driven' or prompted system, the searcher is presented with a list of options. The search type is selected and the user then enters the search term(s). The results may be in the form of number of records retrieved with options to start again, refine the search, display or print the records. In some packages the results are displayed on the screen immediately. This type of interface is best for the occasional user, but is often slow for the regular user and rarely allows full use of the search facilities.

User-friendly searching is an area where much development work is underway. The use of windows for browsing through indexes, and the function keys for choosing search and display functions are becoming increasingly common. Expert system techniques are still rare in commercially available packages, although Harwell Computer Power, who market Status have launched Status/IQ, a front end which will accept searches in natural language and then rank the results according to how closely they match the search criteria. Personal Librarian will also give ranked displays, in this case in the form of a bar chart as a pictorial representation of the spread of items relevant to the search strategy.

Thesaurus/authority control

Many information units develop their own thesaurus or authority list to exert some control on the number and range of subject terms and names used in the database. Some of the packages (e.g. Cairs-IMS) offer linked online thesaurus programs to assist in both index creation and searching. A few of the systems assist at the data entry stage by allowing the user to browse through an authority file or thesaurus, select and mark a term which is then lifted into the new record. The systems which offer full document storage and retrieval can often accommodate synonym control. The information manager would need to define the synonyms for a particular term, the system then automatically searches on all terms, which saves the user specifying alternative terms for a search. The ability to display authority files, a thesaurus or at very least, the inverted index files, helps the user choose appropriate terms when entering a search strategy.

Data output

The result of a search can be displayed on the screen, printed on an attached printer, or copied to a file on the disk for further processing or manipulation by another software package (e.g. word processing) or another database system. As a general rule, flexibility of output increases with the price of the system. The cheaper packages may offer only one output with a single level of sorting the records. Others will allow sorting on many different fields to produce author–title listings, subject–date listings, etc. With some packages, there is a special program called a 'report generator' for creating various formats for printing. The fields to be printed can be specified, as can their layout on the page, including the page width and length, print enhancements, additional stored text and headings. User-defined formats can usually be stored on disk for future use: these are often used as the basis for printing off subsets of the database in a variety of different formats for particular purposes, e.g. producing reading lists or a current awareness bulletin. Reports can be written onto a disk for further processing by a word processing package or desk top publishing. Some text retrieval packages offer arithmetic calculations on numeric fields.

Stored searches

The ability to store search strategies for current awareness purposes can be very useful. The stored search can be recalled by a search 'set' number or a label. It can be modified as needs change or limited by date or accession numbers for search database update.

Record import/export

Many of the packages can import files prepared by word processing software or other text editing systems, provided the records have the appropriate field tags and that the files are in an ASCII text format. Data downloaded from a remote database, CD-ROM or diskette data distribution service is another useful source of records for an in-house database. Some packages e.g. Bib/Search, and the more specialist packages, Pro-Cite and Reference Manager, include conversion programs to reformat incoming data into the appropriate data structure for the database. Several packages form part of a suite which caters for the whole procedure of doing an online search, reformatting the data, and loading it into a database for subsequent use: Head Software International's Headline, Headform and Headfast; Personal Bibliographic Software's Pro-Search and Bibliolinks for use with Pro-Cite, are examples.

IR packages for library management

The IR packages offer more facilities for text databases than does the framework of the DBMS, but they do not have library management written as part of the system. Their flexibility is such that the user can add simple housekeeping facilities to them and there is now one library management system based on a microcomputer IR package, Cairs-LMS. Inmagic has a different approach: users have the option of purchasing Biblioguide, a set of formats for library housekeeping routines which individual users can tailor to their own needs. Other packages, LibraryPac and Headfast, have optional circulation modules which may be purchased as add-ons. However, traditionally IR packages have had a number of drawbacks if applied to library housekeeping routines. Many have allowed only batch updating of records and of indexes; even if available as an online option, the index updating (usually re-inverting the whole record) is such that it offers poor performance in a dynamic system where data is constantly changing. Some packages do, however, incorporate a number of features which make them more amenable to use in a housekeeping context. For example, more online data entry and indexing is available, there is provision for linking to other files interactively, and the command-driven interface is being replaced by menu options or more friendly, user-definable interfaces. IR packages are self-evidently most suited to cataloguing and catalogue-related activities, especially if there is a requirement to handle documents, reports or abstracts. They are weakest in the areas of serials check-in and routing, and circulation control in cases where a high volume of loans transactions is involved.

LIBRARY MANAGEMENT SOFTWARE AND SYSTEMS

Library management systems are more commonly referred to as library housekeeping systems. They cover the following functions or application areas: cataloguing of different types of library materials, including catalogue creation, and catalogue enquiry, in hard-copy or online form; acquisitions – this mainly relates to the purchase of monographs; circulation control, providing lending routines; and serials control, including subscription management, check-in, and distribution or routing to users. More recently suppliers have begun to introduce inter-library loans systems and also communications and interface software which permit records from external sources to be imported. The range of applications provided and the number of packages have increased dramatically over the past two years.

The common approach is the integrated library system (ILS): some ILS were developed from the outset as multi-functional systems whereas others have evolved from a single application. Most ILS are modular, so that software for each of the different applications is available separately as well as part of a total system. A small number of applications-specific packages is available, primarily for serials control and inter-library loan.

Functions and facilities provided

The following paragraphs give an overview of the facilities to be expected from the current range of systems.

Cataloguing

This is at the core of most of the systems with the bibliographic record also used to support acquisitions and circulation control. Records will be structured and this is where the special library needs to make its first decisions on what system(s) are going to be suitable. At one extreme will be systems with a relatively basic record, able to accommodate one or two authors, brief title and either subject keywords or a class mark; at the other will be systems using entirely variable-length fields, allowing the user to define his or her own fields and capable of storing larger quantities of text such as abstracts. In between, of course, are many with a mix of basic, fixed-record structure and additional fields offering more flexibility and text-handling capability. The advantages of the brief, fixed approach are the system's immediate usability, easier support and maintenance because it is a standard product, and, often, its relative cheapness. On the negative side, it may not be able to accommodate the information required, particularly if the library has a collection of reports and technical literature. The major advantage of the more flexible approach is just that – flexibility to cover not only standard monograph cataloguing but also to include other types of information files on the system.

As well as offering flexibility in determining the record structure and content, many systems also allow the user to define which fields are to be indexed and the type of indexing to be applied. This typically applies to the generation of keyword indexes.

Data entry is online, usually to formatted screens or, less commonly, in response to field-by-field prompts: suppliers will normally provide default versions of these (so there is limited set-up required by the user) but, depending on the package chosen, there will also be facilities for the user to modify the records and the screens. Editing is screen based, using features such as cursor control, insertion, overtyping etc. – effectively most of the facilities of a word processing package, including in some cases automatic word-wrap at the end of lines. Files and indexes are updated online, either on a record-by-record basis or after a batch of records has been created.

Catalogue enquiry and output

The majority of systems on the market today assume that access to the catalogue will be handled primarily by online enquiry, either by library staff on behalf of the user or by means of an online public access catalogue. It should be said at this point that some systems which are directed towards the special library do not have a public catalogue for the casual, untrained user. Most offer quite complicated and powerful searching, often using commands or functions keys, and requiring some knowledge of the system.

The minimum enquiry supported is author, title and class-mark, in addition to some form of control number. The more basic systems employ phrase indexing from the beginning of the field up to a maximum number of characters, with, therefore, implicit right-hand truncation. The more sophisticated systems have keyword indexes, with words taken from title field(s), subject, abstract, as specified by the library; often there are additional retrieval facilities such as Boolean (usually AND and OR), wild card characters and truncation.

Output is normally on card or print in a variety of sequences and levels of sort, though, again, the extent to which the user can define these will vary from system to system: they will not normally offer the flexibility of output available from the information retrieval software.

Acquisitions

Systems should use the catalogue file and/or allow bibliographic details to be copied from the order file to the catalogue on receipt. Other standard facilities are:

- support for a suppliers' file, so booksellers' data is easily input and retrieved by a simple code;
- ability to handle item costs and totals;
- production of and printing orders, usually in supplier order batches;
- production of chasers and claims notices, possibly as exception reports;
- handling fund allocation and budgets for monies committed and spent;
- fast recording of receipts with use of defaults to reduce keying;
- and a couple of packages have also introduced automatic currency conversion.

Circulation control

Circulation modules maintain borrowers' files with at least one address for mailing and with status information on the borrower. They provide speedy entering of book and borrower, either by keyboarding but increasingly by light pens and barcodes. Online checks are carried out on entitlement, on book and borrower status: these may simply warn or may inhibit the transaction. Once a transaction has been accepted, all files are updated immediately. Overdue notices are printed and some form of reservations control is provided.

Serials control

Serials systems currently available allow the library:

- to record titles with multiple locations;
- to control subscriptions, both costs and renewals, for these copies;
- to check in copies and issues of a title (probably with some element of prediction included in the system);

- to produce claims for missing and overdue issues, to control distribution or routing round borrowers;
- and, in some cases, there are even routines for binding control.

As an alternative to the serials modules which form part of complete library housekeeping packages, serials management systems are now available from many of the subscriptions agents. These often have the benefit of data supplied with the system, but they can be expensive unless the library does a lot of business with the company.

Serials automation is a highly complex area and full automation requires very sophisticated systems employing prediction algorithms, multiple-linked record and copy handling etc. For the small special library which does not have a large number of serials titles, most of the systems represent overkill. There may be other solutions: distribution lists usually require the ability to reproduce lists quickly, to maintain them easily, probably incorporating a global change facility so one name can be replaced in all lists by another as new members of staff arrive. A simple DBMS, or even possibly a word processing package, can solve this without the expense of a full serials package. The same is true of subscription renewal alerts.

The foregoing may read like a library's operational requirements. The functions described are, however, taken strictly from the facilities of the packages in the present market place and, therefore, do relate to what libraries should expect. However, most packages will not provide all the functions in all the areas. Those with special library origins – such as Soutron Library System, BookshelF, CALM – have a stronger emphasis on retrieval and in particular on use of keywords, of Boolean searches and of thesaurus control to subject terms. They also have serials control and routing, though not necessarily binding control. On the debit side, circulation control may often be limited, and not well adapted to the needs of the special library, with perhaps one single overridable loan period, and with severe restrictions on the options to control borrower entitlement and to implement differing borrower categories and privileges. However, recently some packages of this type have introduced 'high level' circulation modules expressly to cater for the needs of the college market.

The integrated systems which have evolved from academic library needs (usually small college) offer more generalised retrieval, often via simple menus, and frequently targeted at known-item searches. On the other hand, circulation control is more parameterised with varying loan periods, with provision for borrower categories to influence loans policies, and with fines control.

Before buying a package, it is obviously advisable to find out as much as possible about the features it offers and how it works in a live situation. Attending a supplier's demonstration is a good way to see a package in depth. To get a feel for a package in a live working situation, it is helpful to visit an existing installation with similar requirements to your own. At the initial stages, it can help to see a range of packages to develop an impression of what you can expect from software of a certain type. The Library Information Technology Centre's series of Introductory Information Packs contains a detailed checklist of functions and system descriptions for those wishing to investigate systems more closely. We offer demonstrations on a consultancy basis to show a representative sample of systems currently on the market. The LITC can be contacted at: South Bank Technopark, 90 London Road, London SE1 6LN (Tel: 071 928 8989 Ext. 2729 Fax: 071 261 1865).

SUPPLIERS OF SYSTEMS FOR SMALLER LIBRARIES

System	Supplier
Access	Dolphin Computer Services, 5 Mercian Close, Watermoor, Cirencester, Gloucestershire, GL7 1LT. Tel. 0285 659291
Advance	Geac Computers, Hollywood Tower, Hollywood Lane, Cribbs Causeway, Bristol, BS10 7TW. Tel. 0272 509003
Alice	Softlink Europe Ltd, 1 Thorncliffe Road, Oxford, OX2 7BA. Tel. 0865 311902
BLS	BLCMP Ltd, Institute of Research & Development, Birmingham Research Park, Vincent Dr, Birmingham, B15 2SQ. Tel. 021 471 1179

BookshelF   Specialist Computer Systems & Software,
                   4th Floor, Goodson Building, Goodson St,
                   Hanley, Stoke-on-Trent, Staffordshire, ST1
                   2AT. Tel. 0782 201201

Cairs-LMS   Leatherhead Food Research Association,
                   Randalls Rd, Leatherhead, Surrey, KT22 7RY.
                   Tel. 0372 376761

CALM   Documedia Systems, 11 Colthrop Way,
                   Thatcham, Newbury, Berkshire, RG13 4LW.
                   Tel. 0635 876800

Diderot/Polybase   Polyphot (UK) Ltd, 56 Queens Gate Terrace,
                   London SW7 5PJ. Tel. 071 6360440

Dynix   Dynix Library Systems Ltd, Quay House,
                   Park Lane, Harefield, Uxbridge, Middlesex,
                   UB9 6NY. Tel. 0895 824091

Heritage   Logical Choice, 3 Newtec Pl, 66–72 Magdalen
                   Rd, Oxford, OX4 1RE. Tel. 0865 200200

Libertas   SLS Ltd, 3/4 York Court, Upper York St,
                   Bristol BS2 8QF. Tel. 0272 420613

LIBMAN   Amtek Computer Systems Ltd, Intersection
                   House, 110–120 Birmingham Rd, West
                   Bromwich, West Midlands, B70 6RX.
                   Tel. 021 525 8903

Librarian   Eurotec Consultants Ltd, 143 Hythe Hill,
                   Colchester, Essex, CO1 2NF. Tel. 0206 572538

LibraryPac   Information Systems Design, 31 Penarth
                   Grove, Coventry CV3 2PH. Tel. 0203 650285

Licon   Floyd–Ratcliffe, 2 The Crescent, Leatherhead,
                   Surrey, KT22 8EE. Tel. 0372 376423

Manager Series   Datatrek UK, Dugard House, Peartree Rd,
                   Colchester CO3 5JX. Tel. 0206 369233

OASIS   Dawson Technology, Cannon House, Park
                   Farm Rd, Folkestone, Kent, CT19 5EE.
                   Tel. 0303 850537

Oracle Libraries	Oracle Corp. UK Ltd, The Oracle Centre, The Ring, Bracknell, Berkshire RG12 1BW. Tel. 0344 860066
PROGEN Library	Limrose Software Ltd, Llay Industrial Estate, Wrexham, Clwyd, LL12 0TU. Tel. 0978 855555
Soutron Library System	Soutron Ltd, Jerome House, Hallam Fields Rd, Ilkestone, Derbyshire, DE7 4AZ. Tel. 0602 441664
Supermax Library System	Dansk Data Elektronik, Great Britain Ltd, 2–4 Oxford Road, Newbury, Berks, RG13 1PA. Tel. 0635 550 909
TECHLIB PLUS	Information Dimensions (UK) Ltd, Centre Point, 103 New Oxford St, London, WC1A 1QT. Tel. 071 497 1403
TINlib	Information Management & Engineering Ltd, 140–142 St John St, London, EC1V 4JT. Tel. 071 253 1177
Unicorn	Sirsi Ltd, Daneway House, Darkes Lane, Potters Bar, Hertfordshire, EN6 1AQ. Tel. 0707 47039
URICA	McDonnell Douglas, Information Systems Ltd, Maylands Park South, Boundary Way, Hemel Hempstead, Hertfordshire, HP2 7HU. Tel. 0442 232424

SUPPLIERS OF SELECTED MICRO-BASED INFORMATION RETRIEVAL PACKAGES

System	Supplier
Assassin-PC	Associated Knowledge Systems, Amen House, Bedale, North Yorks DL5 1XA. Tel. 0677 425101
BIB/Search	Information Automation, Penbryn, Bronant, Aberystwyth, Dyfed, SY23 4TJ. Tel. 097 421 302

BRS/Search	BRS Software Products, 11 Weymouth St, London, W1N 3FG. Tel. 071 580 5271
Cairs-IMS	Leatherhead Food Research Association, Randalls Rd, Leatherhead, Surrey, KT22 7RY. Tel. 0372 376761
Cardbox-Plus	Business Simulations Ltd, 30 St James St, London, SW1A 1HB. Tel. 071 925 0636
CDS/ISIS	Institute of Development Studies, University of Sussex, Falmer, Brighton, BN1 9RE. Tel. 0273 606261
Extract	Software Solutions, 70–72 St Marks Rd, Maidenhead, Berkshire, SL6 6DW. Tel. 0628 781135
Folio Views	Soft Options, Dean Clough, Industrial Park, Halifax, W. Yorks HX3 5AR. Tel. 0422 368612
Headfast	Head Software International, Oxted Mill, Spring Lane, Oxted, Surrey, RH8 9PB. Tel. 0883 717057
Idealist	Blackwell Scientific Publications, Osprey Mead, Oxford OX2 0EL. Tel. 0865 240201
Inmagic	Soutron Ltd, Jerome House, Hallam Fields Rd, Ilkestone, Derbyshire, DE7 4AZ. Tel. 0602 441664
LibraryPac	Information Systems Design, 31 Penarth Grove, Coventry CV3 2PH. Tel. 0203 650285
Personal Librarian	Systematic Upgrade, 58–60 Edward Rd, New Barnet, Hertfordshire, EN4 8AS. Tel. 081 441 9792
Pro-Cite	Personal Bibliographic Software, Woodside, Hinksey Hill, Oxford, OX1 5AU. Tel. 0865 730275

Reference Manager	Silver Platter, 10 Barley Mow Passage, Chiswick, London, W4 4PH. Tel. 081 995 8242
Status/PC	Harwell Computer Power, Curie Ave, Harwell, Oxfordshire, OX11 0QC. Tel. 0235 834606
Strix	Microbel, Institute of Research & Development, Birmingham Research Park, Vincent Drive, Birmingham, B15 2SW. Tel. 021 414 1814
Textmaster	Bytesmiths Ltd, 12 Redden Court Rd, Harold Wood, Essex, RM3 0XA. Tel. 04023 345150
Topic	Verity Inc, European Operations, 5A Surbiton Hill Rd, Surbiton, Surrey KT6 4TW. Tel. 081 3903330

REFERENCES AND FURTHER READING

Kimberley, R. (ed.) (1990) *Text Retrieval: A Directory of Software* (3rd edn) Aldershot: Gower.

Leeves, J. (1990) *Library Systems: A Buyer's Guide* (2nd edn) Aldershot: Gower. This covers large and some small library housekeeping systems.

LITC Information Pack on Information Retrieval.

LITC Information Pack on Library Housekeeping Systems for Smaller Libraries.

The LITC's journal, *VINE*, covers systems suitable for libraries.

Chapter 5

Online searching

Louise Amor, Independent Consultant

Information retrieval has always been an important area of activity for special libraries. Pre-1970s information retrieval was done with the aid of printed abstracts and indexes and could be a cumbersome and time-consuming business. In the 1970s publishers of these abstracts and indexes began to use computers in batch processes to produce the printed copies. It was a comparatively short step from there to make these available in electronic form direct to users and so the era of online searching was born which has so revolutionised much of library and information work.

In essence, online searching means accessing remote databases of information, using a personal computer and the telecommunications network. These databases may be numeric or bibliographic, and can contain, for example, newspaper or journal articles (either in full text or summary form), original market research reports, product information, conference papers, research reports, trade statistics or share prices. This information can be searched and retrieved in a very flexible way, and captured electronically onto a file. It can then be edited with word processing software, if required, and printed according to in-house specifications.

Whereas the earliest databases in common use covered scientific and technical subjects giving access to the literature in these areas (journals, articles, technical reports, conference papers, books) and were mainly of a reference nature (i.e. providing a reference to a source usually accompanied by a summary or abstract), the pattern has changed considerably over the last twenty years. There are now databases covering every subject area and the humanities and social sciences are well covered. There has been a particularly spectacular growth in the area of business databases which are sometimes bibliographic databases but increasingly full text (news items) or numeric (company accounts or statistics).

Most information managers in special libraries will already have experience in online searching but for those who do not or those who are wanting an overview of the area including the latest developments, this chapter looks in detail at online searching. It covers areas such as the reasons for using online databases, what systems are available, hardware, software, costs, how to start an online service and new developments such as CD-ROM.

REASONS FOR THE USE OF ONLINE SYSTEMS

There are a number of reasons to explain the growth of online usage. Among the most significant are:

Single point of access for a wide range of databases

The number and range of databases which are available today is vast and growing rapidly. According to the latest edition of *Computer Readable Databases* (Marcaccio 1991), there are over 5,000 publicly available files world-wide. 33 per cent of these cover business subjects.

If we take the area of company information alone, there are over 100 numeric databases (ie containing company accounts information) accessible through four of the main online services used in the UK, and at least twice as many with textual (i.e. news) information on business and companies.

These statistics are not meant to alarm, but to inspire potential users of online. In practice one might regularly use up to fifty databases, but have access to many more if needed, at no extra cost.

Individual databases are loaded onto a host computer system e.g. the US host Dialog, or Data-Star, the major European system. Some are loaded onto both systems and the implications of this will be discussed later. Each system uses a common command language by which the user can interrogate the system (albeit not the same one, but the principles are generally the same) and this is used to search all that host's databases.

The speed at which new databases are being loaded onto hosts

(Data-Star loaded over fifty files during 1990) means that more and more potentially useful information is appearing online. By signing up with the five most popular hosts, the user has access to almost 1,000 databases.

It would be impossible to have access to such a wide range of information and so many new sources if only hard-copy sources were used. With online, the task is relatively straightforward. It is possible to make rapid use of information which is needed only occasionally and which it would be hard to justify purchasing in hard-copy form.

Timeliness of information

It is essential to have information which is up to date and hard-copy information sources, particularly directories, are out of date before they are published, which is a major disadvantage.

In the news and financial areas some databases are now updated several times a day; the full text of the *Financial Times* is accessible on Profile just after midnight – before the hard-copy version is easily available. This also applies to foreign news sources; the COMLINE database provides early access to the Japanese press, and there are a number of newswire databases on Dialog which are continuously updated. Virtually all online databases have increased their updating speeds in recent years in order to meet the demand for current awareness searching.

Speed of retrieval

Most information managers and librarians work under extreme time pressures. Not only is it essential to have up-to-date information, it is essential to be able to produce it almost instantly at times.

Let us take two typical examples. Ten minutes before a meeting the chairperson wants a profile of a particular company, including all the news about it during the past few days – a task which would be impossible in the time using hard copy sources but relatively easily achievable using online sources.

A manager wants a list of the top ten UK furniture manufacturers, ranked by turnover, together with their profits and return on investment. This type of information can be retrieved in minutes, and adds real value to the service which can be provided.

The availability of online sources provides a sense of security, in that many such requests can be dealt with very quickly when necessary. There are of course some users who will then always leave requests until the last minute, but they have to be quietly educated at a more appropriate time.

Flexibility of search software

The sophistication of search software has improved tremendously in the last few years – this is not to say that it is particularly complicated, but it is extremely flexible.

This means that it is relatively straightforward to go online and retrieve only the information which is required – to be very specific about what is needed, and the form in which it is retrieved. A search strategy, carefully set up before going online, can be executed rapidly.

The result of a search can be printed in a user-defined format, i.e. containing only the fields of information which are required. It can then be output in a particular order – for example, using the Kompass file, companies can be listed by country and within that, ranked by turnover.

Databases can be searched singly, or in user-defined or pre-defined groups. This enables searches to be carried out more quickly. Identical bibliographic references from different databases can then be checked and deduplicated automatically.

Searches in numeric databases (e.g. of company accounts information) can be manipulated into a spreadsheet format instead of a text format, making them more comprehensible to the user.

Alerts or SDIs (the selective dissemination of information) are another useful feature. These are stored searches which can then be run automatically, at an interval specified by the user, in order to provide current awareness on a particular subject. The results of searches can be sent directly to the individual user, by post, or by electronic mail. Most of the main host systems have electronic mail facilities, which can be used to communicate with the host, or other users, and to receive the result of searches which have not been captured online.

Presentation of results integrated with office software

The results of searches can be either printed out while the user is online, or printed from the host computer at night and sent in the post – offline.

Offline is cheaper, in that less time is spent connected to the system, but some databases now charge more for offline than online prints to compensate for this. It is inevitably slower, and usually not very practical. A compromise between the two is to have the results sent to an electronic mailbox, where they are usually received within 24 hours.

The usual practice is for searches to be downloaded, i.e. captured electronically and written to file. With the faster transmission speeds used now, this makes it cost-effective to print the results online. Furthermore, the information is still in electronic form and can be copied into a word processing system for editing. This also applies to searches sent by electronic mail.

This ability to edit searches is a very important advantage of online, but can be easily overlooked. The result of the hard copy search for our chairperson, giving a profile of a company, could look fairly messy, especially when carried out at short notice. It might consist of a number of photocopied pages, some A3 and some A4, plus an Extel or McCarthy card. An extract from a directory may not have been able to be copied at all, and has been handwritten or typed. If the information then needs to be faxed to someone the situation is even worse; it will have to be photocopied onto A4 paper, and this all takes time and resources.

The online user, however, can access a number of databases to obtain the information. The results of these searches can be contained in a single file, which can then be manually edited and annotated, and printed in a house style on good quality paper. The overall effect is highly professional and more acceptable for the user.

In an organisation where many users are not on the same site as the information centre and fax is used extensively, it is therefore possible to provide a better quality service. Online searches can be presented in a uniform manner, but also personalised to reflect the needs of individual users.

However, if searchers are intending to download large amounts of information from online databases it is wise to check the copyright situation with the individual host or database producer. In general, online search results can be downloaded without extra charge if they are for internal use only and will not be kept long term on a computer system.

Other types of manipulation can be carried out with online information. It is possible to use software to reformat biblio-graphic records automatically to a house style, e.g. for an internal bulletin or database. It is also possible to download numeric information directly into a spreadsheet, thus giving even more value to the end user.

AVAILABLE HOSTS AND DATABASES

There are a number of useful sources of information to enable potential users to decide which hosts and databases they need to access.

The quickest way to get a feel for what is available is to scan through a number of directories of online databases available, the best known of which are listed at the end of this chapter.

Some of the sources (e.g. *Directory of Online Databases*) are available online but these are probably best used when trying to identify specific databases rather than to get a general overview of the area.

Professional bodies (Aslib, Library Association, Institute of Information Scientists) are also useful starting points as are exhibitions and conferences. The most important of these is the annual International Online Information Meeting held at Olympia in London each December. This is the online industry's trade fair, and well worth visiting.

The main hosts in use in special libraries are the following:

Dialog

The oldest established host, based in California, has over 300 databases spanning business, science, technology and the humanities. Its bias is towards US sources, but it has many databases with European and Pacific information.

Data-Star

The main European host, which has grown rapidly in recent years, and is the market leader in healthcare and biomedical information, as well as European company information. It has over 200 databases.

FT Profile

Owned by the Financial Times, the system specialises in the news and market research sectors, offering many FT publications, and Euromonitor and Mintel market research.

PFDS

This system has some exclusive databases, mainly in the business sector. It also holds company files and technology databases.

ESA-IRS

This is the Information Retrieval Service of the European Space Agency. Owing to its origins, the emphasis is on databases in the science and technology areas. However, it does also offer a gateway to FT Profile and PFDS. In October 1990 the British Library Science Reference and Information Service took over responsibility for ESA-IRS in the UK from the Department of Trade and Industry.

Textline

The historical database product from Reuters is an extremely valuable service, giving access to over 2,000 individual sources. Its main advantage is that it is very strong in world-wide press and trade journal coverage, mostly full text and mainly exclusive, and also has some original foreign language sources. Recent changes have meant that distribution of Textline has passed to the major hosts such as FT Profile, Dialog and Data-Star, with Reuters retaining editorial control.

All the host systems produce comprehensive information packs about their databases and may also offer free demonstration disks or seminars. It is worth contacting each of the main ones and comparing their coverage.

The greatest overlap of databases occurs between Dialog and Data-Star. It is a good idea to sign up for more than one host as in most cases there is no charge for going online. It is always useful to have an alternative source of information and users often prefer to search a particular file on one host rather than another. The same file can be structured differently on different hosts, and this can be useful.

HARDWARE, SOFTWARE AND OTHER COSTS

Computer terminal

Almost any make of computer terminal should be suitable, as long as it has a serial interface in order to connect it to the modem. A hard disk is preferable, though communications software does not take up a great deal of space (normally less than 1.5 Mb).

A printer which is next to the terminal is important, even though it is better to download search results rather than print them simultaneously. It is also a good idea to have the online search terminal dedicated to that type of work if possible, and set in a relatively quiet area of the information centre. It is often necessary to carry out an online search at very short notice, and this can be disruptive or even impossible if there is only one multi-purpose terminal available.

Modem

The modem physically connects the telephone line to the terminal, and interprets the information sent between the host system and the computer. It can be either external or internal to the computer. There are a number of features which are important to check including:

- autodial so that the logon procedures can be carried out automatically;
- speed. Most searches nowadays are carried out at 1,200 baud which means that data is sent at 120 characters per second. A number of hosts now offer 2,400 baud speeds and it could be useful to have this capability;
- duplex. This refers to the transmission and receipt of data, and is either full or half duplex. Most online services use full duplex, but some operate in half duplex and it is useful to have a modem which can switch between the two.

The host companies can give precise details of the type of equipment needed to access their services. Nowadays it is possible to buy an appropriate modem for around £100–200.

Telephone line

The telephone line should be a direct one, i.e. not going through a switchboard. This may be an extra cost, but it is much safer, as it avoids the risk of having the line cut off during the search. A separate line also enables telephone calls to be made or received while online. This may sound impractical, but it enables the searcher to call a helpdesk while searching, and enables users to contact the searcher. Having a dedicated line also means that it is easier to monitor telecommunications costs.

Communications software

There are many software packages which can be used for online searching. Some common ones are Smartcom, Mirror, Procomm Plus, Crosstalk, Headline, Dialoglink. The prices are usually between £100 and £200, depending on the number of features, although Procomm Plus is a shareware product and costs around £50.

The use of a communications package enables the searcher to logon automatically, with all the passwords, phone numbers and protocols stored in the software. It also allows searches to be set up before going online, and transmitted rapidly once connected instead of typing them in. Also, search results can be downloaded to the PC. These features should be standard in the package, and are essential in order to make full use of online, to minimise the time spent connected to the host and therefore the costs.

It is only fair to warn that there can be a phenomenal waste of time and effort expended in setting up a communications package. It is in theory very simple to set up the software with all the necessary information. However, it usually means that users have to know their way around the package, and unlike other types of software, there are few helplines or training courses available. The software is relatively inexpensive, and therefore not worth supporting, relatively few users purchase it, and the dealers rarely know about online searching. Most of the packages (except Dialoglink and Headline) were designed for file transfer and not online searching and are therefore not quite as straightforward and focused as a beginner needs.

The Library Information Technology Centre provides a very useful service in offering demonstrations of communications packages and it can advise on setting up the software (see end of chapter 4 for details). The hosts will also be helpful but they will not necessarily give detailed instructions for all types of software.

For users who are having trouble setting up the package, and who cannot get free help from their supplier, it is well worth paying for a day or two's consultancy from a software engineer to set up the system and to give guidance on its maintenance. It may be necessary to change passwords etc., or sign up with new hosts which have different technical specifications, and it is important to know how to do this.

The UK Online User Group (UKOLUG), a special interest group of the Institute of Information Scientists, can also help in this area, and it is worth joining it in any case.

Training

It is essential to have proper training for the host systems which are used on a regular basis, and there is a wide range of courses to cater for complete beginners or for users in a particular discipline. A one-day course costs around £100, and all the staff who will be using online need to attend.

All the hosts also offer helplines, and can usually provide the answer to specific search problems. It is also useful to receive training from a database supplier (e.g. Predicasts), if there is regular use of a particular source. A number of independent organisations (e.g. Aslib – The Association for Information Management – and the Polytechnic of North London) also offer online-related training.

Manuals

Manuals cover two areas – the search software used on the host system, and specific databases held on that system. It is useful to have the former for the hosts which are used very heavily, but it is not essential to have the manual for each host. There are quick search guides available and these can be quite adequate.

Similarly, with specific databases, the host will provide information sheets showing record structure, searchable and indexed fields and output options. These can be very informative, but in order to use a database to the full, and especially an expensive one, it is well worth buying the appropriate manual. This particularly applies to the Predicasts series of databases with their detailed codes. These are invaluable to anyone seeking market and business information, and the manual is essential and very well written. Some database providers offer free manuals and search guides.

Search costs

Many potential users of online are worried by the perceived cost of searching, and it can indeed be very expensive. However, much information – especially business information – is expensive to retrieve in any form and accessing it online does not make it more expensive. Rather, it enables more precise, flexible and rapid retrieval to be carried out.

Unnecessary expenditure comes from inefficient use of databases, perhaps by untrained users, or where searches have not been adequately prepared before going online. The pressure of time can make it tempting to go online without doing enough preparation, but this is a very false economy.

There are a number of elements to be taken into account when discussing online costs. It is a very complex area, and much has been written on the subject. Each host system has a different cost structure, but, broadly speaking, there are charges for connecting to the host via a network (often international), for the time spent searching the database and for the amount of information retrieved.

However, there have been some major changes to this time-based charging policy, notably by the Chemical Abstracts database, and the host system ESA-IRS. In these cases, connect time charges have been lowered and output charges raised. This frees users from the need constantly to minimise the time which they spend online, and does not penalise slow or inexperienced searchers. The change is a positive one, but so far other hosts have not made any move towards a new structure.

The different components of costs are as follows:

Network charges

These are the charges for connecting to a host via the international data networks. There are usually a number of different 'routes' into a host – the traditional one is via the national network (e.g. PSS [now part of British Telecom's Global Network

Services] in the UK) and thence on to the host. There is a charge for registration with PSS, and the average cost of using it is around £6 per hour at the 1,200 baud rate. Once a password for PSS has been obtained the network can be used to link up to most of the online services in a variety of countries.

Users can now also access Dialog directly. They do not have to sign up separately with the national network, and the charge is roughly the same as PSS. This service is an advantage but it is not possible to use other hosts on the same network. In any case, it is always useful to sign up with PSS in case of telecommunications problems, even if Dialog is exclusively used.

Up-front charges

The advantage of online searching is that in most cases there are no costs for registering with the host. There is an administration charge for using Dialog, and FT Profile makes a charge which includes a training session, but these are exceptions.

Connect time

This is a charge for the time spent connected to each database, most usefully quoted as price per minute. This varies greatly depending on the type of database, but as an example for business users, on Dialog Dun & Bradstreet's Million Dollar Directory costs US$1.80 per minute while Predicasts Promt, the market information database, costs US$2.10 per minute.

Print charges

There are also charges for the amount of information retrieved while searching. These costs depend on the different elements of the record, e.g. title, abstract, full text, citation. In most cases users can either define their own formats or use predefined ones. As an example, a full record from the Million Dollar Directory costs US$2.40 to print – either on or off line.

Offline prints are still available and can be output to the user's electronic mailbox for faster receipt. This can be a very cost-effective way of using online where there are not severe time pressures for results. However, for most business databases the cost of prints is identical whichever method is used, and other factors determine whether offline would be better.

Staff time

The staff time required to set up and run an online service should never be underestimated. As well as training and familiarisation time, a lot of time is needed simply to investigate new hosts and databases, to administer the services and to keep up to date with developments in this fast-changing area. In order to keep in practice and therefore use the services efficiently, searching needs to be regular – preferably daily.

Most organisations have one trained individual who is responsible for all the online searching and associated operations. In many cases of course this means the information manager, who may often be working alone.

GETTING APPROVAL

The overriding consideration for many information managers is the cost of online searching and the need to get approval for the expenditure.

First, the benefits rather than the costs of online services need to be conveyed to the appropriate authority. The benefits have been outlined already, but it is clear that more and more hard copy sources are now available online and their usefulness is greatly enhanced by this.

Online databases are essential to the information service, providing access to thousands of sources world-wide, and used and paid for as they are required. This can make estimating a fixed budget somewhat difficult, as it is often the case that online usage develops rapidly as users discover what is available to them. However, it also means that the information manager can know what is being spent on each search and look at the value of the information retrieved.

Certainly, some directories can be completely replaced by online – but not straight away. Many people feel alarmed by the disappearance of traditional user-friendly books through which they can browse, and there is still usually a need for these.

Specific types of information which may more easily be

replaced are company accounts, either fiche or hard copy, Extel cards and back copies of newspapers and journals. Factors to be examined are the usage made of these, the existing expense of providing the information through hard copy sources and the possible saving on floor space if such items are no longer needed.

If there is already a PC in the library, it is probably easier to get approval for online services; approval for the capital expenditure on equipment can be more difficult. However, almost any low-cost PC can be used, and the modem and software can be purchased very reasonably. They do not need to be highly sophisticated.

A preliminary budget and trial period should be planned for – say six months over which to try one or two host services and use them regularly. The important thing is for the information manager to have control of the online service and to be able to choose which databases to use and when.

Exact situations where online can be of use should be described, giving specific examples of recent searches, or potential areas of work. There can be very great time savings when using online instead of hard copy sources.

The timeliness of online sources should be stressed, applying it to specific instances when information was needed rapidly but could not be obtained. Highlight which databases could have been used, and also what a difference they could have made to the presentation of results.

The information unit may be using external sources such as information brokers (expensive) or public libraries (time consuming). Use of these might be cut down by offering in-house services instead.

GOING ONLINE – PREPARING TO START

This section is a quick checklist of what needs to be organised:

Equipment

Is the external telephone line in place? Is the communications software properly set up? What is the process for copying downloaded search results into the word processing package?

Passwords

For PSS or other international networks (this can take a few weeks). For the host systems (almost instant). Keep an up-to-date record of all passwords, and keep it secret. Change the password if there is reason to think that it might have been copied, or if the online searcher has left the organisation (just a precaution!).

Manuals

Have the necessary manuals been obtained? Have their contents been filed ready for use?

Training

Have staff attended the relevant training courses?

Environment

Is there space around the terminal to put a manual? Even if the search strategy has been prepared and uploaded, it is useful to have the manual to hand in case of emergency.

Miscellaneous

The searcher must know how to disconnect quickly from the system, or leave it temporarily if they are interrupted by a telephone call. They must also know how to send a break signal to the host system. This is vital if the connection needs to be broken suddenly while still remaining online. This can happen when searchers find that they have asked the system to print some records which are particularly long, or they then find that they do not want to wait and see them all. The break key sequence is usually modem-dependent.

OFFERING THE NEW SERVICE

It is a good idea for the searcher to use online for a week or so until they become familiar with it and are confident enough to offer searches on demand to users. The searches which they practise with may be real enquiries, but they will still want to practise search strategies, downloading and reformatting of the results. A certain amount of free time is given by most of the hosts, and this can be used for trial searches. Alternatively, on Dialog there are many inexpensive practice files with the same structure as their live equivalents.

There is a certain amount of preparation to do when starting to offer online services to users who have very little idea of what to expect. Write a brief paper explaining what online services are and how they can help the information unit to access more types of information. Describe in very practical terms some of the main databases which will be used, but do not give costs at this stage. A cost of X per minute is meaningless to a user who has no idea how many minutes the search might take, and it is impossible to give average costs of searches. Each one needs to be assessed separately.

However, if a company accounts database is going to be used, it could be stated that the full format data (profit and loss, balance sheet, ratios, directors' details etc) costs X, and that could be compared to the cost of a Companies' House search. Stress too, that information can be obtained in a matter of minutes. Similarly, brokers' reports on companies can be costed, and these would normally be much harder to obtain than a set of accounts.

Stress the very wide range of information which can be accessed, both geographically and in terms of subject, and the fact that it is kept up to date.

Send individual copies of the paper to key users, and other departments who perhaps do not use the information unit fully. Invite them to discuss their requirements, and arrange to meet them to follow up the paper.

Carry out the follow-up meetings as soon as possible, and when users have had a chance to read the paper. Even if they say that they have no time to read it, organise a meeting with them anyway to discuss the service.

Think of specific areas of application for different users:

• Would a current awareness service such as daily or weekly headlines on a particular topic be useful?
• Does the organisation need to monitor competitor activity, and how does it do so at present?
• Does the marketing department access market research information effectively?

- Does the organisation need information on the European Single Market regulations?
- Do senior executives, or sales managers have regular meetings with individuals and companies? How do they prepare for these?
- Do sales or marketing departments need target lists of companies meeting certain size or geographical criteria?

There can be a great deal of education required to acquaint users with the latest information sources which are available. In most cases they will not remember much about them, but it is important to raise their level of awareness about online, so that they regard it as a normal part of the information service.

Set a start date for the service, and stick to it. Do not wait to be asked to use online; it should be used like any information source, as it is needed, and funded from the information centre's budget.

However, it is sometimes essential for users to pay for their own online searches when these are particularly expensive, or time consuming to set up. This is a matter of internal policy and common sense.

Certain users often want to carry out searches for themselves, but it is not usually practical to encourage them, at least to start with.

Keep users up to date with developments in online databases. Do this either across the board, with regular update bulletins, or selectively to different users as items of interest appear.

Once a successful online service is established, demand for its products will grow rapidly and new ways to use the information will be found in all areas of the organisation.

KEEPING UP TO DATE

This is not always easy as there are so many new databases and new features appearing all the time. Users should make sure that they are on the mailing list of all the hosts which they use, and receive all their new database sheets. Many individual database providers also have mailing lists and offer search guides and regular newsletters.

The Dialog monthly journal, *Chronolog*, is full of useful information and also available online if users need to search back through it. There are often free offers of search guides, and tips for searching.

Users in the business information area can subscribe to *Online Business Information*. This is a very practical journal, with excellent product reviews. There are a number of other relevant journals; *Information World Review* is particularly good for news of what is happening in the whole area of electronic information.

It is also worth joining UKOLUG (the online user group of the Institute of Information Scientists) which also operates a number of local groups.

If the organisation is an Aslib member, staff can use their library for review articles, directories of databases, journals etc. They also publish an online review journal, *Online Notes*.

Attendance at conferences and exhibitions is also useful for finding out about the latest developments, especially the International Online Information Meeting (IOLIM).

ALTERNATIVES

Finally, there are some alternatives to using the host command language to search online databases. These can be described variously, if not very elegantly, as intelligent front-ends or knowledge gateways. They range from simple menu-driven versions of databases to systems which aim to provide full search support for users who have no previous experience.

Menus are now available on a range of Dialog and Data-Star databases. The connect time charges are the same in most cases, but it is necessarily much slower to search using a menu. It could be argued that menu-based databases are not appropriate for the regular online user who wants to make best use of the system. They are time consuming (which simply costs more) and not specific enough.

Both Dialog and Data-Star have launched end-user services: the Dialog Business and Medical Connections and Data-Star Focus respectively. These offer groups of databases in defined subject areas and a series of menus or prompt screens leading users to the specific information which they require. There is a flat rate connect charge and different output charges depending on the databases used.

For end users who need simple access to only a few databases, and will make regular use of them, it may be worth looking at this type of searching. It would enable them to control their own usage, and free the information manager to do other things. The Dialog Medical Connection has been particularly successful in this respect, with researchers using the system for most of their basic information requirements. The original command language is also available for users who wish to become more proficient.

There are a number of other products which claim to add intelligence to the retrieval software while also making it simple to use, usually through menus. They are designed to allow users to go online without knowing which databases they need; the software then guides them through the system.

These products are not host-specific; they cover broader subject areas, and also frequently co-ordinate administrative tasks for connection to the different hosts which are used.

Infotap, based in Belgium, offers a system called Intelligent Information, which gives access to twelve hosts, using a single search procedure. Direct searching is also available. The Keyword Menus feature helps users to identify the appropriate database.

Some products have offered much more search support than this, but there are a number which were launched with great enthusiasm and are now no longer in operation. It is not possible at present to devise a practical system which can cater for all types of search across a wide range of subjects. The systems which have failed have underestimated the complexity of online searching, and the needs of users.

However, it can be very easy for users to be enthusiastic about doing their own searches, and then find that they are spending far too much money. The whole concept of online then falls into disrepute. But a recent success story has been that of a merchant bank which provided all its executives with personal access to FT Profile (Hamilton 1991). They were trained to use the service, and found it very easy and helpful. It would certainly be easier for end users to access FT Profile than most of the other hosts, but such an experiment needs to be carefully planned, and targeted at appropriate users. The bank in question spent over £60,000 setting up the system.

The managing director of Data-Star was quoted as saying that easy-to-use, menu-driven systems will take a greater share of the online searching market. This is undoubtedly true, but at the moment such systems cannot adequately replace a skilled searcher using a command language.

In the longer term a convergence of the two methods may well come about and at last make online searching more widely available, to the benefit of anyone who needs information. Until then, it is up to the information professionals to make the most of these services.

CD-ROM

The most fundamental alternative to online searching which has emerged over the last few years is CD-ROM.

CD-ROM (Compact Disk-Read Only Memory) is a publishing medium which utilises technology originally designed for CD audio. It is an ideal medium for distributing databases – a database can be loaded onto a master disk and that disk replicated and distributed. It can then be read by a normal PC provided that it is fitted with a CD-ROM drive which can be stand alone or internal.

Understandably, the new technology does not come cheap. A CD-ROM drive will cost in the region of £350 to £750, with a storage capacity of 630 or 560 Mb. Major manufacturers are NEC, Hitachi and Panasonic. A year's subscription to a CD-ROM disk can be anything from a couple of hundred pounds to several thousand pounds.

There are now an increasing number of CD-ROM products available which in some cases are online databases in CD-ROM form (sometimes with enhanced facilities). In other cases they offer alternatives to hard copy sources such as encyclopaedias, and sometimes both.

Among the most common and well-established CD-ROMs are: Medline (medicine), Books in Print, Compendex (engineering), ABI/Inform (management), FAME (company accounts).

The main advantage that CD-ROM offers is its ability to hold a vast quantity of information (about 250,000 pages of text on a single CD-ROM) and the ability to manipulate and retrieve information quickly and flexibly. In this it is very similar to online searching – the difference is that the cost of CD-ROM is a one-off cost and not related to use. Instead of online searching where minutes and money can tick away inexorably without anything very useful being retrieved, once a CD-ROM has been purchased it can be used as many times as required without any extra cost. Interfaces are usually more user-friendly, browsing is easier because it is detached from the pressures of cost and the system can be used effectively by end-users and non-experienced searchers.

The main disadvantages of CD-ROM are the following:
- the cost of disks and drives;
- although they are large capacity, large files cannot be put on the same disk and to do a comprehensive search it may be necessary to use more than one disk;
- they are updated usually monthly or quarterly and are therefore not as up to date as online sources;
- direct access by end users can paradoxically cause problems. These can be problems of access arrangements (only one person at once can use the CD-ROM unless they are networked), security, damage to equipment and training. Despite the relative ease of use, much training and documentation need to be provided and the hidden costs of this can be significant. In the short term it probably outweighs the savings in time brought about through less mediated online searches being carried out by library staff.

Because of these factors CD-ROMs are more suited to some kinds of library than others and their use has been spearheaded in academic libraries. Academic libraries are ideally suited to CD-ROM – they have an extensive stock, usually including a wide range of printed abstracts and indexes; a large number of staff; an existing emphasis on user education; a known and well-educated localised clientele; and pressures on budgets that make it difficult to carry out a large amount of online searching for users.

These assumptions are born out by figures in recent surveys. Of sixty two UK libraries using optical products and responding to a survey carried out by FID (Federation Internationale d'Information et de Documentation), 45 per cent were academic libraries, 31 per cent public, 16 per cent special and 8 per cent government (Chen and Raitt 1990). A British Library survey looked at ninety four libraries using optical products, consisting of academic libraries 50 per cent, public libraries 31 per cent, special libraries 15 per cent and government libraries 4 per cent (Royce *et al.* 1989).

The takeup of CD-ROM in special libraries is at the moment

slow as will be seen from the case studies at the end of this book. The special nature of special libraries means that the disadvantages of CD-ROM often outweigh the advantages, whereas the reverse could be said to be true for academic libraries.

For those information managers in special libraries who are considering the introduction of CD-ROM it may be useful to list the factors they should consider in making a decision:

Frequency of use

Unless CD-ROM covers a subject that is of a constant and high level of interest to the organisation and will therefore be frequently used, the costs of a subscription may be more than the costs of carrying out online searches on the same database. However, an additional factor to be taken into consideration is whether buying the CD-ROM could mean cancelling a hard copy subscription, resulting in a saving of money.

Nature of use

Unless customers of the library are likely to use CD-ROMs themselves on a regular basis the investment may not be worthwhile. Obviously, if most of the users are remote from the library (e.g. company libraries with other sites, professional bodies with a scattered membership) and do not visit in person, CD-ROM is unlikely to be useful (unless networked). Also, if the library's clientele is made up of a large number of infrequent users, they are unlikely to be able to get the best from only occasional use of CD-ROM.

Currency

How vital is it that the information is absolutely up to date? CD-ROMs are updated less frequently than online databases. This is more crucial in some areas (e.g. company information) than others and a possible way round it is to use CD-ROM for historic data and then top it up by obtaining the latest information from an online search.

Historic data

To what extent do users want only current information rather than historic information? If they want to go further back it may be necessary to use more than one disk and do separate searches, which will be irritating for users. Index Medicus, for instance, includes only six months' data on one disk.

Charging

If the library charges for some or all of its services (either re-charging to internal departments or charging for outside use or both) a charging policy for the use of CD-ROM will need to be developed.

Training/user education

Does the library have the resources for training and education in the use of CD-ROM that will be necessary? The resources needed can be considerable and whereas they will be concentrated in the introductory phase, there will be an ongoing need for training for new users and in the use of new CD-ROMs.

FURTHER INFORMATION

Hosts

Data-Star, D-S Marketing Ltd, Plaza Suite, 114 Jermyn St, London SW1Y 6HJ. Tel. 071 930 5503

Dialog Europe, PO Box 188, Oxford OX1 5AX. Tel. 0865 326226

ESA-IRS, British Library Science Reference and Information Service, 25 Southhampton Buildings, Chancery Lane, London WC2A 1AW. Tel. 071 323 7951

FT Profile, PO Box 12, Sunbury-on-Thames TW16 7UD. Tel. 0932 781425

Pergamon Financial Data Services, Paulton House, Shepherdess Walk, London N1 7LB. Tel. 071 490 0049

BT network (PSS), British Telecom Global Network Systems. Tel. 0800 282444

Help/advice/training

UK Online User Group Membership Dept, Institute of
Information Scientists, 44 Museum St, London WC1A 1LY.
Tel. 071 831 8003

Aslib – The Association for Information Management,
Information House, 20–24 Old Street, London EC1V 9AP.
Tel. 071 253 4488

Polytechnic of North London, School of Information Studies,
Ladbroke House, 62–66 Highbury Grove, London N5 2AD.
Tel. 071 753 5155

Database guides

CD-ROM Directory, TFPL Publishing. Annual.
Cox, J. (1991) *Online Building, Construction and Planning Databases*, Aslib.
Cox, J. (1991) *Online Environment Databases*, Aslib.
Desmarais, N. (ed.) (1992) *CD-ROMs in Print 1992: An International Guide*,
    Meckler. (Also available on CD-ROM.)
Directory of Online Databases, Gale Research (previously Cuadra
    Associates). Two issues per annum.
Hanson, T. (1991) *Going Online*, Aslib.
Lyon, E. (1991) *Online Medical Databases*, Aslib.
Marcaccio, K. Y. (ed.) (1991) *Computer-readable Databases* (7th edn) Gale
    Research.
Marchant, P. (1989) *Online Patents and Trademarks Databases*, Aslib.
Nichols, S. J. (1991) *Law Databases*, Aslib.
Online Business Sourcebook, Headland Press. Two issues per annum.
Parker, N. (1991) *Online Management and Marketing Databases*, Aslib.
Parkinson, H. (1991) *Online Business and Company Databases*, Aslib.
Pilkington, S. and Rhodes, R. (1992) *Online Engineering Databases*, Aslib.
Sibley, J.F. (1992) *Online Patents, Trade Marks and Service Mark Databases*,
    Aslib.

Journals

Information World Review, Learned Information. Monthly.
Online Business Information, Headland Press. Monthly.
Online Notes, Aslib, Ten issues per annum.

Journal articles

Bates, J. (1990) 'Hooked on Comms', *PC Magazine*, October: 54–76.
Efthimiadis, E. (1990) 'Online searching aids: a review of front ends,

gateways and other interfaces', *Journal of Documentation*, 46 (3): 218–62.

Eskola, P. and Sormunen, E. (1990) 'Cost comparison of online searching in four hosts: Data-Star, Dialog, ESA-IRS and STN', *Online Review*, 14 (5), October: 303–16.

Hamilton, F. (1991) 'Current awareness at everyone's fingertips', *Information World Review*, May: 14.

Robinson, M. R. (1990) 'Dialog business databases: an informal survey of prices', *Online Review*, 14 (5), October: 318–26.

Reports

Chen, C. and Raitt, D. (1990) *Survey on the Use of Optical Information Products in Libraries and Information Centres in Europe*, FID.

Royce, C. et al. (1989) *CD-ROM: Usage and Prospects*, British Library, R & D Department.

Chapter 6

Relationships with users

Fiona Henderson, Head of Information Services, Norwich and Norfolk Chamber of Commerce and Industry

Previous chapters have concentrated on the design, choice and implementation of IT in special libraries. Implicit in all these should be the underlying philosophy of the special library – to provide a good and comprehensive service to its users. IT is a means to this end and not an end in itself. Unless IT can offer enhanced services to users it is worthless. This chapter concentrates on that all-important aspect – special library users and their relationship to IT. It looks at what benefits and services IT can offer the user, what kind of access should be provided, how IT should be marketed and promoted by the special library and what type and level of training is appropriate.

Decisions in these areas for the special library will depend on the type of organisation and the type of users – and also on the level of IT awareness and use generally within the organisation. The special library does not operate in a vacuum and its introduction of IT and the services offered will to some extent be dependent on how advanced the organisation as a whole is in these areas.

A large proportion of library users are likely to have some familiarity with IT already, although it is difficult to get a real idea of how widespread that might be. Recent EC figures (Information Market 1991), indicate that most workers do not use computers or word processors. Figures for the percentage of workers not using IT were given as:

54%	office employees
55%	mid-level executives
62%	salaried professionals
60%	self-employed professionals
73%	high-level executives

It seems likely that the comments in a Financial Times survey (Bradshaw 1991) are most likely to reflect real usage. The comments centre on the fact that use of office technology is not integrated but planned in a piecemeal fashion. 'Many companies introduce word processors . . . and then the managers believe the task is complete and sit back complacently.' The article goes on to describe some of the piecemeal uses of technology: a printout is obtained from the central database and then this paper product, the printout, is circulated for comment, annotation etc.

This means that if users do have access to, or knowledge of IT, it is quite likely to be of one particular function. There is no reason to suppose that their use of IT will have anything to do with their library or information department. Of course there are flagship organisations where work is being done on integrated systems but these are probably small in number.

Users with some familiarity with IT are likely to have access to client databases and records and perhaps to internally generated technical information databases. The most common uses will be for housekeeping/administrative functions such as word processing and budgeting packages.

It is possible, although not likely, that information personnel have been involved in advising on the setting up of specialist databases such as client databases. This will give them a technology-related link with their users and so they will have some credibility in the area already.

When users visit their information departments they will find IT used in different functions – first of all, in access to external information (either online or on CD-ROM), and second, in access to specialist internal information such as internally generated files, bibliographic records/catalogues and library housekeeping activities such as journal circulation, loans or acquisitions.

BENEFITS OF IT TO USERS

Since most users are likely to be familiar with some uses of IT, information personnel will be able to build on the advantages that users already know about.

Advantages which can be stressed to users include:

* speedy access to information – no more wading through paper copies of Research Index if Textline or Profile are available;

- greatly increased flexibility e.g. more access points; the poss-ibility of combining different criteria, so that users can locate firms in Redditch, with 10–20 employees, making nails;
- remote access so the user does not have to visit the department in person. This is double edged – the department may lose a lot by not actually meeting clients; for example, it might lose the possibility of add-on services;
- round-the-clock-access – the basic systems can function even though the staff have gone home;
- access to much more information – the choice becomes more difficult for the user. Here there is an even greater need for the information specialist to guide the user to the best source. This is where a specialised knowledge of sources and of the organi-sation is essential;
- facilities for reformatting and combining data from different sources without paper shuffling so the users can have their information downloaded and can then work on it at home on their own PCs.

These advantages should produce measurable benefits for the user population.

- Improved access results in more information being available on a pay-as-you-go basis. This means that budgeting can be more precise and that cost can be passed on to the client or to the job in question, if appropriate. Individual pages of market research reports can be downloaded so the user need only pay for the information that he or she really wants. There is no need to buy a complete item where only a few pages are needed.
- Information should be more up to date. Real-time data can be provided and there should be no need to make do with an old annual report if a newer one has been filed – nobody can walk off with an online database! Therefore, users are more likely to find that the information they need is actually retrievable.
- Regular products can be created much more cheaply and effec-tively. For instance, a regular search on competitor names can be run every day across the press of different countries. Updates of new sources of information in a particular field can be automatically produced for interested departments.
- Specialised internal databases on competitors or on perfor-mance of the company's own products can be built up. Users

can combine data sets to produce their own analysis, so information becomes more flexible to use and can be fitted to individual requirements.

ADVANTAGES OF IT FOR INFORMATION STAFF

An integrated use of IT offers staff opportunities to develop their role and range of services in relation to their users. If time-consuming but routine jobs can be automated then staff should have more time for development. For example:

* The possibility of developing the analysis and interpretation function and of becoming specialist in their subject areas rather than being seen as curators. Where there is a team it should be possible to develop particular areas of expertise – e.g. competitor information, local information.
* Allied to the previous paragraph, the possibility of improved status. IT can be used to enhance the image as well as the actuality of the department.
* A new marketing opportunity. Often information staff feel they need a reason to go out and see their clients. A new service, or an old service which has a new angle because of an IT development, can provide a very good reason for some marketing approaches. Proactive departments will probably be doing this already, in the form of a personal meeting or via an inhouse magazine or newsletter.
* An opportunity for feedback. In the same way as it can be used for a marketing opportunity, IT can be used to obtain feedback from users. Indeed an effective department will have some organised feedback system as well as making use of less formal opportunities.
* An opportunity to link in with other departments which have information that users need. This is also an opening for forming new alliances and groupings and another way of emphasising the place of information as a corporate resource.
* Improved links with computer departments – this is very important if systems are to work well for the benefit of users rather than for the benefit of system designers. It is sometimes possible for information staff to build on this relationship and to offer themselves as a link between the technical areas of their parent organisation and the end-users.

POSSIBLE DISADVANTAGES OF IT FOR INFORMATION STAFF

However, it would be foolhardy to claim that IT can only bring benefits to users and to information staff in their relationship with users. Among the possible problem areas are:

- Unreasonably high expectations – there is nothing quite like disillusioned users who have had an enormous build-up on what the information department can do for them only to find that budget cuts means that their own questions cannot be answered. It is important that publicity to users keeps services in perspective and a lateral-thinking information person should be able to think of alternative strategies for answering the question. It may be a question of a special project which will need to be set up or it may be best answered by briefing the department concerned. Often user groups are not aware of the implications of their query and, of course, it may turn into a completely different query once it has been discussed!
- Inadequate budget – if a department has to make cuts but at the same time sees that it is essential that it introduces new services to stay ahead of the competition, then it is important to review the whole basis of the department. For example, how important are the housekeeping tasks? Should users be persuaded to take these into their own departments? There is no reason why a library or information department should have a monopoly of expertise on journal circulation, for example. So why not put it out to the users to deal with?
- Danger of being made to fit in with the firm's IT strategy rather than sensible decision-making as to what is best for the department. In this case the department will have to build on the alliances previously made and rally its users.

STRATEGIC IMPLICATIONS: INTERMEDIARIES AND END-USERS

The argument about intermediaries versus end-users has been going on for some considerable time and shows no sign of abating, although the ground is shifting all the time with the introduction of new technologies such as CD-ROM. The basic argument is: to what extent is it practical or even advisable for users of library systems to carry out their own searching of databases (internal or external)? Should this be encouraged or should it be done by information staff acting as intermediaries?

While there has been some shift towards more end-user searching in the past few years, the practice varies greatly from organisation to organisation, often depending on the type of organisation.

Organisations with sizeable research departments or with technical or manufacturing products that require a lot of research and development seem to be much more amenable to end-use. Professional service organisations, on the other hand, are not devotees of end-user searching. In these firms the predominant culture is that of fee-based advice, time is charged out by the hour and it is likely that information personnel are also income-generating and so seen to some extent as fee-earners. In this situation one of the deciding factors is the most cost-effective way of doing a task. So if it is seen as more cost effective for an information professional to carry out some research involving online searching it is likely that the decision will be made on a cost basis.

The perception is likely to be that end-users are not information professionals, their job is elsewhere and they do not have the time or interest to devote to learning about databases and how to search them effectively. The time to keep up to date with new developments and facilities is hard to find for information people so end-users are even more unlikely to be able to spare the time.

There is room for discussion as to whether or not this state of affairs is nurtured by the information professionals in these firms and how the situation may change. It may well be that the idea of information access has not been well marketed or that the marketing was not appropriate.

The recession has curtailed end-user searching of online but has encouraged end-user searching of CD-ROM products. It could be argued that this will give users valuable experience of searching that they will be able to transfer to online. But this may depend on how the users are trained – if they tend to develop their search strategy while actually in the system, rather than preparing the strategy beforehand, they could have developed some bad habits. It is really too soon to tell what effect this kind of learning will have on online use.

Researchers will often be used to looking for information

themselves and will have an in-depth knowledge of their field. This should make them good candidates for online searching because they will be familiar with the terms used and the way that their particular source talks about their subject. This will not necessarily guarantee a good online searcher. We must all know people who have a good grasp of their chosen field but who cannot transfer this knowledge to an online search. Like most information and library skills, it is assumed that online searching is easy to learn and that anyone can do it. This is what database hosts would like us to believe but this is not how the process really works.

For successful online searching it is important to know how the selected source or sources will express that idea that the user is interested in. Some searches are relatively straightforward, depending on the reliability and the indexing policy of the host. Company names, for example, should not present a problem. More complex questions, such as searching for material on demographic trends, can be very difficult. These require analysis and lateral thinking on the part of the searcher. They also require some persistence and knowledge as to whether the information sought is likely to be available or not. We must all have seen end-users give up with a search that we are sure could have been run successfully with a little fine tuning.

So this area of end-user searching is still up for debate. It could be argued that end users are not being paid to keep up to date with new sources and new search facilities. Information professionals are being paid for this activity. We are also being paid to make informed decisions about which databases to use in which circumstances and, indeed, whether or not an online search is the most suitable answer to a query.

It is perhaps significant that some early attempts at maximising end-user access in the UK have not done well. The Institute of Chartered Accountants in England and Wales (ICAEW) introduced a gateway to several major hosts in 1975. This was intended to give accountants, particularly those in smaller firms, the access to information that personnel in larger firms already had. At the time of writing it seems that this gateway is now defunct. Cost has been cited as one of the main reasons for non-use. The ICAEW felt that it was too easy for users to run up a large bill without realising what was happening and without retrieving any useful information. Often staff time on research can be written off – but a bill from an online host cannot!

TRAINING

However, in all organisations there are going to be some keen would-be end-users. The information department needs to cultivate this group and to train them well. Resources need to be allocated both in terms of money and staff time.

Departments need to decide whether to run training courses themselves or whether to use the hosts. Usually an internal course is best because it can be tailored to meet the needs of the participants and their organisation. It will also help the Information department to develop their relationship with the users and get a better idea of their information needs.

If the organisation has internal systems that are compatible with those used by the information department then it may be helpful to integrate the training on both internal and external systems. Like all training, this will take more time to plan than can possibly be imagined. It may be that information personnel decide that there will be too much to cram into the time available. In this case a regular training programme may be required with different sessions for different kinds of information.

When identifying likely pilot groups, the information department should be able to identify some sections which would find training particularly useful and would be able to put it into practice quickly. It would be helpful to involve someone from the target department early on so that they can participate in the planning stages. This should help the information department to develop a user perspective which will be useful both for planning the course and for writing the course documentation.

MARKETING THE SERVICE

Any new facilities or services give information personnel an opportunity to go and talk to users about the new service being introduced in addition to other services. Information staff can use this to review their users' knowledge and awareness of the department's services in general.

The department will need to decide whether or not it is going to market IT in the information department as a separate area or whether it is going to form part of an integrated marketing plan. It is probably better to market an integrated service although it can be useful to have a new IT-related service as an introduction.

The best marketing methods are the face-to-face ones. During a presentation information staff can adapt the subject matter if they need to and have the option of following up on current topics of interest or on a particular line of questioning.

Other methods can be useful as a back-up, e.g. for people who never seem to have time to come to a presentation. So the information department could make a video or send out some direct mail with an option to arrange a personal visit if necessary.

The marketing strategy needs to be tailored to the needs of the target groups and should be carefully paced. A pilot is useful to test the content of the presentation/letter/brochure or whatever is being used. The organisation's marketing department might be a good place to start as well as being an obvious user group.

When marketing an IT-related service or any other information service it is important to make the content of the presentation as real as possible. So the presentation should include some 'real' information which will be of relevance to the group being addressed. It is particularly easy when talking about an IT-related service to become fascinated by the technical details – it is equally easy for a user group to find these same details extraordinarily boring! For most users the technicalities of service delivery are not nearly as important as the benefits to them.

REFERENCES

Bradshaw, D. (1991) 'Need for an overall plan', *Financial Times* (Survey on Office Technology) 8th October: i.
Information Market (1991) 67, July–August.

Part II

Case studies

Chapter 7

The use of computers in the Information Services Unit at the British Gas Management Centre

Russell Gain, Support Services Manager, British Gas Management Centre

The British Gas Management Centre (BGMC) consists of two residential training centres, one located near Stratford-upon-Avon, and the other at Burcot-on-Thames, near Oxford. The purpose of the centre is to contribute to the improved management of British Gas plc, the sixth largest company in the UK. This it does largely by designing and running a range of training programmes for senior managers of the company. The Information Services Unit (ISU) is an essential part of the centre's resources, providing an information service to the tutorial staff of the centre and to course participants. In addition the unit acts as a central information source on management for the whole of British Gas, and its stock and services are available to all British Gas managers, many of whom use it as a source of business information relating to current projects, and as a resource for continued self-development.

The stock of the unit covers all aspects of management and business information, as well as an extensive section on energy and information relating to British Gas itself. As well as books and journals the unit uses a wide range of audio-visual material including interactive video.

PLANNING FOR IT

Part of my brief on taking up the post of information officer in October 1985 was to examine ways in which the unit could make wider and better use of information technology. The situation on my arrival was that while some use was being made of computers, there was little or no integration between the various areas of work which was being done. A Commodore Pet microcomputer was being used to produce lists of some categories of library material. This machine was situated in the ISU and was also used by course members for computer familiarisation (this was at the time when every self-respecting manager thought that they would have to learn to program computers if they were to survive the 1980s). More complex word processing was carried out on a Philips machine at the opposite end of the building to the ISU. Some online searching was being done using a Northern Telecom Displayphone – a neat little device, but with no storage memory for downloading.

There were clearly good reasons for developing our use of IT and trying to achieve greater integration between our various systems. Having worked with an internal computer database in my previous job, I knew that replacing our conventional card catalogue with a computer database would mean less time spent on catalogue maintenance, more thorough indexing and better use of our stock. With little prospect of additional staff recruitment, and with an increasing workload, we also needed to get better control of routine tasks such as stock ordering, overdues, and keeping accounting, borrower and loan records, all of which were being done manually with varying levels of efficiency. To get the full benefits from online searching we needed to download information and to be able to word process the results, and perhaps add them to our own databases. Finally, all ISU computer applications needed to be concentrated in the ISU itself, not carried out in some remote part of the building well away from our customers.

All this was important not only in relation to our own efficiency, but as a part of the image of the BGMC, which in trying to instil the best management practice cannot afford to be seen using antiquated techniques, especially in a company like British Gas which is constantly seeking greater productivity through technical advances. Total integration of all our computer applications – databases, library housekeeping, word processing, spreadsheets, communications, mailing list was not, and is probably still not, a practical possibility. However, an integrated library-management package could bring together our two biggest applications – database and library housekeeping, and it was therefore decided to look for such a system to form the basis of our IT plan. Our intention was to run the system on a network of terminals, allowing both staff and customers access to it.

My predecessor at the BGMC had already drawn up a detailed specification of what the ISU would require from computer software. Such specifications can be a useful guide when it comes to software choice, although certain points must be born in mind when formulating them. First, you must think about your services and your hopes for their future development from scratch. Do not just write a specification to automate your existing systems, think about how automation might improve and increase the services you offer. Second, once you have a specification, unless you are having software custom-written, beware of allowing it to become a strait-jacket which too rigidly limits your flexibility of choice. By all means use your specification as a guide-line, especially in areas that you regard as key to your require- ments. But if you are looking at off-the-shelf packages you will not find one which satisfies every detail of your specification. The trick is to find the one which most closely fits your needs, and then to make the most of it.

We did briefly give consideration to having software written in-house, but it soon became apparent that this option would be more expensive, much more time-consuming, and unlikely to lead to a successful result. A library-management package is a complex piece of software, and very few systems people have sufficient grasp of the concepts involved to write such a package.

So, the search was on for a suitable off-the-shelf package. As every expert will tell you, the right way to proceed in such a situation is to look for software first and then to find a machine to run it on. Sound advice, but corporate life is not often that simple. The number of organisations today who are starting computing with a completely clean sheet must be few indeed, and not many information departments have the power, or would find it advisable, to go outside hardware guidelines set by their companies. In the case of the BGMC at that time, we were committed to using IBM or IBM-compatible equipment. Even more limiting, the ISU already had an IBM PC XT which had been bought as part of a package to form the basis of our automation set-up. Fortunately, as I will describe, this limitation was later overtaken by events, but it could have been a considerable block on the route to a successful project.

With this in mind I started to attend exhibitions, conferences and demonstrations in order to survey the market. Having already been through one library automation project in my previous job, and having kept reasonably up to date with new developments, I already had some idea of what was available.

The necessity of working in an IBM environment and initially on an XT excluded some packages, but still gave us a reasonable choice. Among the packages examined in some detail were CALM, Inmagic, Ocelot, TINlib and Soutron. In each case we were looking not only at facilities offered and user-friendliness (the plan was eventually to make the system available to tutors and course members, so ease of use was important), but also the sort of maintenance and support which would be available, what future development of the system was likely to take place, and what sort of training was given. These latter factors can often only be judged from your subjective impressions of the suppliers, aided of course by contacts with libraries who are already using their products. We were fortunate that price was not an overriding factor in our purchase decision, providing very clear benefits for the BGMC could be identified.

Eventually, after several months of work, numerous demonstrations and consultation with existing users we decided to go for the Soutron Library System, which had been introduced to the UK from Canada some months previously. As with most software decisions there was a certain amount of risk in making the choice. Soutron was new on the market at that time, and its existing customers were all in the fairly early stages of working with it. Nevertheless, initial reports were favourable and we were particularly impressed by the range of facilities offered – the software seemed to have been written by people who understood information work and had allowed for most situations which are likely to arise in the library. The database part of Library System was also very powerful, quick to search and easy to use, and the built-in thesaurus control for subject headings and other authorities was impressive. At just this time, we also discovered that a group of librarians in British Gas's Research and Technology division had been carrying out similar investigations and (to my great relief) had come to the same conclusion with regard to software.

MAKING A CASE TO MANAGEMENT

The next step was to justify the purchase to my own management. Naturally, I had been preparing the ground for such a proposal for some time, in meetings and conversations, so it was only a question of bringing the arguments, facts and figures together into a formal document. This began with a summary of my proposal, followed by some background on the need for automation – increasing workload, the need for higher productivity, and the possibility of improving levels of service.

I then went through each part of our work which would be affected by computerisation, outlining the weaknesses of the existing system and the expected benefits of automation. The main expected benefits were as follows:

Cataloguing

- More thorough indexing and more flexible searching;
- Once-only data entry, no laborious cross referencing;
- No misfiling;
- Easier, quicker production of bibliographies, additions list etc.

Acquisitions

- Easier chasing and claiming of overdue orders;
- Integration of catalogue and orders records;
- Automatic compilation of accounting information, leading to better budgetary control and more management information.

Circulation

- Flexible loan periods with fuller control;
- Quicker, easier production of overdues, therefore more intensive use of stock;
- Fuller borrower information available;
- Search of database would reveal loan status;
- Automatic production of statistics.

As a very small unit in staff terms (consisting of myself and one assistant) we did not have the clerical time available to ensure that our manual systems were always fully effective, so the benefits of automation were probably proportionately greater than for a unit with an army of library assistants. This was followed by a brief explanation of the reasons for preferring Soutron to other systems, and then a full breakdown of the anticipated costs over the following three years.

While being as clear as possible about the areas of improved efficiency and enhanced services, I was careful not to make any specific statements about savings in time and money which might result, knowing that such benefits might only accrue after quite a lengthy implementation period.

Most of the discussion of the proposal revolved around cost/benefits. Management was used to the idea of microcomputer software costing a few hundred pounds, but needed some persuasion that the complexity of a library system justified expenditure of £6,000 on software alone.

IMPLEMENTATION

Authorisation for purchase was duly given however, after which the proposal had to be approved by staff at British Gas's London Computing Centre. After consulting with them we agreed that it would be better to install the software and build up the system on a single machine first, moving to a network later, when any initial problems had been overcome.

The software was installed first on our IBM PC XT, our plan being to add a small number of records to the database, and then to carry out tests and familiarise ourselves with the various parts of the software before starting the full implementation. We learnt a tremendous amount during this stage, being able to make mistakes and experiment with various ways of setting up our system, without committing ourselves irretrievably. Indeed, there is much to be said for keeping such a test system indefinitely in order to test ideas without affecting your main system files.

At around this time both my assistant and myself attended the one-week training course provided by Soutron Ltd as part of the purchase price of the software. It is impossible to overstress the importance of training in ensuring successful implementation, and fortunately the training in this case was well carried out, taking place at Soutron's offices, well away from the interruptions of normal work.

One slightly disturbing by-product of the training course was that it was obvious that the software was running much more slowly on our PC than on the Novell network in Soutron's offices. This would have been corrected in any case when new hardware was installed for our network, but fortunately external circumstances came to our aid even sooner.

It had been decided that the BGMC was to absorb a smaller library which had been located at the company's HQ Training Department. Fortunately, I had made clear in my report to management that the PC XT would limit us to a database size of about 7,000 records, and this merger took us well above that figure. I was therefore able to justify the purchase of a new Olivetti M28 with 1 Mb of RAM, a 40 Mb hard disk and a built-in tape streamer for backup. This machine gave us substantially quicker performance. The Soutron software was installed on this machine, and we began building up the system in its final form. It was now January 1987.

It was only some months after this that the one major error in our planning became apparent: it was taking much longer than anticipated to add all our catalogue data to the database. In order to minimise costs in the original proposal I had undertaken that we would ourselves carry out all the data entry from the keyboard, allowing only for one additional temporary member of staff for three months to help with this task. All new material was being added from the acquisitions module at the time of ordering, but progress with the retrospective cataloguing progress was proving slow. Some librarians, especially those working in fast-moving subject areas, have avoided retrospective cataloguing altogether, perhaps wisely. I felt that it was necessary for our collection and in retrospect feel that I should have found some way of automating the process, perhaps using Soutron's MARC interface to read MARC records into the library system format. Having already persuaded management to part with more money than they really wanted to for library automation, it was impossible to ask for supplementary expenditure so soon. It eventually took until mid-1988 to complete the retrospective cataloguing.

The software itself worked very much as anticipated, with no unpleasant surprises. Naturally there were a few problems in the early stages, caused mainly by our own lack of experience with the system. Most problems were sorted out over the telephone helpline, which was generally satisfactory, though not always as speedy as we would have wished. Only one problem caused us real difficulty – an inability to get the software to print certain reports in the correct format. This took some time to resolve, and eventually necessitated reloading the software to achieve the right result. All in all, however, I feel we made the right choice of software for our particular situation, and five years later I still hold to that view.

IMPACT OF IT

Our administrative procedures have been completely transformed by the new system. I do not propose to give a fully detailed description of the software, as this is available from the supplier; but I will describe some of the basic features as they have affected our daily operations. The card catalogue has been replaced by a computer database. Instead of being searchable only by author or class mark it can now be searched via a whole range of keys. These can be combined using Boolean operators ('AND', 'OR'). Searching is very quick, comparing favourably with the speed of external online databases.

Most items are added to the database at the ordering stage via the acquisitions module, further details being added once the item arrives and is classified. Items on order appear on the main database with their status clearly marked. There is a fixed format for records, which we find adapts quite easily to our type of stock. Field labels can be changed but the order and length of fields is fixed. Authorities, i.e. authors, corporate authors, series title, conference title, subject headings are added at the cataloguing stage, terms being selected from an online thesaurus for each category. This lengthens the cataloguing process slightly but ensures good control of the use of subject terms, forms of authors' names and so on. Number of copies at various locations can be shown on the one record. The system prints labels for each item for use on spine, book card and the item itself.

The acquisitions module holds a database of suppliers' details. It prints orders, will print claim letters on request for those items which have passed their anticipated arrival date, and will interact with the circulation module to earmark items on order for certain customers. The system keeps all our accounting records, broken down by category of stock and various expenditure codes. Our accounting is simple, as none of our expenditure is recharged to customers or other departments, so we only scratch the surface of what the system is capable of in this area.

The circulation module holds a database of all our customers' names and addresses. We still use our old self-service system for short-term loans within the centre, but longer loans and all loans outside the centre are recorded on the computer by entering borrower and accession codes from the keyboard. A barcoding facility is available, but the volume of our loans does not justify using such a system. Overdue notices are printed on request, laid out for use with window envelopes. In just this one instance, a process which used to take several days can now be completed in a couple of hours.

BENEFITS FOR USERS

So what does this mean to our customers? It is all very well to make existing procedures much more efficient, which is generally the aim of initial computerisation. This has certainly been achieved. It might be seen as the equivalent of a large company automating its accounting procedures in the 1960s. Thinking on the application of IT has now moved on however. The aim for the 1990s is to achieve competitive advantage through IT, i.e. to make a real impact on service to the customer.

The majority of small special libraries were passed over by the first wave of library automation, mainly because the technology at that time was not economic for small-scale applications. It was only with the advent of compact and powerful microcomputers in the mid-1980s that the application of IT in the small special library became a practical possibility. This was a great opportunity, but as people's expectation of what could be achieved by IT had moved on, we really needed to make in one step the progress which had taken the rest of industry up to thirty years of development. How have we fared by this criterion?

The customer coming into the ISU today and making any enquiry about the stock now has a much better chance of getting a satisfactory answer, especially in cases where he or she only has incomplete information about what they want, e.g. only part of a title. The customer also gets more information (Is the item on loan? When is it due back?) much more quickly, and can have a printout of any search of the database within seconds. Areas of our stock which were only indexed in a rudimentary fashion previously, such as our collection of papers and reports, are now fully accessible to customers via the database.

Customers are also better informed about additions to the stock. We had always produced an additions list, but the production of it has now been automated, and the time needed to produce it substantially reduced; we now produce an additional, more frequent update for use within the centre, highlighting new stock which is of particular interest to BGMC staff. We produce a whole range of reading lists on management topics, which are produced from a combination of online databases and our own resources. These are now indexed on the database and kept on a word processor for easy updating.

The use of online databases is the subject of other chapters in this book, and therefore I do not propose to say much about them here. It is sufficient to say that online databases make a vital contribution to our information service, and it is difficult now to imagine operating without them. The use of online databases in conjunction with word processing has allowed us to:

• widen vastly the range of resources which we can access; and
• present that information in a much more professional manner.

Most of our online search results are downloaded to files on our own computers. These files are then called up on Wordstar (though not the most sophisticated word processing program, Wordstar has the advantage that it will accept files in most formats). We then add headings and explanatory notes and remove unwanted records and codes which will be unintelligible to the customer. We may then add material from our own database, or photocopies of key articles from our own stock, the end product being a package with much more added value than a standard online printout.

Additionally, value can be added at the delivery stage by the use of electronic mail. For some time Telecom Gold was used quite widely within British Gas and customers would ask for search results to be delivered to their electronic mailbox. Because Telecom Gold is based on what might be termed lowest-common-denominator technology, there was usually no problem in it accepting online files and transmitting them. British Gas, however, is now in the process of installing a company-wide network based on DEC equipment and All-in-1 software, including electronic mail, word processing, diary management, spreadsheets, graphics and other office automation facilities. Interfacing the online files with this more advanced software has proved more difficult, but will no doubt be possible in due course. In other cases, where urgent delivery is required, facsimile machines can also be useful, though they are laborious for long documents, and not suitable where high-quality printed output is required.

In February 1988, as had always been our eventual intention, we moved the system onto a network of three terminals with a dedicated file server. This allows simultaneous use of the system by myself and my assistant with one terminal still available to tutors and course members. I saw demonstrations of three networking systems, but as Novell Ethernet software was recommended at that time by both Soutron and British Gas, the decision was not a difficult one. The network, using an Olivetti M380 file server with two Olivetti terminals and one IBM PC, was installed by Soutron and has been largely trouble free. It has also further improved the system's operating speed, the Novell software allowing more efficient use of the computer's RAM than in stand-alone mode.

About a year after this, British Gas carried out a major review of its management training, and a new Management Training Framework was introduced which resulted in an approximate doubling of the amount of training which the centre had to carry out. To enable us to do this, the BGMC was allocated a second residential centre located at Burcot-on-Thames, near Oxford. Although this had previously been operating as a training centre, the building needed re-equipping in many areas, and library facilities had to be provided from scratch. It was decided to set up and staff a small satellite library which, as far as possible, would be able to link and share resources with the more extensive Information Services Unit at Stratford, fifty miles distant. Part of the solution to this problem was to provide a PC in the ISU at Burcot which is linked to the Novell network via a dedicated telephone line (private circuit) to the file server at Stratford. This is done by connecting a small diskless workstation to the network which acts as a communications server. This and the PC at Burcot both run Carbon Copy software and are each connected to a Dowty Quattro modem. The result is that after logging on through the Carbon Copy software, the PC at Burcot will act exactly the same as the terminals in the ISU at Stratford. Performance is slightly slower, but not sufficiently to be inconvenient. With this facility, and with the extensive use of electronic mail, telephone and fax we have been able to minimise the duplication of materials at the two centres. The two sites share a single database which shows the location of each individual copy of an item. Any operation which can be carried out on the network at Stratford can also be carried out at Burcot.

All the PCs on the network are able to run other software apart from the library program. We use both Wordstar and WPS+ (a DEC product) for word processing. The printed output from Soutron, while adequate for basic bibliographies and catalogues, is not very flexible, so we usually spool files to be printed and tidy them up on the word processor before printing. Other software used includes Dbase III+ for our publications mailing list, Lotus 1-2-3 for recording and manipulating our statistics, and Aldus Pagemaker for desktop publishing of guides and other documents. The network is linked to a Hewlett Packard laser printer which gives a high-quality printed output when hard copy is needed.

FUTURE DEVELOPMENT

While the major part of our computerisation is now complete, there are plenty of areas for continuing development. We have been assessing CD-ROM for some time but have not yet found an economic application for it. We do not use any one database to such an extent that using CD-ROM would ever be cheaper than online charges, and as many of our customers are at the end of a telephone line, the ability of CD-ROM to give access to databases for very large numbers of users for a known price is not a major consideration.

The advent of the company-wide network offers many opportunities, but serves to illustrate of one of the main problems we will face in developing our systems further. E-mail gives us the ability to deliver information to the user's desk very quickly and in a form which allows the customers to carry out further work or manipulation of the data themselves on their own PCs. Nearly all the staff of the centre now have a terminal on their desk, so we will soon be able to give them direct access to our database from their own office. After that we will aim to give remote access to BG users nationwide and even overseas. CD-ROM may find a role here in giving direct access to databases for large numbers of users across the network. The principle behind any future developments will be to provide an increased range and level of service to customers without a commensurate increase in costs, which has been the reasoning behind all our computer developments from the beginning.

The problem that I referred to is basically one of compatibility. The new DEC-based company network is not compatible with our current Novell network; a way will have to be found of bridging between the two networks. The new company-standard word processor is not good at handling online files without complicated reformatting. As other new technical developments come along, they too will probably have hardware or software limitations which will make it less than straightforward to graft them on to existing systems. There will be technical solutions to all these problems, and eventually the best solution will be to completely redevelop the library system and start again. We certainly have not reached that point yet, and I would not expect to do so for some years. But the challenge for the rest of the decade will be to carry on extending the capabilities of the system, while maintaining a reasonable level of compatibility between its different parts.

Chapter 8

Developing a computer system for an NHS hospital library

Ian King, Librarian, Bradford Royal Infirmary

This case study is based on experiences in automating the library service at Bradford Royal Infirmary. I shall begin with a brief outline of the structure and background to the project and then proceed to a description and evaluation of the system as it stands today.

There has been a Medical Library at Bradford Royal Infirmary for many years and we have a collection of books dating back to 1658 and journals such as *The Lancet* dating back to the 1800s. However, when I was appointed in October 1977 I was the service's first professional librarian and it was necessary to reorganise the library from top to bottom. The service is now organised on District Health Authority-wide multidisciplinary lines, with two major libraries and two smaller collections which we call satellite libraries. The largest library is at the Bradford Royal Infirmary (BRI) and serves as the district's major resource for clinical and management information, while the other main one is based in the Airedale and Bradford College of Nursing and Midwifery at St Luke's Hospital. Both of these are staffed by a professional librarian and there is a further half-time 'peripatetic' professional and three clerical assistants (working for a total of 24 hours per week in the BRI Library and 6 hours at St Luke's). Both of these libraries hold about 10,000 books. The BRI Library takes about 225 current periodicals while the Nursing Library only takes around 30. The staffing provision is extremely inadequate for this level of stock and I decided fairly early into the 1980s that automation was the only way in which to continue to develop the service.

FIRST STEPS

In about 1984 the City of Bradford Libraries and Information Service was planning to update their computerised service with a change from a Plessey to an ALS system. As I am officially on their staff (and seconded to the Health Authority) I was asked to consider participating in the same way as the conventional branch libraries. This would have involved the installation of at least one, and preferably two, terminals which would be linked to the Central Library's minicomputer by a dedicated telephone (leased) line. On closer investigation, I found that the capital outlay would be in the region of £12,000 for each terminal plus a high recurring cost for the dedicated phone line. I concluded that, not only would this be an expensive way to automate a relatively small library, but that it would be extremely unlikely that I could persuade the Health Authority to fund it! Accordingly, I decided that it would be better value for money to develop my own system.

Throughout the development stages, the guiding principle has always been to obtain the best deal for the modest funds likely to be made available. Applications for any microcomputer application within Bradford Health Authority had to go through a committee which was then known as the Computer Working Group and whose members were either in-house computer experts or interested representatives from various hospital departments. The Group was allocated a small capital sum each year and had to decide between a number of differing bids from all sectors of hospital life. (For the previous two to three years the total costs of the bids received had exceeded the group's budget by 600 per cent.) Accordingly, I looked around for the most inexpensive package that would do the job required, and eventually received approval with the minimum of lobbying or political manoeuvring.

There is, of course, the contrary argument that one needs to put in an expensive bid for any capital expenditure in order to prove the seriousness of one's case and to impress management with the needs and status of the library services – but I am not at all convinced that it would have worked in those days of severe budget limitations.

As with all automation projects, the first step has to be to sit down and decide what you want the system to do. My priorities were to:

- automate the book catalogue;
- control the book ordering process;
- provide an online literature searching facility;
- automate the issue system; and
- consider additional tasks which might lend themselves to automation – such as inter-library loans, journal subscriptions and circulation, etc.

The next stage was to find appropriate software on which as many of the above options as possible would run. I started with visits to two local computer suppliers who attempted to demonstrate that standard business software would meet all my requirements. However, I remained unconvinced because it was quickly apparent that they knew as little about libraries and the organisation of bibliographical information as I did about computers. In particular, one of them tried to persuade me to choose DBaseII which is a relational database with a strong and powerful programming language of its own on which very effective databases can be constructed. However, it was clear to me that this would involve a considerable amount of tailoring to meet my needs, and I certainly did not possess the necessary programming skills to undertake it myself, preferring to choose an existing programme that had been specifically designed to cope with bibliographical retrieval. (Experience in Bradford since that time has convinced me that this was the right approach. A small research centre was set up in the early 1980s in the building in which I work, and one of its tasks was to set up a specialist database using DBaseII on a Sirius microcomputer. The research officer never got to grips with the system, and they must have spent several hundred pounds over budget in consultancy fees in attempts to get the database working, with minimal success.)

So, I then had to look further afield. I read around the subject in the professional press and sounded out opinion in the 'invisible college' – that body of friends and colleagues that one collects in the library profession by attending meetings, conferences, etc. At that time there was a limited choice of suitable software and I finally came down to two alternatives – Inmagic or Micro-Cairs. I had already seen the former demonstrated and knew that it was running at a neighbouring hospital library – Pinderfields General Hospital, Wakefield – where it was used for the compilation and management of the National Demonstration

Centre's Rehabilitation Bulletin (a current awareness service distributed nationwide). However, the deciding factor was again the price, as Inmagic was cheaper by over £2,000. At that time, Head Computers Ltd (now Head Software International), who then held the sole European licence for Inmagic, had just started to promote an all-in package deal offering a microcomputer, dot-matrix printer, modem and all necessary leads plus the Head Collection of software. This was very attractive both financially and as an easily identifiable, almost turnkey system which could be sold to the Computer Working Group and to hospital management. (Later experience, as reported by other users, would suggest that this might not always be the best course and that there is a lot to be said for buying your software separately and obtaining the hardware from a local supplier, as this makes it easier to obtain repairs and to apply pressure when necessary. But I certainly found it easier to persuade management by presenting a package deal).

THE HEAD COLLECTION

Inmagic

At this stage, I will describe the programmes which constituted the Head Collection as I purchased it and indicate their uses within my library service. The central programme is Inmagic, a database management tool specifically designed for text retrieval applications, which makes it particularly useful for library catalogues and other textual information services. (Apart from the library applications that I shall describe later, I also use it for the maintenance of a membership list for an association of which I am chairman which gives me the ability to list out subsets of members and produce addresses directly on to self-adhesive labels.) The advantage that I see in using Inmagic is that it is very flexible. Rather than buying a turnkey system which will only perform specified activities, Inmagic can be used for almost any database function within a library which may benefit from auto-mation – with the principal exception of issues or stock circulation for which it is not really suitable. That said, Inmagic Inc. now publish a *Biblio-Guide* which includes a variety of data structures and report formats which can be adopted and adapted for use in various library functions, including loans and serials management. However, I have not tried any of these out, so am unable to comment on their efficiency.

There is a fair amount of preparatory work to do before a database can be used in Inmagic. The first step is to draw up the data structure – which is a list of all the types of information which are to be included (see figure 8.1). These types are known as fields and might include, for example, author, title, publisher, etc. Then, decisions have to be made on whether each field is to be indexed, and, if so, the type of indexing which will be appropri- ate. For example, unless you are in a very specialised library, it is unlikely that you will want to search a database to find out how many first or third editions may be in stock. However, you will want to be able to retrieve authors, or words from the title or subject keyword fields. Inmagic has two types of indexing – keyword or term – and you can choose to apply either or both of these to any field. Keyword indexing creates an index of indi- vidual words while term indexing looks for a group of words. For example, with a book entitled *Introduction to Medicine*,

---

INMAGIC – DEFINE Data Structure

Enter name of stucture: CAT
Enter description line (optional): STOCK CATALOGUE
Enter retrieval key field(s): ACCESSIONNO
Enter order key field(s): AUTHOR

LABEL	NAME	INDEX	SORT	EMPHASIS
AN	ACCESSIONNO	T	1	1
AU	AUTHOR	Y	5	1
TI	TITLE	Y	9	1
SE	SERIES	Y	9	1
ED	EDITION	N		
PU	PUBLISHER	Y	5	1
YE	YEARPUBLISHED	T	4	1
PR	PRICE	N		
IS	ISBN	T	1	1
LI	LIBRARY	K	1	1
DA	DATEADDED	T	4	3
CL	CLASSIF	T	7	1
NO	NOTES	N		
SU	SUBJKEYWORDS	Y	5	1

Figure 8.1 Drawing up the data structure

a keyword index would list the words 'introduction' and 'medicine' separately in its index while the term index would store the whole phrase. As can be seen from figure 8.1, I have used both types of indexing (indicated by Y in the index column) for most of the important fields in my catalogue database. This means that I can search either for individual words (e.g. Smith, or medicine) or for complete phrases (e.g. Smith, J. A.). The final decisions in setting up the data structure are the types of sorting to be applied to the different fields. The UK version of Inmagic has a total of nine different sorting types from which to choose. Examples include letter-by-letter alphanumeric with the leading articles ignored, chronological, word by word, ASCII collating sequence, and numerical, including UDC and a special one for Library of Congress (and, therefore, National Library of Medicine) classification numbers.

All of this probably sounds extremely complicated but it does, in fact, only take a few minutes' thought and use of the manual to accomplish. In addition, Inmagic users tend to be a helpful lot and are more than willing to share their experience and exchange copies of their data structures. There is also a very useful Inmagic User Group which has an annual meeting and which is planning more and more opportunities for the exchange of experience.

My first step was to devise the data structures for the catalogue and on order files. The majority of the fields are identical, as the same information is needed for both buying and tracing a book, but different ones are appended to each to satisfy their particular needs. For example, in the order database there is need for information on the source of information, and date ordered, while in the catalogue one needs the classification number, subject keywords, etc. When new books arrive, they are identified in the order file and the records written to a separate file on the hard disk. This is then processed in Headset to delete the unnecessary fields, amend any incorrect details, and add in any new data – such as classification numbers. The amended file is then batch-added to the catalogue database; and, finally, the records are deleted from the order file. This reflects the situation as I devised it in 1985. Subsequent thoughts have suggested that it might have been better to put both categories into one large database to reduce the time spent searching for any one particular item. However, there is also some merit in maintaining them as separate clearly identifiable files, so I have never felt it was worth the effort necessary to change the structure and rebuild both databases into one.

Another essential requirement for a database programme is the ease and flexibility of its output – i.e. the printing (or displaying on the VDU) of required sections of the database in a desired layout and format. Inmagic's Report Generator is one of its major assets, being very powerful and flexible, though somewhat difficult to grasp at first. Among other report formats, I use one which prints book orders on to 5 inch × 3 inch printed slips which were originally designed for handwritten information within predefined boxes – and Inmagic can be instructed to print out the appropriate field into its box with a good degree of accuracy. It is also easily able to cope with the printing of catalogue cards if these are still considered necessary once the catalogue has been computerised. As mentioned earlier, it can also be used for a mailing list and can mail-merge a standard letter so that it appears to have been written to each individual recipient. Other report formats can be devised for almost any need, and those I use include book lists, memoranda concerning items on the database and the printing of standard request forms for local inter-library loans.

Inputting

One of the most important points to consider when planning to automate a library catalogue is the inputting (or typing in) of the data. It is essential to include a costing for this in your initial estimates as it is almost impossible to undertake such a major operation while continuing to run a library service. For my book stock of nearly 6,000 books (at that time) I estimated that it would take one of my part-time library assistants (a trained typist) about one month's full-time equivalent work to input a very minimal level of catalogue data (author, title, edition and classification number). This did turn out to be something of an overestimate, but it is important that it should not be underestimated for the reasons already stated. It is also important to consider how much of your older book stock needs to be included in the automated catalogue. Do you really need 100 per cent coverage or would it be justifiable to apply a cut-off date before which you would only include important items that are unlikely to go into a later edition; or maybe, only include items as and when they are borrowed from the library. In 1985, when I was planning this system, I decided on a cut-off date of 1980. It should be remembered that the information supplied from a hospital library service needs to be very up to date; and it is standard practice to dispose of earlier editions and outdated books.

Nowadays, it might also be worth considering the use of an outside organisation as the source of your original cataloguing data. Some large organisations, such as BLAISE (the British Library's Bibliographic Services automation wing) can offer the possibility of downloading relevant cataloguing data into almost any type of computer readable media. For the small School of Nursing Library there is a firm in Taunton, Somerset which maintains and sells on subscription a database of books relevant to nursing and which is about to introduce a library management package for a very modest price which will permit the transfer of records from the books database into the catalogue database by using a light pen. It could also be worth enquiring about larger, automated library systems which might be willing to sell a copy of their database, which could then be adapted to your own requirements by selecting out the relevant records and amending them to reflect local information. Finally, there are a few specialist firms that will take away your catalogue drawers and create a computer catalogue in a short space of time for reasonable fees.

If, however, you are forced to rely on your own resources, it is equally important to choose a quick, easy and safe way of inputting the data. The second part of the Head Collection, which is useful here, is called Headset. This is a word processing package specifically designed for the creation of data for inputting to database programmes such as Inmagic. It can be tailored to the requirements of any data structure and provides prompts to the typist for each field. This speeds up the inputting operation considerably; and it also has facilities for formatting and checking on the data as it is typed. For example, Headset will check the ISBN field, both to see that it contains the correct number of characters and by verifying the final check digit. It will also convert all typing into uppercase (e.g. for author fields) and generate and keep control of running numbers. This latter function can be very useful for accession numbers or for inter-library loans (particularly as the later upgrades of Headset allow for the inclusion of lettered prefixes before the numbers, thus allowing the use of British Library request form numbers). This feature is especially useful when the same series of running numbers is carried over more than one database. For example, a number is applied to each book ordered in the ORDer database, and transferred to the CATalogue database as the accession number when the book arrives. Similarly, in the Inter-Library Loans system, each request is given a unique number which can be used in either the current or the archive databases.

Headset is not essential to the use of Inmagic or any other database program, but I have found it extremely useful for the preparation of data. One of the problems of Inmagic, and, I presume, other database programs, is that it is vulnerable to corruption of the database while information is being fed into it. A power cut, or a sudden surge in the supply, can seriously damage the contents of the database. This threat cannot be entirely circumvented, except by the purchase of expensive electronic equipment, but there are two major ways in which its impact can be lessened. First, one should stay in the data creation mode (Inmagic's Maintain Environment) for as short a time as possible. Using Headset, or any other compatible word processor, and batch-adding records is the best way of minimising this risky period. Second, regular backups of the databases should be taken onto floppy disks or a tape streamer and, preferably, stored well away from the library's computer in case of fire damage.

Inter-library loans

The ordering and cataloguing processes have been run on Inmagic since the system was initiated in late 1985. The latest development, inaugurated in the summer of 1988, has been the control of inter-library loan borrowing. The previous manual system relied on the completion of two separate forms for each ILL request, one for our own records (a two-part slip, separated and filed manually in two separate locations) and the other to send to the supplying library, whether it be the British Library Document Supply Centre (BLDSC) or a local source. The same bibliographical details are included on both forms and it seemed to be an extremely time-consuming and yet drearily routine procedure. In the new system, the requests are entered onto Headset using one of two prompt files – one for British Library requests and one for the rest. Each request is given a unique number which is generated sequentially by Headset itself. The British Library prompt file also keeps control of the BL request numbers, allocating them in turn as needed. The Inmagic data structure is quite long (see figure 8.2), but is usable for all types of ILL request, whether book, journal or photocopy. Once a number of requests has been fed into Headset it is batch-added to Inmagic. From the select (or searching) programme one can then sort the requests into their different types and, for British Library ones,

INMAGIC – DEFINE Data Structure

Enter name of stucture: ILL
Enter description line (optional):
Enter retrieval key field(s): REQUEST_NO
Enter order key field(s): REQUEST_NO

LABEL	NAME	INDEX	SORT	EMPHASIS
REQ	REQUEST_NO	T	1	1
BLR	BL_REQ_NO	T	1	1
TYP	TYPE	T	5	1
TI	JNL_BK_TI	Y	9	1
AU	AUTHOR	Y	9	1
ART	ARTIC_CHPT	N		
VOL	*	N		
PT	PART	N		
PP	PAGES	N		
PUB	PUBLISHER	N		
ED	EDITION	N		
DA	DATE_PUB	N		
IS	ISBN	T	1	1
SO	SOURCE_REF	N		
LI	LENDING_LIB	T	9	1
NA	NAME	Y	5	1
ADD	ADDRESS	Y	9	1
TEL	PHONE	N		
DAT	DATE_REQUESTED	T	4	1
REC	DATE_RECEIVED	T	4	1
DUE	DATE_DUE	T	4	1
EXT	RENEWAL_EXTENSION	T	4	1
RET	DATE_RETURNED	T	4	1
NO	NOTES	N		

Figure 8.2   Inmagic data structure

write them into a separate computer file using the powerful report generator to put them into the format suitable for transmission to the BLDSC using the ARTTel (Automated Requests Transmission by Telephone) procedures (see figure 8.3). These can then be sent via a telephone call to the BL using Headline.

On receipt, photocopy records are transferred to an archive file which uses an identical data structure and which can subsequently be used for identifying management information – such as the most commonly requested titles, the heaviest users, etc. as well as the more usual statistical information which libraries need for their annual returns. For book and journal requests it is easy

---

```
12345
AB3CDEF


TX AB01429 Y   PHOTOCOPY (5800)
BR J PARENTERAL THERAPY
1985 Vol 6 (2) pp 30–42


TX AB01430 Y   PHOTOCOPY (5801)
J ANAT
The late intra-uterine..
MCDONALD M S ET AL
Vol 93 pp 331–341


TX AB01431 Y   PHOTOCOPY (5802)
CLIN PERINATOL
Renal failure..
RATMAN N ET AL
1981 Vol 8 pp 241–250

TX AB01428 Y   HOME READING (5799)
BINES W P (ED)
GUIDE TO RADIATION PROTECTION IN THE USE OF OPTICS
EQUIPMENT. (OCCUPATIONAL HYGIENE MONOGRAPH)
ISBN: 0906927524


NNNN
```

Figure 8.3 Transmission of requests

to amend the records to monitor the progress of the loans procedure and to generate the necessary notification or overdue
notices as required. When these items are returned, the records
are transferred to the archive file as outlined previously. For
requests to be sent to libraries other than the BLDSC, Inmagic can
also be used to print out an appropriate order form (see figure
8.4). Inmagic and its sister programmes have proved themselves
capable of automating my ILL procedures successfully, and has
released the library assistants for other jobs. It has however,
caused me additional work; but this has been offset by the additional contact with readers and their information needs which
was absent when ILL was purely a clerical chore for the library
assistants.

YORKSHIRE JOINT HEALTHCARE LIBRARIES SERVICE

TO: HRI   FROM: BRI (Bradford)   (FOR: F J SMITH REQ 5816)

Please supply the following JOURNAL PHOTOCOPY
Via Second Class Post or JMLS Van.

J LARYNGOL OTOL   1974   Vol 88   pp
139–43

SADE J ET AL

The aetiology of bone..

PLEASE RETURN THIS SLIP WITH THE ITEM.   PTO FOR SPECIAL NOTES.

YORKSHIRE JOINT HEALTHCARE LIBRARIES SERVICE

TO: Wakefield Library HQ   FROM: BRI (Bradford)   (FOR: MR JONES; REQ
5817))

Please may we borrow the following BOOK.
Please send it by Second Class Post or JMLS Van

HEALTH & SAFETY EXEC

HEALTH & SAFETY EXECUTIVE GUIDE TO THE HEALTH & SAFETY ACT

ISBN: 0118837109

PLEASE RETURN THIS SLIP WITH THE ITEM.   PTO FOR SPECIAL NOTES.

Figure 8.4 Order form

Online searching

The other major function required of this system was access to remote computers for online searching of medical and related databases. This has been well established in medical libraries for many years and Medline (the online version of Cumulated Index Medicus), in particular, has led the way in the development of computerised subject searching. Prior to obtaining my own system, I used a dumb terminal at the Central (Public) Library in Bradford for two or three years, and the transfer to a micro-computer was gratifying.

The dumb terminal on which I started was very basic – a VDU, modem and printer – and offered few facilities to the searcher. In particular, when communications are effected using IPSS (International Packet Switch Stream) one needs to input long strings of characters as identifiers and password (eg A931103010002000; NBRADIN123abc) in order to log on, and mistakes in typing lead to great frustration! Using a microcomputer and a communications package such as Headline eliminates all these worries as the required numbers are stored on disk and can be produced at the touch of only two keys. In addition, the search strategy can be prepared in advance using a standard word processor or Headline Entry and then transmitted line by line as required with a single key stroke. This is a boon to slow or inaccurate typists (such as myself), since all the time spent online adds to the costs; so it is important to be as well prepared as possible. Finally, the results of the search can be written to a disk file – the process known as downloading. The advantage here is that one is not tied to the speed of the printer which is often slower than the baud rate for online searching (120 characters per second). The results can then be printed out after logging off, which is another cost saving. In addition, one can load the search onto a word processor and tidy up the results before sending it to the reader. I have a standard draft memorandum on file (see figure 8.5) which has sections for describing the search strategy, the dates covered and the database(s) used. The downloaded data can then be merged at the bottom of the memo, to give a tidy and professional look to the results of the search.

BRADFORD HEALTH AUTHORITY LIBRARY SERVICE
MEMORANDUM

From: IPG KING BA ALA
        Medical Librarian
        BRI
To:
Date: 1 November 1989

Re: Your request for Information on

I have undertaken a computerised Literature Search of the above
topic. Please note the following points:-

1   The database searched was *Psychological Abstracts* and
        covered the years from 1967 to date.
2   The search was conducted using the following THESAURUS
        terms:
3   The printout is listed below for your attention. If you would
        like to see any of the references please indicate them on
        the list and return it to the Library.

Figure 8.5   Standard draft memorandum

HARDWARE

So far, I have described the software and its operation; and this is,
in essence, the correct way of approaching computerisation. The
software is the most important aspect – once it is chosen one can
then look for an appropriate microcomputer on which to run it.
However, in the real world, where money is tight and librarians
do not necessarily have a free hand in such matters, it may be
necessary to bow to outside pressures. For example, your parent
organisation may have a policy which demands conformity to a
fixed brand in order to take advantage of bulk purchasing con-
tracts; or you may be offered the funding for a computer system
if you can purchase it and pay the invoice(s) by the end of March
– a common occurrence in both health and local authorities; or
someone within the organisation is taking delivery of a new
computer and generously offers their old one to the library. (Treat
such gifts with caution – they may be so old or so limited in
memory as to be unsuitable for most library purposes.) In such
circumstances it may be politic, or necessary, to accept these

limitations on your choice, provided that the proposed system can still undertake the tasks you have planned.

It is difficult to offer advice in the world of computing as development is extremely rapid and what I am writing today may be out of date by tomorrow. However, at present I would recommend that any microcomputer bought should be IBM-compatible as this is now in effect the industry standard by which other machines are compared. The later IBM microcomputers are moving away from this standard, but it is an accepted term for a type of computer which is extremely well established and for which most types of software are now either written or adapted. Unfortunately, I started my system before IBM-compatibility was an option and with an Apricot F10 (which was announced as being withdrawn from production in the same week that I took delivery!). I now use an Amstrad PC1512 which is fully IBM-compatible. The differences are largely internal (i.e. in the way that the machine works) and are not visible in the actual working of any particular program which looks alike on almost any computer on which it can run. Choosing IBM-compatibility at this stage will ensure that there should be useful software available for any future uses you may devise. In addition, the type of chip used as the main processor has a noticeable effect on the speed of operation. The Amstrad PC1512 or PC1640 both use the original 8088 chip but the latest ones are 386 or 486 – and it is highly advisable to go for a microcomputer which uses one of these rather than one of the earlier, and much slower, ones.

PUBLIC ACCESS

So far, I have covered the early development of the system, and the uses of Inmagic. However, it gradually became apparent to me that there was a glaring gap in the whole arrangement. With the onset of automation I rapidly gave up the production and filing of catalogue cards. Indeed, this labour-intensive operation was one of my prime motivations for automating in the first place. However, as the card catalogue became more and more out of date it was increasingly difficult for the readers to find the books they required, particularly as the library is often left open but unstaffed. This led inevitably to the conclusion that there was a need for a separate computer for public use with a user-friendly catalogue of book stock always available. I drew up a detailed

report on the need for a second microcomputer which empha-
sised this lack of publicly available information and argued the
case for its installation in a secure cabinet in the open area of the
library. After some intense scrutiny, not a little lobbying, and a
warning not to ask for anything more for a while, the suggestion
was approved and the Amstrad PC1512 was purchased.

My second area of concern at this time was that I do not really
consider Inmagic to be user-friendly in that it expects a certain
knowledge and logical approach which information professionals are able to provide but which should not really be
expected of the average doctor or layperson! On discussing this
problem with Head Computers I was informed of a new program which they had developed for school libraries which was
called ELROND (Educational Library Resources on Demand).
This is a sophisticated database package which offers a
user-friendly front-end which can be used as a stand-alone program or with existing Inmagic databases. ELROND has since
been developed as a general program suitable for all types of
library applications and has been renamed Headfast.

Database programs are often described as being either
command- or menu-driven. In the former, of which Inmagic is an
example, there is a logical structure that has to be followed in
searching; and an expected knowledge of the required commands.
For example, to search Inmagic for all the books written by anyone
with the surname JONES, one would type 'g au cw jones' (Get
AUthor Containing Word Jones). After a while, such commands
become second nature, and using such a database becomes
extremely quick and efficient. In menu-driven programmes the user
is offered a choice at each stage of the searching process. For example, in Headfast, using the example above, from the Main Menu
one would first choose the option 'Quick Search'. The menu would
change to a selection of the fields available for searching and the
selection would be the Author Field. A small window would then
appear on the screen in which to type the name required – Jones.
Headfast would then display a list of all the records with this
author's name from which could be selected the one(s) required. As
can be seen, this is a slower process than command-driven
searching; but easier to grasp when the system is searched infre-
quently and leading to the same results in the finish.

As I write, the Headfast application is still under development.
An issue (or circulation control) module is eagerly awaited which

should again cut down considerably on the routine chores at present undertaken by the library assistants. At present we use a system of three-part self-reproducing paper slips for our issues, with one set of slips being completed for each book borrowed and filed in two separate sections, by date and borrower. This gives us the necessary control in a library where the clientele come and go with remarkable regularity. For example, in NHS hospitals, junior doctors in training work six month sessions in the various specialties and are as likely to change health authorities at the end of each one as not. To be able to automate this system would be a real advantage.

The last remaining major area of my operations which remained under manual control was journals subscriptions. I take about 225 current titles, and I am yet to be convinced that Inmagic could take over this area of operations successfully. The dedicated journals packages, such as Dawson's SMS Data-Trek and Blackwell's PerlLine, are too expensive to be justifiable for this level of operation, and so I was left considering the options of buying in a stand-alone DBase system, which I had seen demonstrated in London, or commissioning a local programmer to devise one for me. However, when I attended an Annual Conference of the Library Association: Medical Health and Welfare Libraries Group, I encountered a new journals agent – Faxon UK Ltd – at the exhibition which was demonstrating its journals control system – Microlinx – and, for a limited period, offering it free apart from an annual licence fee to their customers. As their costs were extremely competitive with my existing agent, saving enough actually to pay for the licence fee, I had no hesitation in taking advantage of their offer.

CD-ROM

The most recent addition to my computer systems is a CD-Plus CD-ROM workstation for accessing the Medline and CINAHL (Nursing) databases. I had an early opportunity to use a Silver-Platter system with three years of Medline within my own library and it demonstrated that CD-ROM is very useful as a source of immediate information without the frustrations of getting online and the concomitant consciousness of the spiralling costs involved. I usually undertake a search with the client present and this enables me to do a broader search than I would attempt online, with the reader scanning the results on the monitor and picking out relevant items. This is probably more labour intensive in terms of my own time, but more productive for the customer concerned. At that time, I felt that CD-ROM searching was not as flexible and convenient as online, but when I saw the CD-Plus system demonstrated at another LA:MHWLG Conference I rapidly changed my mind. This has been one of the most influential developments in my library service in the last ten years, particularly as a major contributor to customer relations and the respect in which the library is held. The workstation is kept free for clients to use, or library staff can undertake searches on their behalf if preferred. CD-Plus is user-friendly, with a useful facility of mapping the searcher's own choice of search term to the appropriate Medical Subject Heading for greater accuracy in retrieval. Search speeds are comparable with – and often superior to – online speeds and experienced Data-Star searchers can use the same command language while laypeople can follow user-friendly menus. Finally, there is a facility to code each journal title with holdings information – so that each citation retrieved is identified as either being in stock, at a branch or co-operating library or available only on inter-library loan. The Medline database is updated monthly, and the redundant compact disks make excellent coffee mats!

OTHER SOFTWARE

Finally, I should like to take a brief look at other types and sources of software which I have found useful. Word processors and spreadsheets are well established and useful to all types of organisations and individuals. The latter can be particularly useful in the management of budgets. For example, if one is trying to keep control of a journals budget, a change in the price of just one title can have an effect not only on the total expenditure but on departmental or subject breakdowns. On a spreadsheet, changing this one figure will automatically change all the others which are affected without any further input, while maintaining such figures on paper is a time consuming and laborious process. A recent trend is towards integrated software packages which can combine word processing, spreadsheets and, perhaps, an electronic diary and address book. These are useful in that it is possible to produce well-laid-out reports incorporating detailed calculations with the minimum of fuss or duplication of effort.

Another development of potential use to libraries is desk top publishing (DTP). These can improve the layout and design of anything a library may publish, from a library guide to small booklets or journals. They allow the user to divide the page into columns, use several different fonts and include graphics – either in the form of clip art (a variety of simple line drawings stored on disk) or by using a video digitiser or scanner to transfer pictures from any source into computer-readable files, or by producing their own using one of the many graphics packages that are available. DTP is best printed out on a laser printer, but reasonable results are possible on a 9-pin Epson dot-matrix printer using a low-cost DTP programme such as Timeworks DTP, as my own experiences have proved.

I have already mentioned graphics packages in relation to DTP. However, they can also be useful in the smaller library for the production of printed notices, Christmas party invitations, etc. in a faster and more convenient way than using transferable lettering or stencils. To the non-artist, they also offer better spacing and layout, and a smudge-free final product, than media such as lettering machines or transferable lettering. I also use a signwriting program (priced at less than £40) for library notices and it has been so successful that it has generated quite a lot of demand throughout the hospital!

Chapter 9

Making IT work in an industrial information service

John Ellis, GKN Technology Ltd

Library and information services in the industrial sector face two main pressures. Adopting new technology in order to provide a quality service to users who are ever expecting a more sophisticated and rapid response; and adapting to changes in the business strategy of the company concerned. The last decade and particularly the last five years has seen many changes in both of these areas. This case study will concentrate on the use of new information technology and computing techniques. A brief description of the department is necessary first of all.

The Information Services Department is based at the Technology Centre of a multinational engineering company. Its main customers are the engineers at the Centre but a service is also provided to other companies in the group. The bias is towards providing technical information but there has been a noticeable demand for more commercial and business information. The Information Service also provides report production and reprographic services as well as operating the site postal system. The last five years has seen many changes and a major reorganisation. In the mid 1980s the department had a staff of eight, comprising: Head of Information Services, an information scientist, librarian, technical author/liaison officer, two library assistants, a report typist and a reprographics officer. In 1985 these staff shared one terminal connected into the site VAX network, one intelligent terminal and modem for online searches and a stand-alone word processor for report typing. Less than three years later there was one PC or terminal per member of staff all linked to the site network and two laser printers. Through its adoption of computer-based systems and involvement in IT on a site level the Information Services Department has now developed into two separate groups. The library and information service is now operated by just three staff while two staff have transferred from the department to the computing centre where an information systems group has been formed, responsible for developing and supporting the PC network and office automation systems.

Looking back over the last six years there has been a regular series of introductions of new software packages and systems, as the following shows.

1985 Status text retrieval system
1986 –
1987 Personal computer for online literature searching
1988 Desktop publishing system
1989 CD-ROM
1990 Start of PC networking
1991 Computer-based inter-library loan system

These introductions suggest a framework in which to discuss the use of information technology within the information service.

STATUS

In line with the thinking of numerous industrial information services, by the mid-1980s it was considered necessary to introduce a computer-based information management system which would enable information scientists to construct databases of relevant company information, whether they were library catalogues, databases of research reports or technical literature databases. In 1985 following a trial of the software, a licence for the Status system was purchased from UKAEA Harwell. (Status is now marketed by Harwell Computer Power Ltd – a private company.)

Status was chosen for a number of reasons.

1 It ran on the DEC VAX range of minicomputers which was the only computing hardware platform in the company capable of supporting a multiuser software package at that time.
2 Most importantly, the introduction of Status was an initiative of the Information Service at the time. Having conducted a database survey the Information Service identified a number of potential database applications which indicated a need for a

free-text type of system. Naturally this is the type of database most familiar to information scientists, through online literature searching etc. (The alternative of looking at relational databases was not fully considered.)

3 A system was required on which information scientists could design and maintain databases with minimal external support. Inhouse technical and programming support was not available to a great extent due to the commitments of computing centre staff. Status was marketed as a system for use by non-programmers, providing a database framework for which the database manager had just to specify the overall record structure and then create formatted records for input to the database.

4 The database system had to have powerful Boolean searching facilities, and be generally easy to use for developer and user. This latter feature did not come about until the arrival of Status version E in 1988 with its full-screen interface, use of keypad keys for executing commands, and screen-based search panels for making database enquiries. This eliminated the need to write database-specific menu systems using Status macros, and database developers could concentrate more on the database content. The search and display panels are elegant and greatly enhance the product.

The cost factor could also not be ignored and rival systems were evaluated with their software licence costs in mind. The ongoing costs in terms of staff time in creating and maintaining databases, while acknowledged to be significant, were not fully considered. Inadequate provision of resources to develop the databases and market them to users led subsequently to a slow rate of progress.

These were the criteria the Information Service used to select a text retrieval system. A number of commercial packages were considered, including Basis, Cairs and Status. The latter was chosen as it best fitted our requirements.

On purchasing Status the first major application was the development of a hazardous chemicals database by the Environmental Engineering department, a database that was particularly relevant with the introduction of the COSHH regulations in 1989. Development of this database, however, did highlight a deficiency in Status. Although admired as a search 'engine' it has limited in-built facilities for producing high-quality output.

Search results can only be output to the screen or to a file in ASCII text format. A word processor or DTP system must be used to enhance the output to the degree which many users have now come to expect.

Within the Information Service the initial application for Status was to run the library catalogue. Existing catalogue records were taken from an IBM mainframe system (running at the company's central data processing centre) which produced catalogue indexes on microfiche. This transfer involved converting a master file semi-automatically, with the opportunity taken to enhance the records by adding additional index terms and a company specific subject class. The catalogue was converted in 500 record sets, and now has over 10,000 records, referring to publications available from the library.

Originally new input to the catalogue was prepared on a PC but later a VAX command procedure was developed specifically for the database. This inserts the necessary Status markers which delimit fields and records in a Status database. However, experience has shown that a proper forms-based data-entry system is essential. Harwell Computer Power now market Screenmaker which performs this function. It has to be purchased separately however and is not fully integrated into the Status package.

The library catalogue demonstrated that we could develop a multiuser database for the company – but the development effort and sustained upkeep should not be underestimated.

Another application developed involved purchasing external database information and loading weekly updates. This came about through the development of a business/industrial news service in an area directly relevant to our interests. At the inception of this news service subscribers were given the option of receiving it as a printed publication or on a floppy disk. Agreement was obtained to upload the information from the floppy disk and to create our own internal database which staff were then free to search. Considering the large size of the weekly newsletter the database approach was a far better method of distributing the information to a large number of staff and also to provide them with the specific items they needed. To market the database internally a weekly headlines list was produced from the database and distributed to staff. Over a two-year period the database grew to over 30,000 news summaries. Status searches were very effective and the database worked well. The service brought business news to a larger number of staff and the subscription costs were offset by the savings in online searches on commercial hosts. However the news service in this form was discontinued and as the information contained in the database was of short-term interest this Status database is no longer in regular use.

In a wider company context, database management has developed significantly over the last six years. Text retrieval systems such as Status are a specialised sector of the database market and over the last two years there has been much more activity within the company in developing databases using the Focus 4GL system. Focus is designed more for conventional fixed-field, numerical type databases for which there is a great need. The Information Services Department also realised this and appointed an information specialist with a computing/programming background to design applications using Focus. This was in response to requests from departments across the site for databases to be developed.

Status still has a role to play however because text management is still an underdeveloped area in many companies, especially if word processor documents are included within a database structure. However, there now appears to be a much wider range of software available, with ever-increasing capabilities for handling information in many different formats.

Personal computers for online searching

The department purchased its first PC early in 1987 – a modest 8086-based machine (a Tandon) with a 10 Mb hard disk and a monochrome display. This was adequate for its intended purpose – of preparing input for Status databases. A serial link to the VAX network was required and Smarterm240 was chosen as a terminal emulator which also allowed file transfer using Kermit.

The potential of this set-up for online literature searching was rapidly appreciated. Up to then searching was conducted using an intelligent terminal (a Userkit) which could store logon procedures and short search strategies. With the PC these procedures could be automated further, and search results could be downloaded to the hard disk for subsequent editing and formatting. In short an improved level of service could be offered to staff, not least because the search results could be presented easily as an attractive bibliography output from a laser printer.

With the Information Service dealing with approximately 600 major search requests a year and an annual online budget of over £30,000 this advance was an important step forward.

The other technology involved with online searching is telecommunications – a modem to connect the PC via a local dial-up line to the nearest packet-switching node. It is unfortunate that the quality of the local line is variable and line noise can result in spurious characters on screen and on printout. Line noise errors are easily detected in text but can have serious consequences on numerical information. On more than one occasion patent number searches have had to be repeated as the numbers obtained first time around have been displayed incorrectly. Fortunately the situation has improved in recent months and solutions such as leasing a dataline and installing a X.25 card have been avoided.

Packet switching has been of great benefit to the Information Service, and to the company as a whole. There are now many online services which can be called up and the old adage of 'logging on is nine-tenths the battle' is no longer true. British Telecom's Dialplus is an example of an improving user interface to telecommunications.

Having so much information available does lead to false expectations from staff. What we find is that bibliographic information can be obtained on most subjects in just a few minutes. Getting actual factual data and copies of original documents takes longer. The department has experienced increasing pressure to get hold of documents faster from publishers and lending libraries. In turn fax is being used more and more as a document-supply medium.

The success of the first PC led to a second being purchased to support the general work of the information service and also to run the CD-ROM drive (discussed in another section).

Current developments are centred on networking the PCs using DEC's Pathworks software. This provides network printing and superior file transfer facilities, along with server-based disk and file services. Generally information and data can be more easily disseminated around the company which assists the Information Service achieve a key objective.

Desktop publishing (DTP)

One of the tasks of the information service is to handle the final stages of production of research project reports. In an R & D environment the report is often the principal product and the production of attractive, high-quality reports is therefore a priority. By 1988, DTP was fast becoming an established technique and we could see that a DTP system could give us better finished reports. It would also allow us to produce some of the artwork for presentations which previously was subcontracted to graphic design houses.

A stand alone DTP system was purchased consisting of a Compaq 386s personal computer with 1Mb RAM and a 40 Mb hard disk. This was linked to an IBM Personal Pageprinter (postscript) and a Hewlett-Packard Scanjet flat-bed A4 image scanner. This configuration has been highly successful and subsequently another Compaq 386 was purchased along with an HP Laserjet III printer with postscript cartridge. The Compaqs have recently been upgraded with additional memory.

The DTP software chosen was Aldus Pagemaker, at the time when version 3 had just been released. The new version had better support for longer documents; a filter directly to read documents from our VAX-based word processing system (WPSplus); and was generally easy to use through its excellent use of the Windows environment. Pagemaker was chosen ahead of Ventura. An Apple Macintosh system (considered the leading hardware for DTP) was not considered as it was not company policy to support Macintoshs. DTP was therefore PC-based.

At the time of its introduction Pagemaker was for us a revelation in terms of the fonts and typestyles available and the ability to combine text and graphics on the same page. As well as publishing technical reports the DTP system has been extensively used for the production of overheads for presentations etc.

The introduction of DTP had the effect of converting one library assistant into an expert DTP user. Likewise the job of report typist was enhanced through DTP and this is an example of new technology totally changing the work patterns for these two members of the information services staff.

One obvious but often ignored factor in the success of the DTP service, was the provision of training. There is a tendency with computer systems that staff will learn 'on the job' through experience. Properly structured training however means that staff progress up the learning curve far quicker and avoid picking up bad habits.

Until recently, the company used DEC's WPSplus word processing system. Reports drafted in this could be transferred to Pagemaker directly. Again technology is moving on and the company is adopting WordPerfect as its word processing standard. Word processing is approaching DTP in what it can do and WordPerfect has extensive font capabilities and graphics integration. It is likely that all reports will be produced using WordPerfect alone in the future, freeing the DTP system to be used for more artistic tasks.

CD-ROM

On the face of it CD-ROM should be a great commercial success. The ability to store a large bibliographic database on a disk for distribution to subscribers gives database publishers a controllable product to market. Users such as ourselves gain the freedom to search and browse through a database without incurring the cost-of-time penalty associated with most online services. With one notable exception however CD-ROM has not in our case lived up to its promise. The exception is Perinorm, the tripartite standards database published in the UK by British Standards Institution and marketed by Technical Indexes Ltd.

National, international and institutional standards are extremely important to manufacturing companies, even more so to companies operating on a multinational scale. The provision of a comprehensive and up-to-date information service on standards is therefore a key task. Before Perinorm was first released in 1989 we relied heavily on the BSI library service at Milton Keynes. The usefulness of Perinorm was soon recognised because:

- it covers British, French and German national standards in a single searchable database on a single compact disk. This compactness is a key to its success;
- the database is updated monthly, allowing us to provide an inhouse standards updating service for staff, by running standard search profiles against records tagged with the update flag;

As to the system itself, a Sony CD-ROM player is leased from

Technical Indexes. This was deemed appropriate initially when we were uncertain as to how successful the service would be. The lease agreement includes maintenance which has been useful as there have been a few minor faults with the drive.

The search software from Dataware is designed specifically for CD-ROM databases. We have found it easy to use and it provides powerful searching facilities. The ability to browse through retrieved groups of documents at leisure is a great benefit. Indeed the system is sufficiently straightforward for novice searchers to use and there is no reason why engineers should not have direct access to it.

Elsewhere within the company the Occupational Health team make use of CD-ROM services relevant to their subject. Otherwise CD-ROM has not made any further impact. In the engineering sector database services on CD-ROM have been slow to appear. Compendex (Engineering Index online) is now available but as a multi-disk set. A literature search (albeit a stored search strategy) has to be repeated across multiple disks. For us, this inconvenience generally outweighs the advantages of CD-ROM databases over conventional online services.

An interesting development which may swing the database market towards CD-ROM is the storage and display of graphics. This is particularly relevant to patents and the success and usefulness of the Chadwyck-Healey patent CD-ROM images database remains to be seen. Small, restricted subject matter databases appear to offer the best opportunities.

Inter-library loans

Inter-library loans are one of the key activities of the library service, and requests for copies of journal articles, etc. are commonly the final stage of a literature search. In previous years the library has had to deal with up to 3,000 requests a year. The majority of requests are routed through to the British Library Document Supply Centre at Boston Spa, but approximately one in six requests can be satisfied by direct approach to other libraries or through the West Midlands Regional Library Service of which the library is a corporate member. Although BLDSC has extensive stock and does operate an efficient Urgent Actions Service, the latter route is often quicker for getting hold of the original literature.

When online literature searches can identify sources of information very quickly it is often frustrating that it can take days if not weeks to obtain the original document. Pressure on staff time to operate the ILL system and user pressure to obtain documents quicker were two of the main reasons for investigating and developing an automated ILL administration system.

ILL administration is an area of software development which has been slow to develop. Many of the systems suitable for libraries such as ours are PC-based, e.g. the AIMS system initially developed at Leicester Polytechnic. Considering the resources already available within the company for software development we were reluctant to purchase a commercial ILL system which was PC-based as this would introduce another brand of database system. Also by developing our own system we could build in some features specific to our own computer network.

It was decided to develop a VAX-based ILL administration system using the FOCUS 4GL software available. The database is menu-driven and stores data on the requester, the document reference, and the libraries approached. As a part of a multi-user system it is feasible for users to enter their own document request details but this feature is not yet in operation and library staff enter the request information themselves from paper-based requests. Using our VAX network's PSS connection, requests can be sent daily to BLDSC using ARRTEL which is a major benefit. Urgent requests can be sent via our VAX-based fax link to BLDSC or other libraries. Reports, for example request status reports, request letters to other libraries, or database statistics, from the ILL database can be exported and formatted in a wordprocessor.

These facilities have proved to be highly beneficial. The new system is more efficient in staff time as request information only has to be typed in once, whereas the old system which had developed over many years and which admittedly worked well, required the writing out of multiple index cards in order to cross index request numbers and requesters. The new ILL system through its use of ARRTEL is also faster than relying on the postal service.

Human factors

The effect of new information technology has an impact on the expectation of the users of information services and has caused significant changes in the staffing of the department and the skills required.

As the staff of the company become more proficient in the use of computer systems so their expectations of information services have grown more stringent. In particular they look for more rapid access to information, better presentation of the results and, more frequently now, the facility to search databases themselves.

In terms of our Information Department, new staff have been recruited with a more extensive computing background. This has subsequently led to the setting up of a separate information systems group for the company under the direction of the IT manager. Library assistants have become computer users and acquired skills in DTP as well as word processing and spread-sheets. Traditional library skills such as cataloguing are becoming less important. Formal UDC (Universal Decimal Classification) classification has been reduced to the level of a shelf location.

The last five years has seen tremendous change, not all of it under our control. What effect will new technology have on information services in the coming decade?

Index

ABI/Inform 92
academic libraries 93
Access 68
access 99, 100; improved 9–10, 100; software 37–8
acquisitions 32, 34, 53, 63, 99, 113; library management 66; module 115, 116
address book 140
Advance 68
advantages for information staff 101
Aldus Pagemaker 120, 147, 148
alerts 76
All-in-1 software 118
American Standard Code for Information Interchange (ASCII) 35; hospital library 127; industrial information service 144; text format 62
Amor, L. 73–95
Apple Macintosh 28, 41, 53, 147
ARTTel *see* Automated Requests Transmission by Telephone
ASCII *see* American Standard Code for Information Interchange
Aslib 78, 82, 90
Assassin 60, 71
associative expert 38
autodial 80
Automated Requests Transmission by Telephone (ARTTel) 132

backup 47, 115, 130
barcode reader 48, 49
Basis 143
batch 36
Bawden, D. 29
benefits 99–101; information technology 9–11, 117–20
BGMC *see* British Gas Management Centre
BIB/Search 56, 71
Biblio-Guide 63, 125
bibliographic records 57, 99
Bibliolinks 63
BL *see* British Library
BLAISE *see* British Library's Bibliographic Services
BLCMP 2
BLDSC *see* British Library Document Supply Centre
BLS 69
Books in Print 92
BookshelF 67, 69
Boolean logic operands 32, 44, 60, 65, 67, 116, 143
Bradshaw, D. 99
BRI Library 122
British Gas Management Centre 109–21; benefits 117–20; case to management 112–14; future development 120–1; impact 116–17; implementation 114–16; planning 109–12
British Library 35, 129, 131; Bibliographic Services

(BLAISE) 129; Document Supply Centre (BLDSC) 130, 132, 133; Science Reference and Information Service 79
British Telecom Global Network Services 83–4
Brittin, M. 1–11
BRS/Search 71
budgeting: inadequate 102; and installation 21; packages 99
business: databases 74; software 32–3

Cairs 143
Cairs-IMS 61, 63, 69, 71
CALM 67, 69, 112
Carbon Copy software 119
Cardbox-Plus 71
case studies 107–50
casing, hardware 48
casual expert 38
CATalogue database 130
cataloguing 99, 113; disks 47; functional criteria 34; hospital library 127; industrial information service 144; information retrieval systems 55; information sources 9; library management 64–6; retrospective 115; software 53; special libraries 7; system 20, 23; text retrieval systems 32; user-friendly 136
CD-Plus 139
CD-ROM 62, 74, 99, 102, 103, 120, 146; hospital library 138–9; industrial information service 148–50
CDS/ISIS 71
central processing unit (CPU) 45
character set and hardware 48
charges: and CD-ROM 95; online searching 83–5
checklist 42
Chemical Abstracts database 83
Chen, C. 93
Chronolog 89
CINAHL (Nursing) databases 138

circulation 7, 10, 113; control 53, 63, 66, 67, 68; modules 67, 116–17
City of Bradford Libraries and Information Service 123
Cole, I. 38
combined searches 33
COMLINE data-base 75
commercial systems assessment and installation 23–4
communications software and online searching 81–2
Compact Disk-Read Only Memory *see* CD-ROM
company libraries 4
compatibility and hardware 51
Compendex 92, 149
Computer Readable Databases 74
Concord Textmaster *see* Textmaster
connect time 84, 90
controls and hardware 48
COSHH regulations 143
CPU *see* central processing unit
criteria and software 33–7
Cropley, J. 15–27
Crosstalk 81
currency and CD-ROM 94

daisy wheel printer 50
data: entry 40; input and editing 59–60; output 61–2; structure 126
Data-Star 74, 78, 79, 90, 91; searchers 139
Data-Trek *see* SMS Data-Trek
database 32, 34, 47, 110; construction 23; files 33; index and information retrieval systems 58; management systems (DBMSs) 30, 31–3, 53, 54–5, 56, 63, 67; specialised internal 100–1; system 138
DataEase 54
Dataware 149
DBase 54
DBase III+ 120
DEC equipment 118, 120, 121, 142

default menu 39
Delta 54
desk top publishing (DTP) 50,
   120, 140, 144; industrial
   information service 147–8, 150
diacritics 49
Dialog 74, 75, 78, 79, 88, 90;
   Chronolog 89
Dialoglink 81
Dialplus 146
diary: electronic 140;
   management 118
Diderot/Polybase 69
DIP *see* document imaging
   processing (DIP)
directories 75
Directory of Online Databases 78
disadvantages for information
   staff 102
disk: hardware 46–7; speed 45;
   see also floppy disk
document imaging processing
   (DIP) systems 56
documentation and software 44
dot-matrix printer 49, 50, 140
downloaded data 33
Dowty Quattro modem 119
draft copy 49, 50
DTP *see* desk top publishing
dumb terminal 134
duplex 80
Dyer, H. 45
Dynix 69

editing 40
Educational Library Resources
   on Demand (ELROND) 137
electronic: diary 140; mail 76, 77,
   84, 118, 119, 120
Ellis, John 141–50
ELROND *see* Educational
   Library Resources on Demand
end-users 102–4; services 90
equipment and online 86
ESA-IRS 79, 83
evaluation and installation 26
expectations, high 102
experienced professionals 38
external sources of information 10

Extract 56, 60, 71

FAME 92
feedback 41, 101
fields 126, 127; fixed-length 47,
   58; structure 32;
   variable-length 57
files 34–5; free text 33, 56;
   inverted index 31, 32, 58;
   management systems 30;
   multiple 31; on order 127; size
   47
Financial Times 75; Profile 79, 84, 91
flexibility 100
floppy disk 46, 47, 130, 144; *see
   also* software
Focus 4GL system 145
Folio Views 71
free text: files 33, 56; indexing 37
FT Profile *see Financial Times*
   Profile
full field indexing 37, 59
full text data 56
full text indexing 59
functional criteria 42; and
   software 33–4
future developments of
   information technology 120–1
Gain, R. 109–21
government libraries 5, 93
graphics 49, 118
'grey' literature 32
grip feed 51

Hamilton, F. 91
hard disk 46, 47; *see also*
   hardware
hardware 44–51; casing 48;
   compatibility 51; data capture
   48–9; disk 46–7; hospital
   library 135–6; main memory
   45–6; microcomputer 29;
   modems 51; multi-user 45;
   and online searching 80–5;
   paper 50–1; printers 49–50;
   processor 45; single-user 45;
   and software combination 41;
   visual display unit (VDU)
   47–8

hazardous chemicals database 143
Head Collection 129; hospital library 125–34
Headfast 59, 62, 63, 71, 137
Headform 62
Headline 62, 81, 132, 134
Headset 59, 129, 130, 131
health service libraries 4–5
help 41
Henderson, F. 98–106
Heritage 69
'High Sierra' 47
historic data and CD-ROM 94
hospital library 122–40; CD-ROM 138–9; first steps 123–5; hardware 135–6; Head collection 125–34; public access 136–8; software, other 139–40 human factors 149–50; and installation 17–19; see also staff
human resources 22
IBM 28, 114; environment 111, 112; mainframe system 144; microcomputers 136
ICAEW see Institute of Chartered Accountants in England and Wales
icons see WIMP
Idealist 71
ILL see inter-library loans
ILS see integrated library system
image handling 55
impact of information technology 116–17
implementation: of information technology 114–16; and installation 26–7
Index Medicus 94, 134
indexing 32, 36–7, 56, 126; options 58–9
industrial information service 141–50; CD-ROM 148–50; Status 142–8
information resource management 11
Information Retrieval Service of the European Space Agency see ESA-IRS
information retrieval systems 7, 20, 23, 41, 53–63, 73; data input and editing 59–60; data output 61–2; database index 58; indexing options 58–9; for library management 63; micro-based 71–2; record structure 57–8; searching 60–1, 62; thesaurus/authority control 61; types 56–7
information sources and access increase 9–10
information staff and information technology 101, 102
information technology: benefits 9–11; and special libraries 7–9
information timeliness and online searching 75
Information UK 2000 11
Information World Review 90
Infotap 91
Inmagic 112; data 59, 131; hospital library 124, 125–8, 133; information retrieval systems 56, 63, 71; Maintain Environment 130; public access 136, 137; Report Generator 128; searching 60; User Group 127
input requirements 22
inputting and hospital library 128–30
installation 15–27; budgeting 21; commercial systems assessment 23–4; evaluation 26; human factors 17–19; implementation 26–7; management concerns 19–20; planning 15–16; requirements analysis 16–17; scheduling targets 20–1; service maintenance 25–6; specification development 21–2; technical assistance 22–3; time management 24–5; training 19
Institute of Chartered

Accountants in England and Wales (ICAEW) 104
Institute of Information Scientists 78
integrated library system (ILS) 64
intelligent terminal 145
interface design and software 40–1
inter-library loans (ILL) 130–3, 149–50
intermediaries 102–4
internal sources of information 10
International Online Information Meeting (IOLIM) 78, 90
International Packet Switch Stream (IPSS) 134
inverted file index 31, 32, 36, 58
IPSS see International Packet Switch Stream
IR see information retrieval system
ISBN field 129
Ize 56

jet printer 50
journals 54, 99

Kermit 145
keyboard 48
keyword indexing 126, 127
Kimberley, R. 57
King, Ian 122–40
Kompass file 76

labour charges 21
Lanslide 56
laser printer 50, 120, 140
Leggate, P. 45
letter-by-letter alphanumeric 127
Libertas 69
LIBMAN 69
Librarian 69, 72
Library Association 4, 78
Library of Congress 127
library housekeeping 54, 110; software 31–2
Library Information Technology Centre 68, 81
library management software and systems 63–8; acquisitions 66; catalogue enquiry and output 65–6; cataloguing 64–5; circulation control 66; serials control 66–8; see also library housekeeping systems
LibraryPac 57, 63, 70, 71
Licon 70
light-emitting diode (LED) 50
loans 99, 125
Lotus 1-2-3 120

machine readable catalogue format (MARC) 2, 35, 43, 115
Macintosh see Apple Macintosh
main memory and hardware 45–6
mainframe software 29, 42, 51
management concerns and installation 19–20
Manager Series 70
manual indexing 37, 59
manuals and online searching 82–3, 87
MARC see machine readable catalogue format
Marcaccio, K.Y. 74
marketing opportunity 101
Martyn, J. 11
Medicus see Index Medicus
Medline 92, 134, 138
Megahertz (MHz) 45
memorandum, standard draft 135
memory: size 45; and software 39
mental capacity and software 39
menus 90; menu-driven system 60
MHz see Megahertz
mice see mouse
microcomputer: hardware 29; system 53
Micro-Cairs 124
Microlinx 138
Million Dollar directory 84
Mirror 81
modem 146; Dowty Quattro 119;

hardware 51; online searching 80
Moore, C. 53–72
mouse 41, 48, 49; *see also* WIMP
movement, ease of 40
MS-DOS 28, 53
multi-user: applications 53; hardware 45
multiple: database 47; files 31

naive user 38
National Library of Medicine 127
national network 83
nature of special libraries 5–7
near letter quality (NLQ) 49
network charges 83–4
NLQ *see* near letter quality
non-bibliographic information 54
Novell 53, 114, 119, 121
numeric databases 74, 76
Nursing Library 122

OASIS 70
Ocelot 112
offline 77; prints 84, 85
on order files 127
online 36, 99; databases 118; public access catalogue (OPAC) 2, 38
Online Business Information 89
Online Notes 90
online searching 9, 51, 73–95, 104, 110; access, single point of 74–5; alternatives 90–2; approval 85–6; CD-ROM 92–5; charges 83–5; communications software 81–2; computer terminal 80; hardware, software and other costs 80–5; hospital library 134; hosts and databases 78–9; information timeliness 75; integration with office software 77–8; manuals 82–3; modem 80; offering new service 87–9; personal computers 145–6; preparation 86–7; reasons for usage 74–8; retrieval, speed of 75–6; search

software flexibility 76; staff time 85; telephone line 81; training 82; up to date 89–90
OPAC *see* online public access catalogue
Oracle Libraries 70
ORDer database 130
order form 133
ordering system 10
output 143, 144; format 32; requirements 22

packet switching 146
page printer 50
paper and hardware 50–1
passwords 82, 84, 134; and online 86–7; protection 37
Pathworks software 146
perception and software 39–40
performance indicators 22
Perinorm 148
PerlLine 138
personal computers 73; and online searching 145–6
Personal Librarian 60, 61
personal reference managers 56
PFDS 79
Phototracer 56
planning: of information technology 109–12; and installation 15–16
Predicasts 82
price and software 43
printers 120, 140; hardware 49–50; print charges 84–5
Pro-Cite 56, 62, 63, 72
Pro-Search 63
processor *see* word processor
Procomm Plus 81
professional bodies' libraries 5
Profile 75, 99
PROGEN Library 70
prompted system 60
Promt 84
proximity searching 60
PSS 83, 84, 86
public access and hospital library 136–8
pull-down menus *see* WIMP

purchase of software 29–30

Raitt, D. 93
RAM (Random Access Memory) 45, 46, 119
Random Access Memory *see* RAM
range searching 60
Read Only Memory *see* ROM
records 36; fixed-length 58; structure 32, 34; structure and information retrieval systems 57–8; variable-length 57
Reference Manager 56, 62, 72
reformatting facilities 100
regular products 100
relationships with users 98–106
report generator 62
requirements analysis and installation 16–17
resources, human 22
retrieval, speed of and online searching 75–6
retrospective cataloguing 115
ROM (Read Only Memory) 46; *see also* CD-ROM
Royce, C. 93

scanners 56
scheduling targets 20–1
School of Nursing Library 129
screen size and hardware 48
Screenmaker 144
ScreenMaster 60
SDI *see* selective dissemination of information
SDI *see* Selective Dissemination of Information
searching 31, 33, 56, 116; information retrieval systems 60–1; process 57; serial 37; software flexibility 76; stored and information retrieval systems 62; strategy 76; user-friendly 61; *see also* online searching
security and software 37–8
selective dissemination of information (SDI) 10, 55, 76

serials: control 7, 64, 66–8; management 125–6; search 37
service 7, 10; maintenance and installation 25–6; marketing 105–6
shared system 29
sheet feeder 51
Silver-Platter system 138
single user and hardware 45
Smartcom 81
Smith, J.A. 127
SMS Data-Trek 138
software 28–44; access 37–8; business 32–3; criteria for choice 33–7; database management systems, relational 31–3; directories 42, 52; documentation 44; file management systems 30; and hardware combination 41; hospital library 139–40; interface design 40–1; library housekeeping 31–2; mainframe 29, 42; memory 39; mental capacity 39; and online searching 80–5; packages 3, 7, 53–72; perception 39–40; performance 45; price 43; purchasing 29–30; security 37–8; selection 35, 43; shortlist establishment 42; supplier reliability 44; support 44; training 44; user characteristics 39; user, types of 38–9; writing 29–30
sorting requests 132
Soutron 70, 112, 113, 114, 115, 119, 120; serials control 67
special libraries 4; nature 5–7; types 3–5
specification development and installation 21–2
speed of modem 80
spreadsheets 32, 33, 76, 118, 139, 150
staff 8; and online searching 85
status, improved 10–11, 101
Status 42, 61; industrial information service 142–8

Status-PC 56, 72
Status/IQ 61
stop word 58
stored searches 76
strategic implications 102–4
Strix 72
Superfile 54
Supermax Library System 70
supplier reliability and software 44
support and software 44
synonym control 55
system: reliability 22; suppliers 68–70

tagged indexing 37, 59
tape streamer 47, 115, 130
targets scheduling and installation 20–1
TECHLIB PLUS 70
technical assistance and installation 22–3
Telecom Gold 118
telecommunications 51, 73, 81, 146
term indexing 126, 127
text retrieval: packages 31–2; software 33, 42
Text Retrieval Directory of Software 56–7
Textline 75, 79, 84, 99
Textmaster 71
textual databases 74
thesaurus 67; and authority control 61; control 32; files 55
time management and installation 24–5
Timeworks DTP 140
TINlib 70, 112
Topic 72
tractor feed 50
training 105; and CD-ROM 95; and installation 19; online 87; online searching 82; software 44
truncation 60, 65
Turner, C. 4

types: information retrieval systems 56–7; special libraries 3–5

UDC 127
UKOLUG see UK Online User Group
UK Online User Group (UKOLUG) 82, 90
Unicorn 70
UNIX-based system 53
up-front charges 84
URICA 70
use, frequency of and CD-ROM 94
user, 6–7; characteristics and software 39; education and CD-ROM 95; requirements and software 38; types and software 38–9; see also end-user; multi; single; user-friendly
user-friendly: catalogue 136; searching 61
Userkit see intelligent terminal

visual display unit (VDU): hardware 47–8

wild card 33, 60, 65
WIMP 40, 41
Windows 28, 40, 41; environment 147
word processing 47, 62, 99, 110, 118, 120, 150; package 129; system 77; WPS plus 120, 148
word processors 32, 33, 45, 139, 144
word by word 127
WordPerfect 34, 148
Wordstar 118, 120
WPSplus word processing system 120, 148
writing software 29–30

Zyindex 56

S0-DKM-932

THE LOVE FREAK

THE LOVE

CHRIS KAZAN

FREAK

STEIN AND DAY/*Publishers*/New York

First published in 1971
Copyright © 1971 by Chris Kazan
Library of Congress Catalog Card No. 71-178021
All rights reserved
Published simultaneously in Canada by Saunders of Toronto Ltd
Designed by David Miller
Stein and Day/*Publishers*/7 East 48 Street, New York, N.Y. 10017
ISBN 0-8128-1442-8

THE LOVE FREAK

1

"You wrote this book to make money?"

"Well—everyone who writes a book, who publishes a book, is hoping people will buy it."

"But money was not your primary interest?"

"No. Not at all." Tom folded his arms and sat straighter in the plastic chair, quite virtuous.

("Oh, get off his back," muttered Sam, at home, to the interviewer. She bent closer to the tiny borrowed television set, watching the bluish, flickering midgets smile at each other.)

"I was just wondering how somebody set about writing a best seller. Your book is on the list."

"Yes."

"But you didn't just sit down and say to yourself, 'I'm going to put in so much sex, so much violence, so much about drugs,' and so on?" Don Antonio asked.

"Those things are part of life; that's why they're in the book. If I didn't talk about them, I'd be writing a lie."

("That's telling him," Sam said to herself. She thought Tom looked quite handsome, the way his hair curled stiffly to his shoulders. But the skin was drawn tight with nervousness over his face, and his eyes kept bulging toward one side, where, she thought, there must be a clock.)

"Sex, for instance." Don Antonio's expression slid into a

7

leer, crooked in his seamy, wolfish face, seeming to say, Well, we're all out for what we can get, right?

(Electronic giggling subsided slowly. Sam realized that she hadn't seen any audience.)

"Sex is an important part of life. A basic part."

"You can't tell me the average man, the average American, thinks about sex all the time."

"He may hide it from himself. The function of the artist is to expose man's hidden drives."

"But the average guy doesn't know about the artistic end of it. He reads a book like yours, and he says, 'Wow!' That's why he reads books. Sex!" Don Antonio smiled sexily, drooping his left eyelid.

(That doesn't even make sense, Sam thought. Good Lord, what an unpleasant man! She had never seen him before.)

"But that's not why I put sex in the book. I mean, I don't think of it as Sex. With a capital *S*."

"You've got to admit it's good business, anyway."

"Perhaps so."

(Tom smiled; a little sheepishly, she thought.)

"And the title."

"The Love Freak?"

"Yeah. What does that mean?"

"Well, in the colloquial sense, a freak is someone who's preoccupied with, or obsessed with, something. Like someone who watched television all day would be a television freak. And it has the traditional meanings, too: an outlandish person, or a cripple——"

"What I'm getting at is, it sounds to me like a title that was calculated to sell books. Like a combination of Jacqueline Susann and Freud, or somebody like that."

"Well, Mr. Antonio——"

"Don."

"Don."

("Balls," said Sam. The sheep's smile seemed by now to be permanently pasted on Tom's face. If he walks through this

8

door looking like that, I'll pretend I don't know him, she thought affectionately.)

"The title is symbolic of the conflicting demands of a neurotic society, which leads into the major subject of the book—the attempt by the generation in power to mold the younger in its own image, through a sort of emotional blackmail——"

"Just a minute, Tom. We'll be back in sixty seconds with some more lively discussion, after this word. So *don't* go away, people."

Don Antonio's smile turned up full power, warming viewers everywhere; but just before his image faded from the screen, the smile blanked out, leaving the lines of dissipation naked in his face.

(Stupefied, Sam watched as an auto grew in size on the screen, rushing toward her, swerving at the last minute, a terrifying nine inches high, blasting by the camera, leaving its own name in car-high letters; as it vanished, a Scandinavian girl appeared from nowhere, leaning on the name of the car, and began to talk. There go I, almost, thought Sam. She reached toward the coffee table behind her for her little hand-carved pipe, thinking, Maybe it would all make sense if I had a hit. With a tiny gold penknife, she cut a piece of hashish the size of half a pea from the gigantic—two ounce!—block that Tom had bought for her birthday. She placed the dull brown pellet on the wire screen in the center of the pipe-bowl. Lit a match. Sucked the flame, sulfur, hash into her lungs. Was watching the pipe-bowl, cross-eyed, when two Don Antonios appeared on a tiny television screen for each eye. Giggled suddenly at the absurdity, although she could not possibly have been high yet, and lost smoke in a cough.)

"Buy it, people, and don't say I didn't tell you so. With us tonight is Tom Jury, the young—how old are you, Tom?"

"Twenty-two." Tom blinked into the camera.

"—author of the best-selling novel *The Love Freak*. There's an American success story. Read the book, by the way, it's fascinating. If you can't read it, buy it anyway. Make Tom

9

enough money to get a haircut." Don Antonio's face was flaccid and malicious beneath the smiling mask.

("Fuck you," Sam said dreamily around the pipestem.)

Tom's face now was shown on the screen until it became obvious that he was going to make no riposte, only smile sickly.

(As Don Antonio reappeared, Sam felt a strange, hazy urge to touch him; she pressed her palm against the glass screen, which was cold and dead-feeling, and covered his entire face. But the pipe also was cold, and her attention wandered while she lit another match.)

"By the way, Tom is married to Samantha, one of New York's top fashion models." Don Antonio seemed to be reading from a paper on the table in front of him.

("Married?")

"She doesn't model any more. She's a potter."

("Hooray!")

"A what?"

"Potter. She makes pots, dishes, things like that."

"Yeah. Seriously, Tom, what are you going to do with all the money you're making from the book?"

"The first thing I did was pay the rent for a year in advance. Then I got a new typewriter and two dozen pairs of socks, all the same color. And I bought a present for——"

"What?"

"I bought a present for my wife."

("Oh, you sellout! You whore!" The pipe dropped from Sam's mouth. Luckily, it had gone out; it bounced off her leg, leaving the tiny pellet of ash on her thigh. "Wife, is it?" But under the gentle influence of the drug, she could not stay angry. She smiled sleepily and rubbed the ash into her skin.)

"What sort of present?"

"Just something I knew she'd like."

"I imagine she's pretty proud of you. Or is she as unimpressed by success as you say you are?"

"Naturally we're glad to have the money. Sam supported

me for two years while I was writing the book; she believed in me. Now I can support her while she gets her start potting."

"Fascinating. Well, I guess we should get back to your book. I wonder if you could state the thrust in a few words for our audience."

"The thrust?"

"The meaning of the story."

"Oh. Well. It's a story of the conflict between two generations, basically, a story of today. Representing the older is the father in the book. He's an entertainer, a singer, who used to be fairly good, or at least popular; but now his voice is gone, he drinks too much. He's sold himself out to try to hold onto the public approval he needs. The younger generation is represented by his son. The son is an idealist, perhaps a little naïve; he sees the moral bankruptcy of his father, and he's searching for his own answers. He tries all the standard things: dope, sex, politics, drifting. Finally he finds a kind of answer in a girl, a woman."

"That's the heroine of the book?"

"I guess you could say that."

"Isn't she really the main character?"

"Well—from one point of view."

"She takes dope, doesn't she?"

"She smokes a little grass."

"Marijuana?"

"That's right."

Don Antonio peered at the papers on his desk. "And hashish. Isn't that like heroin?"

"Not at all. Hashish is the same as marijuana, except it's more concentrated. An extract, like vanilla extract."

"Are you implying a favorable attitude toward this dope?"

"Not necessarily. But not necessarily critical, either."

"You were comparing it to vanilla."

"I was comparing the extraction process."

"Your heroine is breaking the law by using it."

11

"Yes. But she's not hurting anyone, except perhaps herself. There's an interesting, what I think is an interesting, contrast in the book between her smoking dope, which is a peaceful, self-searching thing, and the father's drinking, which is destructive. The father kills a little girl, you remember, hits her with his car when he's drunk. *That's* criminal."

(As Tom paused, Don Antonio appeared on the screen. Sam, who had slipped into deep concentration, saw strange changes in his face: shock, fear, hatred, a swiftly arranged mask of friendly interest. What?)

Don Antonio's finger pushed at his papers. "This was a hit-and-run incident, right?"

"Yes. He left the child dying."

"But he couldn't have known she was badly hurt."

(What a strange thing to say!)

"The sound of her body striking the car is described. Her scream. No, he couldn't have *known*. But he left her there. That was the act of an animal, a pig."

"I guess that's just the kind of world we live in," Don Antonio said cheerfully. "Not many people would have stopped and let themselves be arrested."

"That's exactly what I mean. What kind of world do we live in, where such a thing almost seems acceptable?"

"It would have ruined his career."

"Career? He was washed up, a drunk. A joke in the industry. He got work in television on his name, for sentimental reasons, that's all."

Don Antonio wiped his forehead with a handkerchief.

(His face was like a ripe melon about to burst its skin. Sam shrank away, afraid it might spatter on her, but the drug had made her limbs weak and she could barely move. She wavered in front of the screen, fighting panic. "Get away, Tom," she said experimentally, but he didn't seem to hear her; he was unaware of any danger. It's my imagination, a dope dream. But still Don Antonio's face pressed against her.)

"Actually." Don Antonio was weirdly insistent. "Actually,

isn't that really splitting hairs?" He cocked his head to one side, nodding heavily, flashing a crooked grin. It was an elaboration of the Italian expression for "You're kidding me." Electronic laughter egged him on.

(Like a dying man parading his illness for approval, Sam thought.)

"To pass judgment on such a man when you yourself favor breaking laws that you don't like. In a calculated effort to write a commercially successful book. Wouldn't some people call *that* selling out?"

"Actually." Tom was as confident as a young stag approaching a hidden pit of sharpened stakes. "There's no contradiction. One has a responsibility to change what one thinks is wrong with the system. My way is writing books. If a book is to be effective, people have to read it. The kind of people who don't agree with my ideas, who I think need to be convinced. Like yourself, actually."

(What is "actually"? Stop it!)

"And you make a lot of money."

"Incidentally. It's not that important."

" 'Incidentally,' Tom, how're the negotiations for the movie sale going?"

"They're not final yet."

"Dickering over the price?" Don Antonio chuckled.

(Oh, God, he's going to kill Tom. He's going to make him into an ordinary bore, a grabby little playboy.)

"I think that's it. I don't have any connection with that end."

"They just send you the money?"

"Right, Don."

(Sam understood the irony in Tom's tone, but no one else would. "Hit him!" she pleaded. But Tom sat, arms folded, with the faintest of smiles, the pose he assumed when things got completely silly. Like a sick lamb. Very pretty. "Oh, Tom, he wants to hurt you—" Tears were blurring her vision. She reached for the pipe, fumbled another brown pellet into the

13

bowl, lit it feverishly. She hadn't watched television since she had left her parents' home; she had never seen anyone she knew on a broadcast. Not being able to touch Tom, to help him, was maddening. Her desire to hurt the wolfish man who was torturing him made her sick, the smoke burned her lungs like fury. On the screen, Tom made some gentle, ineffectual demurrer. The pain in her lungs calmed her a little. How to help him? How to get through? She didn't know anything about electronics. The hash was wonderfully strong, the best she had ever smoked. Tom. Would it work to sniff coke at the same time, together, with Tom? Vaguely she heard the greasy man say something like "I'm just pointing out that this character whose ideas are right in what I would call the mainstream of American thought is portrayed in an apparently unfavorable light which is what I get out of the book but maybe I'm missing something" and Tom agreeing or disagreeing, it was hard to tell which. And the man saying, "There's nothing wrong with making a dollar because that's what this country is all about." Sweet Tom, unaware of the demons that wait hunched beneath the daisies to chew off his toes; he walks apologetically on bare bloody bone and gristle, sorry he's not more graceful. A closeup showed Tom's face so outwardly passive yet so inwardly tortured that the head might have been a dead one mounted on a pole, a trophy for the malicious dark man—The scene on the flickering screen was becoming more and more dreamlike as the drug numbed her.)

Sam was hardly surprised when the door opened behind her and Tom came in at the same moment as his image nodded embarrassed comprehension of some television idiocy.

She stood immediately, overwhelmed with joy as she realized the pictures she had been watching were not at all real. Her feet fumbled and tangled together until she brought the full force of her concentration on Tom and strode to him, unwaver-

14

ing, and wrapped her arms around him. And he was really there, warm and strong, smelling of tobacco and nervous sweat. She squeezed him as hard as she could, willing him not to disappear.

"Hey! What's that for?"

She nodded toward the television set. "I got scared, watching that. It wasn't like you."

"It isn't me. See? I'm here."

"But how is that?"

"It was taped, silly. I didn't think you were going to watch, anyway. Whose set is that?"

"Mrs. Sandusky, downstairs, has three, and I happened to mention that you were going to be on, and she felt so sorry for me that she lent me one——"

Something was wrong.

"Well, thank God it's over. Never again."

The oddest feeling. As though Tom were not completely there.

"At least I know one thing I'm not: a television personality."

She barely heard him. He was only making noises, anyway. No meaning. Not Tom. She squeezed him again. Or was it she who was drifting in and out? He had shaved twice that day, the second time for the television show, so his cheek was very soft; she rubbed her nose against it. And saw behind him in the hall, where the light bulb was burned out, the tormentor.

The dream was real.

Don Antonio's smile was wide, more doggy than wolfish in person, with makeup clotted in the creases of his dark skin, the nose puggish between the jowls. Surprisingly, he was shorter than she. His body was apelike, a series of lumps stuck onto each other, with unnaturally long arms and short, crooked legs, almost a hump to the back—yet with power in it, even a possibility of some grotesque charm. Like an ugly boxer dog she'd like to scratch behind the ears to see his bulging eyes droop; or

15

perhaps a bloodhound, she thought nervously, about to bring down a deer. There was a brute sureness about him, a frightening self-approval, that made her want to look away.

The hollow laughter from the television set seemed to be directed at her. She stepped away from Tom and offered her hand resolutely to Don Antonio.

"I am Sam."

His handshake was powerful but unpleasantly slippery; he prolonged the contact a second too long. His breath stank faintly of liquor and peppermint. "I'm Don Antonio." He nodded at the set. "I guess you knew."

His eyes were goggling at her, darting over her body like mice. She mastered an urge to spit at him, realizing why he was staring. "I know that must look strange. I had to shave for a bikini ad, and it takes the longest time to grow back."

"It's very becoming," he said heavily. "You watch my show all the time?" he added, as if trying to calculate how many naked girls were among his audience.

"I've never seen it before."

"Ha-ha." His eyes darted greasily at Tom and lit with malice. He looked at Sam again. "You got a gorgeous build."

"I think I'd better get some clothes on. I'm making you nervous."

"Don't on my account." He made a Groucho Marx expression with raised eyebrows. But he seemed relieved. In another moment he would have had to leap upon her to fulfill the foolish threats of ravishment.

Sam turned away, trying to concentrate on where she had left her clothes. The apartment was one gigantic room, almost a loft, and they had never divided it into areas of use, so she might have put the clothes anywhere. There was a pile of things by the potter's wheel, thrown over a carton of clay, but she thought those had been there a long time. Anyway, the blue china cat on the stove was trying to catch her eye. Sam winked at him. I really ought to get my clothes on, in case I want to take them

16

off again, she thought. She scanned the room. The skirt and blouse were draped over the old gray easy chair by the bed. Exactly where she had left them!

She found herself walking toward the chair and wondering if her behind looked too skinny—and damned the dark man for making her think that way. Tom is quite fond of it, and that's all that matters. She sat on the chair when she reached it, forgetting for a moment why she had come. Her foot came to rest on a pair of panties, and she shook these out and drew them on, observing the men across the room. Don Antonio was talking to Tom in a low, phony tone, darting automatic glances at her. Tom was smiling stupidly, as though flattered by the attention.

"Hey, you got anything to drink?"

"Sorry, Don, I bought a bottle of wine a couple of weeks ago, but I'm sure somebody drank it. We ought to keep something around."

Why should we?

"Don't worry, kid, I got plenty."

Sam fished under the bed with a toe and found a sandal. To her delight, the other was right next to the first. She slipped these on and circled back toward the men, wondering what they were up to, tucking her shirt neatly into the short skirt. Much like a schoolgirl. Which is what they remind me of: boys in high school. She walked behind Don Antonio to see if he really had a hunch on his back. And leered at Tom to see if he really was taking this hunchback seriously. But to her disappointment, it didn't seem to be a real hunch. And Tom said, like a schoolboy volunteering information in class, "Don was wondering if we'd like to come out to his country place for the weekend."

Don Antonio smiled proudly as Sam arrived on the far side of him. She felt a vague stirring of anger, remembering. "You and your charming wife?"

She was pleased to see that Tom blushed; he still had a spark of decency. "Actually—Don, Sam and I aren't married."

"I suppose that's not unusual these days." But Don Antonio's social smile came a little unhinged. What a fake! Sam leered at him. He addressed Tom earnestly: "It's a good thing you didn't say that on the air. The show has a family audience. We might have had to cut the tape."

"What a bother!" Sam agreed.

"Yeah, it means more time in the studio." Something was troubling him. "We can give you separate bedrooms for the weekend, if you like. If you'd feel uncomfortable."

Sam considered this strange suggestion. There must be some purpose behind it. Don Antonio was staring at her with apparent seriousness, but the maliciousness was still clear. To her. But her head was not clear.

"Mr. Antonio——"

"Don. Please. Or DA. My friends call me DA."

She was about to say, No thanks, Tom can go if he wants, by himself, that's the way it is between us. But she had a sudden image of Tom lying tied to a tree with his throat cut, sacrificed like a sheep, blood pouring onto the grass. So she said instead, "I don't want you to think you have to invite me, too, just because Tom and I live here together. We're not really a *couple*." As she said this, she smiled at him in a peculiarly warm way.

"Not at all, not at all," he said hurriedly. "I don't want you to think I'd invite you for that. I don't know why a good-looking broad like you would think so."

"Now, if you're inviting me just because you think I have a pretty face——"

"Not just the face. I mean, the woman behind the face. I always say, a woman can't be really good-looking unless she's got class, I should say personality, behind the looks. Which I can tell you've got."

"Thank you, I'd be delighted to come to your country home for the weekend." You mutton-fisted troll. You slayer of small, warm children.

18

"Good, great." He rubbed his hands together, his eyes flashing in triumph.

Why, the dum-dum really wanted me to come, Sam thought. How did he talk me into it? I'd better watch him, he's not half so simple as he thinks he is. Wants me to think he is.

"Might as well get going." Don Antonio moved toward the door.

Wants me to get going, too. The great thing about dope is that it teaches you the relevancy of words. Irrelevancy.

"Wait a minute. What kind of clothes should I bring? Bathing suit?"

Don Antonio shrugged suavely. "We have everything you'll need. Even a toothbrush." He chuckled. "Everything is disposable nowadays."

This was so ludicrously sinister that Sam laughed a little with him. "Well," she observed, "that just depends on your point of view, now doesn't it?"

He grinned, bobbing his head deeply with a complicated and meaningless series of facial tics ending in a wink for her.

This can't be real, Sam thought. I'd better stay high all weekend, because whatever is the way things really are might be not even as nice as this.

That she could comprehend such a complicated idea gave her confidence. Bring on your trolls, she thought, bustling around the apartment and sweeping things into her huge leather handbag. To spite Don Antonio, she packed the bag with whatever came to hand: matches, a can opener, two dissimilar candles, a small jar of peanut butter, a waxed packet of crackers, a peach, Tom's razor, Tom's toothbrush and her own, mint-flavored toothpaste, a twenty-nine-cent disposable raincoat no larger than a pack of cigarettes, John A. Krout's outline of *History of the United States Before 1865* which she was rereading, a hairbrush, and other things. She noticed Don Antonio watching her with a puzzled frown as he chatted idly with Tom at the door; deliberately, she added a stainless-steel fork and a red velvet mouse to the bag. She carefully rewrapped the block of hashish in tinfoil and rolled it, with the tiny pipe and pen-knife, in her bikini, which she wadded on top of everything else. And stepped to the door, prepared.

"You pack like you're never coming back." Tom seemed annoyed; perhaps he was just embarrassed.

Sam pulled his hair aside and kissed him beneath the ear. "You can't ever tell. Innocent city girl corrupted in the wicked suburbs. Fresh concrete in the carport. Disposal Slaying Bared. All that. Missing potter found checking out groceries; white-slave link aired. It happens all the time. I had a friend who went to a party in Mamaroneck and was married by a real-estate salesman. No, really," she assured Don Antonio, who was looking as though he had a fat insect caught in his throat.

"I think you got the wrong idea. This isn't the suburbs we're going to. Not by a long shot. I've got a hundred and one acres. All of it landscaped."

"Oh, yes. You said the country."

"My wife even raises vegetables. Tomatoes and garlic. She gets the biggest goddamned garlic I've ever seen."

"Really."

"It's great. Too early in the summer now, but maybe she's got some frozen from last year."

"I bet that's good. Fresh garlic."

It was true that Tom liked garlic, but every time he said something tonight, he seemed to be sliding out of himself into some vast, gassy area of agreement with Don Antonio. Out of her range.

"Yeah, the country's great. You'd be amazed if I told you some of the people we've had out there. Entertainment stars, congressmen, even a senator from New York once. People who really count."

"We might as well get going," Sam said, and led the way through the door.

As the lock snapped into place behind them, she became aware of the faraway, insincere murmur of the television set in

20

the apartment. "Wait a minute; I forgot to take that thing back to Mrs. Sandusky."

"That's all right; she can watch the other two tonight." Tom was impatient.

"But at least I ought to turn it off."

Don Antonio shook his head decisively. "Worst thing you could do. What wears out a set is turning it off and on all the time. Heating up the tubes and cooling them off. A TV repairman told me that, and ever since then we always leave ours on. Haven't had any trouble at all."

Now Don Antonio was in the lead, drawing them down the dusky stairwell with unnatural speed. Tom smiled palely back at Sam as he pulled her along. "This is a terrific opportunity to meet some people," he whispered. "And I'm getting great material. Isn't he a fantastic character?"

No. Sam concentrated on keeping her footing. The heavy leather bag thumped dully against her leg.

The door of Mrs. Sandusky's apartment opened a crack as they sped across the landing. The old woman peered out suspiciously, her purple knit cap pulled low on her forehead; her eyes opened wide as she discerned Don Antonio in the lead. Sam, wanting to leave some message, some directive for rescuers to follow her, saw that Mrs. Sandusky was about to shriek something at the television star. Frantically, Sam put her finger to her lips, winking. The old woman nodded comprehension—of what, Sam did not know—and edged the door farther shut, leaving only enough opening for one yellow eye to follow their progress.

As they continued, at a dizzying pace, the crack of light was left far above. Sam stumbled and began studying the rhythm of her feet on the stairs, seeing nothing else until they burst into the cool, sooty night air and halted on the pavement, Sam panting heavily, because if there is one bad thing about smoking dope, it is that your wind suffers. If you smoke a lot.

They were paused on the sidewalk, apparently, for a chance to admire Don Antonio's car. This was a gigantic, flabby British

21

limousine whose cabin was painted pearl gray with pinstripes, while the extensive hood appeared to be pure chrome wrought with Greek figures. The rear window was a contemptuous six inches square, masked by a tiny velvet curtain.

The car reminded Sam of a woman crouched on her paws, buttocks in the air. She looked at Don Antonio. He nodded knowingly, appreciating the effect the car must be having on her, acknowledging that this wonderful machine was his. But this was purely automatic; his attention was on Tom.

The author was examining the car dreamily; he was, Sam knew, translating the reality into his personal literary style, a habit that annoyed her. "Go ahead," Don Antonio said to Tom. "You didn't get a good look at it before. Examine it. Take your time."

Huh? Some pregnancy of meaning here bloated and burst over their unknowing heads. Sam would have liked to stamp her foot in annoyance, but knew she was too tall to get away with things like that. Also too high. She discovered that the tiny, grotesque figures on the hood were gathered trompe-l'oeil into large scroll initials: DA. She giggled slightly, which Don Antonio took as a new sign of admiration.

"It's a Norbert Thundersweep. Custom, of course. The factory only makes two a year. I had my name on the list for five years before I could get one. I'd hate to tell you what I paid for this baby."

Sam nodded; she didn't want to know.

"Sixty-six thousand, plus change."

Assuming she could sell all the pots she could make at forty dollars each, twenty-five per thousand—her head gave up.

She walked to the nose of the car to get away from Don Antonio, who followed her, saying "zero to sixty in eight-point-six seconds" and other things. His initials were repeated on the front grille in massive metal letters bolted to the vertical bars. "And still gets over six miles to the gallon cruising."

"Your headlight is broken," Sam said. Tom had joined

them at the front of the car. All three stared at her finger, pointing, then at the glassless right headlight.

"Ha-ha," said Don Antonio. "I was wondering if you'd notice that." His voice was so wonderfully flat, so suppressed, that Sam looked and saw him staring at Tom with a murderous light in his eyes. Tom seemed oblivious, cataloguing the car's grotesqueries with gentle amusement. Don Antonio's look would have scalded anyone else. "Ha-ha," he repeated. "All repair parts have to be custom made, also, of course."

"How did it happen?" Tom asked absent-mindedly.

"I've had this headlight ordered for a long time."

"Bit of a scratch on the bumper, too, isn't there?" For the first time all night, Sam detected a faint sharpness in Tom's voice. Why, he's up to something, she thought with relief. He knows something. He's just playing dumb.

"No one seems to know anything about it." Don Antonio's glance was wary now. "Sotto claims it didn't happen while he was in the car. And of course I haven't driven for years."

"Of course."

"Who's Sotto?" But in the vast dimness of the driver's compartment Sam now discerned a set of teeth smiling phosphorescent in the center of a darker shadow. She had not noticed him before because his bulk was so enormous that she had not perceived it as a human being's. Childishly wanting to get this large person on her side, she went to the driver's window and stuck in her hand. "I am Sam."

A swarthy hand the size of a ping-pong paddle gently swallowed hers, moved it up and down a few millimeters, and released her. The hand had a curiously dry, tough quality, like leather. It dipped into a pocket and emerged with a tiny card between two fingers. Sam took the card and read in the purple streetlight: "I Am a Deaf-Mute." Beneath this was rubber-stamped blurrily: "Sotto Toppolo." Then, printed: "Learn Manual Alphabet to Communicate with Your Deaf-Mute Friends. Give this Card to Somebody Else." Sam peered at the reverse side; it bore twenty-six line drawings of hands demonstrating the letters of the alphabet.

"Thank you," she said. "I'll try to learn. Oh, dear." She stopped in confusion.

The huge man smiled and patted her arm, nodding at the card. She nodded back, with an exaggerated smile, pointing at her head and the card. They nodded in rhythm, in fellowship; but the moment dragged on, Sam did not know how to break it off. Finally, still nodding, but looking at her as if she might be a bit loony, Sotto reached back and opened the door to the passenger compartment. Why do I affect people that way? she wondered.

The compartment was the size of a Pullman; two long leather seats faced each other over a low, polished-wood console. As Sam sat, facing front, Tom got in from the other side of the car and sat beside her. Don Antonio entered frowning. "Hey?" he said to Tom. "Does it make you sick to ride facing backwards?"

"No. Why?"

"It does me."

"Oh." Tom slid around to the other seat. Don Antonio edged next to Sam. His thigh touched hers. His smile at this moment was so putrescent that Sam, having nothing sharp or heavy with which to hurt him, smiled back, nervously scratching the seat at her side. His face stank with lust; it was absurd, a fulsome parody of the pleasant human letch. If that expression were authentic, which I don't grant for a moment, she thought, he is totally insane. Because no normal person—it is crazy to be fixed so completely on one single source of possible——

Despite herself, in the midst of her disgust, she began to tremble slightly in some sort of response. Looking away, she noticed that Tom was studying her critically, and felt an unfamiliar twinge of shame. He really was very acute, always aware of what people were thinking. Sensitive.

With the air of a magician, Don Antonio pressed three buttons on the console: curtains slid across the outside windows and the glass partition behind the driver's seat, completely enclosing the cabin; soft recessed lights at the junction of the sidewalls and the roof lit the interior; there was a faint sway as the car began to move.

Don Antonio pointed at the third button. "This is the intercom. Wired to an electrode on his neck. We have signals for all the usual places. Once is for the country house." He chuckled at Sam's expression of dismay. "It doesn't hurt him. I don't think anything could hurt Sotto."

"He's a strange person. So enormous, and so gentle."

"Gentle with people he likes. But he's completely loyal, like a dog. I think he would kill without question." The car came gently to a halt for a few seconds, apparently for a traffic signal, as Sam considered the unlikelihood of Sotto's harming anyone, and then started again.

"Loyalty." Don Antonio tapped his forefinger on the console. "I don't like to philosophize, but that's what the younger generation is missing. The kids question everything. They don't know the meaning of self-sacrifice."

"You make yourself pretty comfortable," Sam said.

"But I *made* sacrifices. I *fought* for this. And I didn't have anybody to wipe my nose, either. Your young people don't know about that. Rich kids."

Tom laughed.

"What?"

"I was just thinking about my own childhood, DA. Pretty far from 'rich kids.' "

"Kid, you wouldn't have lasted a day in the place I grew up. You ever have to fight for your life? Against some bastard that wanted to kill you only because you were a guinea wop?"

"Tom's family is mostly Welsh," Sam said inanely.

"Yeah." Don Antonio sneered. "It's all Anglo. Unitarians. Don't know anything about prejudice." A red light on the console blinked seven times. "Damn! Forgot all about her." He pushed a button three times. Immediately the car swerved to the right, apparently to the curb, and halted. A blue light blinked three times in confirmation. Don Antonio mashed another button with his thumb, holding it down. "This is a real convenience. Rings a buzzer in the apartment. It was Miggie's own idea."

"Miggie is Don Antonio's wife," Tom explained.

"Yeah. What a fantastic broad. Wait till you meet her." But Don Antonio's tone was flatly indifferent; as if to make up for this, he added: "She's dying of cancer, you know that? There's nothing they can do about it. But you'd never figure it to talk to her. She's as cheerful as a bedbug in a whorehouse."

"Inoperable?" Tom's tone was that of one physician to another.

"Hopeless," Don Antonio insisted. "One of those female parts, you know? She can't even have normal sex any more. It's a terrible thing for a vital woman. No matter what they say, a woman's got to have it just like a man does." He glared at Sam, as though challenging her to dispute this enlightened viewpoint. She found herself nodding agreement. "Her especially. What a gift for life that woman has!"

They sat in the belly of the car, each apparently considering the gift for life of Don Antonio's wife. The enforced intimacy of the thought, the heaviness of the velvet curtains, began to stifle Sam. She imagined she could see their three breaths mingling obscenely in the impossibly tiny cubicle. "Do you suppose we could open a window? For some air?"

Don Antonio, with a superior manner, nodded at a grille in the ceiling. She touched it and felt a clammy caress of chilled air.

"Complete ventilation system. Changes the air in the compartment every two minutes. I never open the curtains when I'm in the car. It's better to keep them guessing."

"Who?"

"I don't know. That's the thing, you never know who's watching." He studied her expression suspiciously. "You don't think I'm paranoiac, do you?"

26

"I don't know. I don't know you."

"Let me tell you, when you're at the top of the mountain, there's people coming up behind you fast. I could tell you some unbelievable stories about people in the industry, television. Cases of food poisoning. Strange tropical fungus diseases. Actual unexplained deaths—automobile accidents."

Tom blinked slowly. Don Antonio took this as a challenge. "Ha. You laugh. One guy, they got together and everyone mumbled around him for a month, never said anything he could understand. One month is all it took. The guy went nuts, had a breakdown. You'd be amazed if I told you his name. He's a household personality. They'll get you any way they can. I even gave up having a live audience for the show. Too risky."

"I'm sure," Sam said politely.

"Then there was a famous actress, not only television but stage and screen also. I worked with her. A delicate woman, too nervous for situation-comedy work. She got into it with another girl on the show. The other one bugged a toilet seat in the women's can and got a tape of this actress taking a dump. Incredible! I heard it myself. At the big moment, she made a noise just like a woman in bed. They arranged it so she overheard the tape once, just once, and she was gone. Never set foot inside that network again, bought the contract and everything. Can you believe it?"

Sam shook her head. He didn't notice. Leaning forward intently toward Tom: "They'll *kill* you if you give them a chance. That's why this thing about the headlight worries me." He screwed his eyes almost closed. "Frame-up. The oldest trick in the game. A piece of glass left in the wrong place—you know how it'd look to the police. I've got some real friends on the force, but there're others——"

The right-hand door burst open and the head of an overripe blonde woman appeared. Her cheeks and nose were pink, firm as the rest of her face must once have been; but there were deep bags under her eyes, and her slack mouth, caked with pink lipstick, was framed by cynical wrinkles. A slight wattle hung

27

beneath her chin. Tiny white scars next to her ears gave evidence of a futile lift-job. Her eyelids seemed to be struggling against sleep and boredom or self-indulgence; the eyes peeping out beneath them were bloody and bruised-looking.

Been screwing, Sam thought approvingly. Oh, no. That's not right. She can't.

The woman's hair swung dryly across her face in artificial waves. Her body, as it followed her head into the compartment, was made up of large chunks of flesh, breasts and hips, waving beneath a fuzzy pink dress. Sam liked her smile. It had a very open quality.

"Oh Donnie, I'm so sorry, you caught me asleep." She planted herself next to Tom, closing the door and twisting to look him over. "Who are these exciting young people?"

"You missed the show, hah?" Don Antonio asked sourly.

"Oh, no, Donnie, I saw almost all of it. You look much better in person," she added, to Sam.

"Not her. The guy was on the show."

"Oh, my goodness, that must have been when Francine called. You know how she talks. I've told her not to call when you're on."

Don Antonio growled, cutting her off. "Tom Jury. Sam—what's your last name?"

"Street."

"Samantha Street. This is Miggie." Whom he looked at without favor. He pushed the third button once, holding it down. Sam winced at the thought of the electric shock on Sotto's neck. Don Antonio smiled automatically as he noticed this, but he was beyond cheering up now. "Jesus, the least you could do is watch me," he told Miggie as the car slid smoothly into motion.

"I try, Donnie, really I do." She focused on Tom. "I'm sure it must have been fascinating, if you were on. What do you do? You must be an artist or something. How interesting."

"I'll get them to run the tape of the show for you."

She ignored her husband. "Writer, then? Not one of those

28

pop music freaks; you look much too nice." Tom nodded agreement. "Donnie had one of them out to the country once—you are coming out to the country with us?" Sam nodded. "—and you wouldn't *believe;* actually, he was trying to rape me, you have no idea how frightened I was. If Donnie hadn't come into the bedroom at just the right moment, I don't know—I was so surprised, shocked by the whole thing, I could hardly struggle——"

"Shut up," Don Antonio said quietly, and instantly she was silent.

There was only the slightest vibration to show the car was moving. Don Antonio, for once, seemed sullenly withdrawn; he toyed with a cookie-sized gold watch, snapping it up and back on its expansion band. Miggie sat like a schoolgirl, straight, with her arms pressed against the seat back, palms flat on the seat next to her thighs. Her eyelids were drooping now as though in remembered pleasure, and her lips sagged in a small, crooked smile; every now and then she flickered a look at Don Antonio, who did not seem to notice. Once she looked at Sam, and her smile grew brighter, conspiritorial, for a moment.

They must have been on a parkway or highway now, because the sounds of other cars were few; only now and then they passed another, leaving the noise quickly behind them. Tom leaned back with arms folded, as though drinking in this sterile situation. Big fraud, Sam thought. Why did he ever get involved with these people? Going on television is one thing, but trying to pretend to be enjoying himself with these absolutely——

"Know what a geek is?" Don Antonio spoke in a low tone; Sam thought he must be talking to her, and shook her head. Miggie raised her eyebrows despairingly. Don Antonio studied Tom scientifically.

"What?"

"A geek."

Tom shook his head.

"Hell." Don Antonio resumed playing with his wristwatch.

29

"What is it?"

"What?"

"A geek."

"Oh. It's a guy in a sideshow that bites the heads off live chickens." He consulted his watch. "We ought to be there in thirty-five minutes."

"But why did you want to know?"

"It's a joke he made up," Miggie explained, when Don Antonio looked puzzled. "Geeks baring grifts. But it's no good because nobody knows what a geek is."

"I'd like to hear the joke sometime," Sam said politely.

Don Antonio looked at her with a trace of contempt. "Why? You just heard it."

"Oh. That was all of it?"

"No, of course not. There's a story you have to tell to lead up to it. But after you heard the punch line, you could make up your own story."

"Oh. All right." She closed her eyes, leaning against the seat, and tried to think of a story. She opened her eyes again. "What's a grift?"

"A cheat. A con game."

"Thank you. That's what I thought." She closed her eyes, but the joke seemed so silly that her mind wandered to the block of hashish in her bikini. She studied Don Antonio and his wife through her eyelashes. Better not, she thought. People who were ill-tempered and erratic were often liquor freaks, and they were the ones who were the most vindictive about dope. But I'll have a hit when we get there, she promised herself.

"How long have you been doing the show?"

What do you care, Tom?

"Oh, let's see, about five years and eight months, more or less. My fans are loyal. The show has the highest Continuous Acceptance Rating of its type, and any ad man'll tell you a good CAR means product transference."

"Doesn't it get monotonous, doing the same thing over and over every night?"

"Yes," Sam agreed.

"Never. There's always something new."

"I'd think it would be frustrating because it's such a one-way street." Tom pulled his earlobe. "There you are, in front of the cameras, saying things, singing a song, and never seeing any of the people the whole thing is addressed to."

"How is that any different from writing a book? Do you talk to your readers? Do they slap you on the back and say, 'Nice work, Tom!'? The hell they do."

"I see, that's true. But I feel when I put an idea on paper that I'm expressing myself, that——"

"I express myself every night. To millions of people."

"But the purpose of your doing that is to sell things, *products*. That's the motive behind all the machinery, the cameras, the transmitters, the wires, and tubes. It's to get across the ads, to make money. If you didn't sell things for the sponsors, the process would collapse."

"If no one would buy your books, who would publish them? You and your publisher probably feed yourselves a lot of crap about art, right? But if you wrote the greatest book in the world, what would be the difference if no one would buy it? If no one would publish it?"

"I'd know the difference."

"Sure. There's probably a thousand people convinced this minute that they've written the best book anyone ever wrote, only they can't find anyone to agree with them, so the only way they'll ever get it published is to pay someone."

"The critics agree with me. Most of them, anyway."

"The critics are nothing but the advance guard of the public that buys books. The only reason your book is important, in fact the only reason you're sitting in this car now, is that people are buying the book."

"What about books that are critical successes but don't sell?"

"That just means they happen to appeal to a small part of the book public, the critics, and not to the rest. I could write a

31

book that appealed to another small part of the public, say, guys that jack off into shoes, and if it sold as many copies as one of your 'critical successes,' it'd be just as important. The critics would think it was a lot of crap, but guys who jack off into shoes think the critics are full of crap. Take your pick. The only standard that means anything is totals: how many copies you sell of your book, how many people watch me every night."

"Donnie, do guys really jack off into shoes?"

"Yeah."

"Why?"

"Because they're queer."

Tom looked troubled. "But what you're saying is that nothing is intrinsically better than anything else. I can't accept that."

"Hell, I don't know. I like some books better than others. I like some dames better than others. Maybe you like others. Who's right? It doesn't make any difference. There's no use arguing about things like that, anyway. That's for kids. The only fact is, who sells more books. Or whatever."

Don Antonio looked at his watch: "Ten more minutes." He began snapping it back and forth on the band again, and Sam thought he was suddenly nervous. Miggie flicked the nail of her middle finger with her thumbnail, examining the cuticle. Don Antonio rolled his eyes at the roof, seeming casual. But there was a smell of expectancy in the car, as in a lion house.

Tom drew out a pack of cigarettes and offered them around. Miggie shook her head. "Coffin nails," Don Antonio said absent-mindedly.

Sam took one. Tom bent forward with the match to light it. She drew hard on the cigarette, holding the smoke down, filling her lungs, parodying herself pulling on a joint for Tom's benefit. She let the smoke go with a gasp as he was lighting his own cigarette; he exploded with laughter, blowing out the match, which made him laugh louder as from outside the car came a brief scream, high like a child's, and a dull thump like a door slamming far away. The car shivered with a light impact.

Don Antonio frantically pushed a button; the car came

32

screaming to a halt, swerving to the right, bumping over something, apparently the curb, first with the right wheels, then with the left. Don Antonio was out of the door in an instant; Miggie after him; then Tom, with his cigarette still unlit; then last Sam, more slowly, wondering what had happened.

Don Antonio was running back along the deserted parkway, searching. Sotto stood by his open door, something black and shining in his hand, perhaps a gun, but it seemed to disappear even as Sam watched. She thought there was a gleam of amusement in the enormous man's face. He made no move to follow Don Antonio.

Miggie stood on tiptoes, peering back along the road. Tom, with a thoughtful air, lit his cigarette. Sam smoked, wondering if she would have time for a pipe in the open air. But no, they were almost to the country place, anyway.

Fifty yards down the parkway, Don Antonio halted. He stood looking down. Sam thought she could make out a dark form at his feet. He seemed to nudge it with his foot.

Surprisingly, Tom put his arm around her shoulder. She looked up at him. He took her chin in one hand and kissed her mouth. And winked at her seriously, almost like a warning.

Don Antonio beckoned to them.

"Does he want us to walk all the way back there?" Miggie asked nervously. "Well, I'm not going to." She climbed back into the car.

Sotto pointed to the car, meaning the others should get in, too. Tom shook his head. "Let's walk."

"All right." Sam threw her cigarette away and followed him along the side of the road. Sotto backed the car down the pavement, keeping pace with them.

It was a deer. The body lay on the grass; the slender neck projected onto the roadway at an impossible angle. There was a little blood, very thick and dark, on the white muzzle. One half-closed eye seemed to roll toward Sam despairingly as she approached.

"Look out!" she called, thinking the tire was about to crush

33

the deer's head. But of course Sotto couldn't hear her. The car backed by and stopped, the wheel missing the head by inches.

At least it doesn't have horns, Sam thought stupidly.

Don Antonio nudged the body with his foot again. The back leg kicked and shivered reflexively.

Sam trembled in sympathy. "Can't you do something for it?"

Tom shook his head.

Don Antonio studied the front of the car. "Didn't seem to do any damage. That's funny." He looked at Tom accusingly.

Tom shrugged. "We must have barely clipped her. Broke the neck."

"Yeah."

Sam knelt by the deer's head. She stroked the neck; it was unyielding, the hair stiff. The eye seemed to be already becoming cloudy. The eyelashes were surprisingly long; they looked false.

"Hey, you know what?" Don Antonio pointed at the broken headlight. "That deer could have done this."

Sam was confused. "How? It was already broken."

"I know, I know. But it *could* have. You both heard the car hit it, right?"

She touched the muzzle. A little of the blood stuck to her fingertips. She wiped them on the pavement.

"Yeah. The deer. It could have happened that way." He nodded to himself.

Sam stood. "Can't you do anything? It hurts her."

Tom shook his head. "She's dying."

"Then shoot her. Put her out of her pain. Isn't that what you're supposed to do?"

Don Antonio paused, getting into the car. He looked at Sam as if she were crazy. "Shoot a deer in the middle of the parkway?"

Sam got into the car after them. Miggie was huddled in the corner of the seat, her face pale. "Can't we go?"

Tom pulled the door closed, sealing them in once more. He

34

held Sam's hand. "There's really nothing we could do. She couldn't live more than a couple of minutes."

Sam took her hand away. And then thought, Of course, he's right. But it ought to mean more than that.

Don Antonio pushed a button. The car started smoothly. "Just one of those things," he said, as if reassuring Sam. "Coincidence."

What?

"I just can't bear to look at things like that," Miggie said to her corner of the car. "There's no reason why I should."

The car rolled to a stop, then started again. The road was more tortuous now, and Sotto seemed to be driving cautiously.

There was no conversation. Once Sam caught Don Antonio's lips moving silently as he nodded to himself.

In a few minutes, they came almost to a halt, made a sharp left turn, and began crunching over gravel. "We're here," Don Antonio said eagerly. "Wait till you see my place."

2

The car climbed a long hill; as it stopped, and the motor was silenced, a ferocious barking, as from several dogs, surrounded them. Paws scrabbled against the metal sides of the car. A white light flashed on and then off, casting the shadow of a huge dog's head with open jaws against the curtain at Sam's window. She shrank away.

Neither Don Antonio nor Miggie moved. Don Antonio smiled contentedly: "We wait until Sotto puts the dogs away. Otherwise there might be an accident."

The light outside flashed on again, casting a shadow of the dog's torso. Sam realized it must be as tall as a man when it stood on its hind legs.

She heard Sotto's door open and then slam shut. A dull thud, flesh on flesh; a grunt of pain from one of the dogs, and suddenly they were silent. Paws clicked on the gravel, moving away. A gate shut. Heavy footsteps returning, moving around the car. The right-hand door opened; Sotto waited beside it for them to descend.

The estate was magnificent; the winding white-gravel drive shone in the moonlight under towering maples, leafy obelisks. The highway was far away, barely visible down the perfect lawn on the hill.

As Sam watched, another white light flashed on and off in a bush near the stone gate towers at the highway. One of the dogs whined eagerly. She turned and saw three spidery black shapes, the dogs standing on their hind legs against a wire fence strung between concrete posts at the side of the house.

"They're trained killers," Don Antonio said. "They know me, but even so I wouldn't get near them unless Sotto was with me. They're taught to attack unless commanded otherwise."

"I've always liked dogs." But Sam wasn't sure she liked these. Any dog will love you if you feed him, she thought. I'll find them something to eat.

The house itself was splendid, in a nightmarish way: a collection of concrete cubes and towers, chunked together, like Don Antonio himself, in a rather haphazard fashion that gave first an impression of overwhelming ugliness, then a possibility of power and charm. Sam realized that although the particulars of the architecture were totally modern, the whole suggested, must have been meant to suggest, a forbidding castle. Its coldness was intensified by large expanses of glass tinted some dark color, which seemed to create voids in the concrete face, swallowing up the car's headlights. There were no trees close to the house. The builder must have torn them down, so that it squatted like a lonely sphinx on the brow of the hill, surrounded only by a pubic fringe of low evergreens around the foundation as far as she could see. It looked less like a house than like an institution, a monument, a factory. There was even a soaring, tapered, round chimney rising from the center of the mass, ready to spew milky poisons into the clean night sky.

As Sam watched, a light appeared behind a frosted window in one of the upper stories. The shadow of a man passed in front of the glass, then sank out of sight. A moment later, they heard the roaring of a toilet flushing, and the light went out. Sam was puzzled; the whole thing had seemed unreal. "You have someone here already?"

Don Antonio laughed. "That's part of the protection system. It's all electronic, uniquely built for this house. You noticed the lights coming on around the grounds?"

"Yes."

38

"They're directed by a small computer. They go on and off at completely random intervals. Even I don't know when. If anybody got by the dogs, the outside lights would scare them off. If they got to the house, they'd see lights coming on in the rooms, shadows moving around. All played at random. There's one that looks like a whole cocktail party. Sometimes I sit out here and watch the show. It's fantastic."

"But wouldn't there be a lot of cars around if there was a cocktail party? I don't think that would fool anyone."

He frowned. "I don't know. All I know is, we haven't had any trouble since we've been here."

Sotto towered patiently next to the limousine. Tom studied the house.

"That's right," Miggie agreed. "And it's so comforting to come home to. Not like an empty house at all."

"Yeah. Watch this." Don Antonio leaned back inside the car and pushed another button.

Floodlights bathed the house and lawn. The interior lights in the central section of the house came on. A fountain in the large entrance courtyard coughed and began playing over the slender marble figure of a girl, while a recording of some tinkling instrument could be heard expressing the theme from the movie *Doctor Zhivago*.

Tom studied it all with sleepy wonder. "That's really something. I thought you must live in someplace like this."

"Yeah. It's us. You got to build a house to resonate with the people that live in it, that's what the architect said. *Resonate* was the word he used."

"He actually lived with us for six weeks before he would start designing the house," Miggie said. "To study us." She giggled.

"He was a faggot."

"He was not!" Miggie was indignant. "He was a very sweet young boy."

"Yeah. Sweet. But I think he really captured me with this house."

39

"Me, too, Donnie."

Don Antonio ignored his wife. "So maybe it was better that he was a fag."

"He *was not!*"

Don Antonio seemed to judge correctly that she was in such a rage that she was about to say something irreparable. He slapped her lightly on the rump. "I guess you'd know, Miggie. Anyway, the kid did a hell of a job. Come on, let's see the inside."

As he led the way into the courtyard, Miggie made a rude gesture at his back with her hand and elbow. She took Tom's arm. "You remind me of him. He had the same soft skin. And gentle personality." Her fingertips brushed Tom's cheek.

Sam turned away, hiding a grin. Get out of this one, she thought. But ahead of her, Don Antonio moved with heavy purpose, as though constructed out of lava. What does he want? Oh, he's just a troll, and this is his cave. She tripped along behind him, listening to Miggie murmur to Tom, noting Sotto's huge silent shadow behind all.

The entrance court was paved with red tiles bearing a fleur-de-lis design. Changing colored lights played around the marble fountain, coloring the girl's figure now flesh, now jaundice, now shivering blue. The concrete sides of the yard were studded with slate, and impossible plastic greenery was set at regular intervals in huge concrete urns.

Behind Sam, the iron gate clanked shut, closing them into the courtyard. Ahead, Don Antonio paused at the front door, which was a slab of dark-stained wood carved with trompe-l'oeil initials, DA, like the hood of his car. He produced an iron key fully five inches long, inserted this in the door, and turned. Oily snap of the lock, and the door swung back noiselessly.

The entrance hall inside was almost identical to the courtyard, giving Sam a queasy feeling that she had been here before. Don Antonio observed her with a slight smile.

The greenery was the same except that here it had improbable bright-colored fruits set at intervals among the plastic leaves. The tiles were slate-colored, and irregularly shaped slabs of rosy marble were set into the walls. The lighting was the opposite of that in the courtyard; there the statue in the fountain had been brightly lit; here, colored lights illuminated the walls, but the statue, in the middle of the hall, was almost in darkness. Looking at the figure closely, Sam discovered that it was a carving of a man, naked, heavily muscled, almost a satyr, but slightly too gross even for that. The water pouring over it obscured the lines, made the heavy flesh seem to run like butter.

The schizophrenia of the two concepts of the space, inside and out, was deeply disturbing. Neither was fully realized; she was reminded of a Picasso painting showing both sides of a face at once. There, the idea was interesting; here, to be inside it, was sickening. The architect had known his business, but she wouldn't have wanted to meet him in a dark alley.

Tom and Miggie, still arm in arm, paused with her at the fountain. Don Antonio watched his guests. "You like it?"

"It's very interesting." Everything was interesting to Tom these days. Sam shook her head. Don Antonio chuckled, noticing her reaction.

A spot of bright yellow caught her eye at the base of one of the plastic shrubs. She picked it up: a little toy kangaroo, with a black-and-white smile sewn on its plush mouth. "What's this?"

Don Antonio took it from her, frowning. "One of those kids must have left that here last week. I gave it to one of them. Nicky, I think. Boy, they don't teach them any discipline out there any more."

"Where?"

He ignored her. "Come on, I'll get Sotto to show you to your room. Freshen up, and we'll all have a drink."

He made a complicated series of arm and wrist gestures toward Sotto, who nodded gravely and preceded them to the left-hand of the two stairways that flanked the hall. Don Antonio and Miggie went toward the other stairs. "See you in the living room in a few minutes." He pointed at a room through glass doors between the staircases. Miggie waved happily at Tom. And Sam smiled at her, clutching the big leather handbag.

The stairs led to the midsection of a second-story hall; at each end of the hall, a smaller flight of stairs led upward again. The hall had a red carpet and gilt light-fixtures; doors faced each other blankly across it as in a hotel corridor.

"This place is a Chinese puzzle," Tom said. "I wouldn't be surprised if they had a Danish modern dungeon."

Sotto led them to the right, down the hall, opened a door, and stood waiting for them to enter. As Sam went by, he pressed a scrap of paper into her hand. She tried to catch his eye, but he was looking the other way. He shut the door firmly behind them.

It was the first time they had been alone together all night.

Sam put her arms around Tom's neck and finished the kiss she had begun when he had returned to the apartment. But still he wasn't quite there. She looked over his shoulder, expecting to see someone, and saw herself, staring at their reflection. The entire wall behind the bed was made of mirror tile. "Christ," she said, and sat on the bed.

She became aware that she still had the scrap of paper Sotto had given her crumpled in her fist. She smoothed it out and read, printed in a large, childish hand, "I AM A FRIEND."

She handed the paper to Tom. He read it, frowning. "The chauffeur?"

She nodded, took the paper back, and suddenly laughed. Tom was puzzled. She laughed harder. "It's so stupid!" He reached for the paper again. "Not this, the whole thing. What people!"

Tom started laughing with her. This made her even sillier. She rolled on the bed, burying her face in the purple spread. Tom kicked off his shoes and rolled with her, tangling them both in the silk. Tensions came bubbling out of her with the laughter. She pictured herself telling Sally or Joan or Hector about it: "The most grotesque people, really, can you imagine? They must have been nearly fifty years old! And the house!

42

Like something you read about, supergothic modern. Both of them so fat and uptight about sex—the woman kept trying to get Tom alone. Sinister, absolutely sinister!"

The bedspread was slick and cool. Sam picked off her shirt and skidded on her back. "Oh, look!" She laughed harder, pointing upward. The ceiling was made of mirrors, too. Her body was white and small on the purple silk; Tom was wrapped up like a mummy; their small laughing faces were like children's.

Sam's hand slid under the spread, inside Tom's shirt. Her hand fitted nicely over the slab of muscle; the ball of her finger rolled over the tiny nipple until it rose. Vestigial pimple. How sad. His hand covered hers, restraining.

"Hey. Did you bring your pipe?"

Reluctantly she broke the contact to rummage in her handbag. Yes, indeed, that will be nice, but——

She was being selfish.

Precisely, she pared a fragment of hash the size of half a pea from the block, placed this in the center of the pipe, and struck a match. She drew hard, welcoming the searing in her lungs. A parody of tears covered her eyes; she blinked. She handed the pipe to Tom, who contemplated it for a moment, pashalike, before putting it to his mouth. As he finished drawing in, she was exhaling and took the pipe back. Three times each they inhaled, and then the hash was gone. Sam applied another match, but it would not stay lit; all she got was biting sulfur.

Carefully she knocked the tiny ash into her palm and examined it. Vacant of all life and juices. How small, and how enormous her hand! With a finger like a huge club, she forced the ashes down, made them crumble into her palm. The heat was of course gone from them, only the dryness was—factual.

Sam smiled sleepily, her eye muscles uncoordinated and relaxed. She drew herself back on her elbows, and her hand turned over like a flower whose petals were her fingers, carelessly dripping ashes onto the bed.

Tom lay on his stomach, his head cradled on his forearms, turned away from her, studying his image in the wall.

In the ceiling, her face was a frozen teardrop.

She stroked Tom's ass. Did he flinch slightly when she touched him? He was very ticklish, though he said he wasn't.

He turned on his back and stared at the ceiling.

She began stroking his belly; the motion of her hand was hypnotic; was it to him, also? So hard to tell! He was half-erect, a sort of dope-dream hard on, and his face was loose and smiling at his reflection—? You never could really get inside anyone's mind. Could you? And how could you tell if you did?

She began laughing to herself at the uncertainty of—? What? Not uncertainty of everything, though that's what she was thinking a minute ago. Because if everything were uncertain, that would be a sure thing. Isn't that right? So in the whole vast thing, the possibilities, most of the results must be unpredictable, but some must be foreordained.

What?

Tom understood, he was laughing, too.

"It's possible. I mean, not possible. Predictable."

By now she had absolutely no idea of what she was talking about, she was entrained in a swamp of variable syllables, discrete as turnips in oil. Yes. Oil. One word, one syll. Short thoughts are best. Though thoughts is too chewy. So's though, actually.

"What's *actually?*"

But Tom was grinning rubberly at his self in the ceiling. Sam squeezed the remaining words from her head, tube from a toothpaste, leaving only *rubberly*. Her mind was as empty as her body. But which should be full. Not with words but with Tom. But his mind was not on her. Only her hand that stroked and held him. Rubberly. Half hard.

Her mind was half an instant away from hating him.

He does not know I am ready for him any time. He does not know how. To be. Like me. Total. But meaning less, or do

44

I? Is that the only time I can be all together, with the dope? *Freak*. But only for Tom.

Be careful. She found herself hating the tiny white image of herself in the ceiling. Stranger with a stiff face. A gulf was beginning to open in a black corner of her mind. She was afraid she would split down the middle, and Tom would be able to look inside, and there would be nothing at all there.

She bent over Tom and took his nipple in her mouth, laving it with her tongue, pulling it erect again with her teeth, gently. Hot central on his chest. The panic deceding. Not now, anyway. But he was required to decode the discording vibrations. Where was he? "Where are you?"

"I was thinking. This house. These people. They're 'slightly gamy.' "

"That stinking review. Forget it."

" 'Slightly gamy first novel.' Hah!"

"What do they know?"

"But that's a good description of——"

"Hey! How much time is passing?"

"What?"

"What?" She laughed. "We're supposed to go down to the living room."

"Grief. We must have been here an hour."

Like guilty children, they scrambled off the bed. Sam pulled on her shirt; why had she taken it off in the first place? She tried a door painted flat white and edged with gilt paint, at the side of the bedroom, and discovered a bathroom.

This was not merely a place where one squatted or soaked for a few minutes every day. The walls were tiled with mirrors with fine, jagged gold lines running through them; her reflection peered at her, and at the reflections of the reflections on the facing wall, as from a smoke-filled cave.

Everyone who entered here would look the same—sexy and mysterious—to herself.

A dim blue night-light hung in the ceiling; there were

switches for other lights, but Sam did not touch them. The toilet was partitioned by a low tiled wall, like a throne. There was no bathtub; instead, one stepped down three tiled steps and through a beaded curtain into a lower tiled section of the room, perhaps six feet square. Sam pushed the beads aside; the enclosure had a faucet and controls set into the wall on one side; overhead a globe the size of a grapefruit seemed to be the showerhead. All the metal parts were yellow: gold?

Sam decided she would spend the rest of the weekend in the bathroom. After the "drink" in the living room. Maybe they would give her a ginger ale. She didn't want her head muddled by drinks. Not muddled that way.

She adjusted the lever over the sink and splashed cold water in her face. If she got very rich sometime, she would have a bathroom like this, perhaps with a strobe light. She pulled her hair straight and gave the room a last affectionate look before leaving. Yes, indeed. Not so bad. Slightly gamy.

She nodded back at the bathroom, indicating it to Tom, unable quite to speak the thought. He hardly noticed; he was ready to go.

Out the door, she went first—and stopped. The barnlike mass of Sotto was there, three paces from the door, waiting patiently. He made a sign with one hand: two fingers outstretched, then the pinky extending upward from the fist. Huh? He repeated the motions. Sam found the alphabet card in the pocket of her skirt. Two fingers extended together: G. No, G was one. Two was H. And the pinky was easy: I. HI. She repeated the motions clumsily: HI, yourself. His face broke into a smile like the morning sun breaking over the Grand Tetons; nodding with pride, he turned to lead the way to the stairs.

"What was that?" Tom whispered.

"Code. HI."

"Hi."

She showed him the card. "See?"

He looked at it briefly. Not his meat.

46

Piqued, Sam tried the A and B, and almost tripped on the stairs. A, B, H, I. Easy. She found the T on the card and spelled out BATH. HABIT. Sotto, pausing to hold open the glass doors to the living room, saw her doing this; his eyes shone. Miggie was drunk. What letter to add next? She discovered the C, which was simply cupping the thumb and forefinger, and slid the alphabet card back into her pocket. CAT, HIT, BITCH.

The living room was another schizophrenic page from *House Beautiful.*

A gigantic room, castle-sized, with each object of furnishing placed at right angles, none with any common motive but expense. At one end, huge logs were piled in a fieldstone fireplace, waiting for winter. Except someone had placed a red light in the grate behind the logs, making them look like plastic. The mantelpiece was one gray slab of cut stone; centered upon it was a wicker basket of plastic grapes, flanked by two red-painted hurricane lamps. Two long couches extended from the sides of the fireplace, geometrically perfect, with low, modern lines; centered between them, too far away for anyone to reach comfortably from the couches, was an apparently Formica coffee table at shin level, with one copy each of *Life, Time,* and *Sports Illustrated* overlapping down the middle.

On one of the couches, Miggie sprawled, one arm flopping over the back, the other hand holding a glass of dark liquor and eroded ice cubes, one plump leg extended on the couch, the other knee bent and tapping a slow, self-centered rhythm against the back of the couch. As if someone had thrown a handful of pink paint into a geometrical, black-and-white painting.

The room's windows were symmetrical, one on each side of the fireplace, three each on the facing walls. The draperies, which were pulled closed, appeared to be made of zebra skins, a pair for each window.

But here the symmetry ended. Having laid out the room

47

thus far so carefully, the architect appeared to have become displeased with his concept; or perhaps here his influence had run out, and the owners had done the rest of the decorating themselves. The remaining available space was crammed with sideboards, lowboys, china cabinets, antique chairs, leather recliners, overstuffed easy chairs, rickety old tables, leopard-fur ottomans, linen-shaded brass lamps, hanging light-globes, a stone Cupid bearing a bowl of stone fruit on his stone head and flanked by a matched modern pair of wrought-iron ibises, all packed so closely that they formed an impenetrable maze; and against the wall by the entrance doors through which they had come, facing the fireplace across the jam of furniture, a gleaming mahogany bar behind which Don Antonio hunched like a gnomish servitor, now in his shirt sleeves, grinning at them nastily.

"We almost gave you up. How'd you like the bed?"

"Fine," said Sam. "We had a hit."

"Ha-ha."

"Givmadrink," Miggie suggested from the couch.

"Well, how about a drink?" He gestured at the rows of bottles on shelves behind him. "We got anything here you could order at any bar in New York, I don't care where. Plus Ballantine ale on tap. Huh?"

"I guess whiskey," Tom said.

Sam was chagrined. What a way to ruin a perfectly good high! She was still floating, her fingertips were tingling, but what it needed was a dark place with some good, loud music. That bathroom would have done fine, with the night light and the water on. She was afraid this living room was going to do something bad to her head. All the glassware behind the bar made her think of Hospital, unnatural, stinging fluids. Turn the bottle upside down with a rubber tube and stick a needle in your vein? How about that? No.

Don Antonio was petulantly mopping the bar with a spotless cloth. "Whiskey. Yeah. But what kind?"

48

"Scotch, I guess."

"Did you know when you spell Scotch whisky, it's without the *e*? *W-h-i-s-k-y.*"

"I didn't."

"Yeah. You ought to use that sometime in one of your books. Anyway, we got all kinds, which do you want?"

"Whichever's the best."

"No, you got to order your brand. Like in a bar."

"Name some of them."

Don Antonio looked disgusted. "Chivas Regal, Old Rarity, Clan MacGregor——"

"That's fine."

"Which?"

"MacGregor."

"Clan MacGregor, coming up. What do you want with it?"

"I guess a little water."

"Right." He turned to Sam. "How about yours?"

"Ginger ale, please."

"Ginger ale?"

"Yes. If you have it."

"It's not a matter of we don't have it. It's a matter of you're sure you know what you're doing?"

"I like ginger ale."

"Okay. Okay." He bobbed beneath the bar. Bottles clinked together. "Goddammit!" In a moment he reappeared, holding a dusty green bottle. "See? I told you we got everything."

"That's very nice," Sam agreed. "I always keep some ginger ale in the apartment myself."

"Sure." Morosely, he began to assemble the glasses, ice, and bottles. What a clown! Sam thought. But then she caught a faint gleam of amusement in his eye, as though he were doing this all to make fun of her ideas about him.

Over the bar she now noticed a photograph of several dozen sad children, posing for the camera like a losing athletic team, all wearing identical dark little suits. The picture was slightly

49

yellowed with age. Below it was a plaque saying Don Antonio, Honorary Father—Orphanage of St. Francis.

Miggie set her glass down sharply on the bar, startling Sam. "How about me, Donnie?"

He filled Miggie's glass from the green bottle of Scotch that he happened to be holding and dumped in two ice cubes, overflowing the glass. She stood for a moment, glaring at him, and then turned to Sam: "When I was a child, I had a pet mouse that died." Her voice was so slurred that Sam had trouble understanding. "I think it was just a house mouse. I kept it in a cardboard box——"

"Nobody wants to hear that story," Don Antonio said. "You've told it a hundred times."

"Well, they don't know about it."

"They won't want to, when they hear it."

She flicked her fingernail irresolutely. Sam smiled at her encouragingly, but after a moment she turned and went back to the couch. "Tell me about it sometime," Sam called after her, but she made no sign that she had heard.

Sam watched Don Antonio fussing with the drinks. She wondered if he had been drinking as much as Miggie; probably, and it hadn't had any effect. She tried to imagine him smoking dope, and failed. He probably didn't even take aspirin. The ape. He probably didn't even feel sick in the morning from drinking liquor.

Don Antonio placed the tall glass of ginger ale in front of her on a paper napkin printed with red slogans. "I may be an Old Goat, but Oh You Kid!" she read. Wrong. What about the goat-troll dichotomy? she thought crossly.

Don Antonio set down Tom's glass and raised his own. "Here's to your book, kid. Every man, woman, and child in the whole fucking country should buy it!"

Sam raised her glass and tried to drink with them, but the ginger ale had a nasty, medicinal taste that made her gag.

Behind them, Miggie said, " 'Ray! Oops!" and there was a splashing noise.

Covertly, Sam spit the stuff back into her glass. Don Antonio noticed, grinning: "What's the matter?"

"It tastes funny."

"Small goddamn wonder, Scotch and ginger ale. You want me to make you a real drink?"

"No. I thought it was going to be plain ginger ale."

"Ha-ha. Plain ginger ale." He looked at her strangely, and turned to Tom. "Seriously, I'd like to read your book. You got a copy with you?"

"I didn't bring anything. What do you mean, you'd like to read it? Haven't you read it already?"

"No, but I got interested while we were talking."

"How could you talk about the book if you hadn't read it?"

"I don't read books, I pay a guy to read them. That's all he does, is read books. Can you believe it? Then he writes up an outline. Page and a half maximum."

"You never read the books?"

"I don't read one a year. Hell, why should I? The whole world passes through the studio. But yours I got to see. Why don't you get the publisher to send me a copy?"

"I could, but it'd be faster and easier for you just to buy one at a bookstore."

Don Antonio frowned. "I don't like to do that."

"What?"

"See, there's a principle involved. You were on the show, right?"

"Right."

"I could have had a dog act, for a little more dough, or I could have sung another number myself, for free. Instead, I had you. That's good for you, for the book, good for the publisher. You got some sales out of it. But if I have to go out and buy your book, that's like saying the whole thing of your being on the show was worthless. Instead, it was an advantage to you."

"That's what the publisher told me."

"So it ought to be recognized."

51

" 'Ray," said Miggie, rather sullenly.

"Shaddup," Don Antonio replied automatically. Miggie kicked her leg defiantly, losing her shoe, which flew in a high arc and knocked over a small lamp with a base like a copper cannon ball. Sotto, who had been standing so still that Sam had forgotten he was there, stepped forward to right the lamp and return the shoe to her. With surprising quickness, Miggie grabbed his ear, forcing his head down, and began to French-kiss him.

"Don't mind her, she'll pass out soon," Don Antonio advised the world.

"Ha," Miggie mumbled. But the position in which she was having to hold her neck made Sam's own ache. Sotto remained impassive, bent at the waist, accepting her tongue in his mouth with eyes politely closed.

The three at the bar stirred their drinks with monogrammed muddlers. Sam tried another sip of hers, but it was too foul to swallow, and she spit it back again. Conversation lapsed.

After perhaps two minutes, though it seemed like much longer, Miggie's head fell away from Sotto's; her hand made a desultory pass at his pants, missed, and wound up between her own knees as a cushion, while the other arm curled beneath her head, her eyes closed, her mouth opened, and she began to snore. Sotto walked away. Oddly, he made no move to wipe his chin, which was quite wet.

"He's impotent," Don Antonio said, smiling with satisfaction as Sotto left the room. "The perfect servant: deaf, dumb, and impotent. That really burns Miggie up. She takes it like some kind of personal insult. But the poor guy can't do a thing, it's true. One time in the city I paid a hooker to try to get a rise out of him. Jesus, she tried everything! And she was a good-looking babe, too. I think I'd kill myself if I couldn't handle a woman." His eyes began flashing a series of complicated, automatic signals at Sam, who ignored them.

"How did he get that way?" she asked. At this moment,

52

Sotto returned, carrying a blanket and a folded newspaper. Sam looked away, embarrassed.

"Don't worry, he can't hear you. You could fire off a gun behind him, and he wouldn't move. I think as a matter of fact it had something to do with the war. Korea." Don Antonio ducked under the bar and joined them, as a customer, his foot on the brass rail. "Did you know I was in the Navy during Korea?" he asked Tom.

"No, I didn't."

"Yeah. Talk about books, if you had my experiences in the service, you could really write one. Hey, that's an idea!"

"What?"

"You ever do any autobiographical writing?"

"No."

"Too bad, I'd probably be better off with someone more experienced. I'll talk to my agent. But maybe you could do it. You're a smart kid."

"Thank you."

"I've done some fantastic things. Did you know I was the only guy ever to shoot down a Commie jet with a rifle?"

"You shot down a jet with a rifle?"

"It was coming over the convoy, and there were other people shooting at it, but I know I got it. I had this old M-1 that I won in a card game in Honolulu, see, and the second time the MIG came over, I bet the mate I could hit it. He was laughing, but you should have seen his face when the goddamn thing blew up."

"That's unusual."

"Yeah." Don Antonio looked at them suspiciously. "I'm surprised you hadn't heard the story. I told it on the air once or twice, maybe more. I even had the mate on the show once to back me up. Had to trace him down through the military records. The guy never made anything of himself, he was mate on some junk freighter. You sure you didn't see that show?"

"Must have missed it."

53

"I never watch television," Sam said. She had been watching Sotto arrange the blanket over Miggie. Now he spread the newspaper on the floor next to the couch and turned her head so her mouth aimed toward the paper. "What happened to the man in the plane? Wasn't there a pilot?"

Don Antonio seemed surprised. "Sure, there must have been a pilot. Those things don't fly themselves."

"Then what happened to him? Did you see him afterward?"

He laughed. "Sweetie, when a few tons of jet fuel blow in the air, you don't look around later for anybody that was in the middle. They're just part of the explosion."

"But didn't it bother you? Didn't you think about the pilot?"

"Maybe I did, I don't remember. But hell, I'd never seen the guy. I was just shooting at the airplane, the machine. It was war. He was doing a job, like me. We were both getting paid. There was nothing personal in it."

"Pretty personal for him, getting killed." She felt a curious kinship with the dead Oriental. "Besides, you were doing it for fun, on a bet."

"Boy, you kids make me sick. We were fighting to save your country."

"Thank you," Sam said gravely.

"I don't care, it takes more guts to fight than to run." He turned on Tom. "How many gooks have you killed?"

"None."

"What branch of the service were you in?"

"None. I'm 4-F."

"You never killed anyone at all? Not even accidentally?"

"No."

"I haven't either," Sam volunteered.

He paid no attention to her. "Then how can you know how it feels?" he asked Tom.

Tom shrugged.

"I'm talking about your book now. You got a part in there

about a guy running down a little girl with his car. How do you know anything about that?"

"You imagine. You put yourself through the experience; you put yourself in the character's place."

"Yeah, but that's not the same as living it."

Tom was thoughtful. "Nothing that's fiction is ever quite like what you've lived through yourself. You synthesize. You build on analogous situations; you take real experiences and work them into the form you want. In a sense you live through the book as you write it; it becomes the same as if you really had all the experiences. It's no more difficult for me to write about how it feels to kill someone than it is, say, for me to write about how it feels to be a woman."

"And the woman in Tom's book is very true to life," Sam said. "I was amazed."

"Yeah." He ignored her. "This scene of the star hitting the girl with the car, that's a central thing, right?"

"It's an important part of the physical plot. Actually, the death scene itself isn't described; it takes place offstage. It's not the actual event that's important, but what it means in terms of the old man's character."

"But something like that, a pure accident, how can it have any meaning?"

"Well. First, although it is an accident, it's brought about by the father's drinking, which in turn is caused by his spiritual bankruptcy."

"You talk a lot like a radical sometimes."

"I'm not political. Anyway, an accident like that, or something similar, could happen to anyone. But the point in the book is his reaction, the fact that he drives on and leaves the girl dying, and his inevitable decay and destruction that follow."

"I didn't get that far in the outline. What finally happens to him?"

"As I say, he falls apart; he loses the last traces of humanity."

"But do they ever catch him?" Don Antonio waited with obsessed attention for the answer.

"He turns himself in."

"Hah!" Don Antonio's breath exploded in anger. "You call that realistic? I'm sorry, kid, but you got no idea. You ought to get someone to do a little research for you before you start writing. You know what percent of hit-and-runs are solved in this country? Eleven percent, that's how many. Straight from the FBI report. What kind of nut is going to turn himself in against odds like that? Almost ten to one he's never going to get caught."

"I wish you'd read the book. That's the whole idea, that he's gotten away with murder. When he realizes that, at first he's relieved. But it begins to bother him. He returns to the scene; he starts to act irrationally; he hears the girl's scream in his nightmares. Finally he turns for help to the son, the son he's rejected and made fun of. The son tells him to turn himself in, and he does."

"Some advice. Some son."

"But giving himself up is the only way for him to relieve the terrible guilt and tension he feels. When he does, his hatreds, his self-disgust, dissolve."

"Yeah. What you're writing is a pipe dream. That's what I mean, you can't know about something unless you've lived through it. If you'd killed people like I have, in the war, you'd know it doesn't make you feel that way."

"How does it make you feel?"

"At first you're scared. You don't know if you're going to be able to do it; you worry about what the other guys are going to say. Then the time comes when some bugger is shooting at you, and you shoot back, and he falls down, and the only thing you feel is you're glad it was him and not you."

"That's a little different from running down a young girl with your car."

"My car?"

56

"One's car. Anyone's car. That's not war; it's murder, or damn close to it."

"Manslaughter in almost every state. Third-degree murder at the most. There's no question about its being an accident."

"Under those circumstances, I call it murder."

"You think you could never do anything like that?"

"I would never willingly hurt another human being."

"Suppose someone was coming after you to kill you. Or your girl. You wouldn't protect yourselves?"

"I'm not sure. I'd try to keep a situation like that from developing."

Don Antonio was beginning to look a little out of control, as though the liquor was catching up with him. He leered maliciously at Sam. "I want to go to bed with her. Your girl. You going to stop me?" He took a step toward her.

"That's up to her."

"You wouldn't fight me?"

"If she wanted to go to bed with you, what good would it do me to stop her?"

"Okay. Jesus, you're weird. Look, now I'm going to hit her. Hard. Because that's the kind of guy I am. I don't even feel bad about it, I'm just going to hit her. I think it'll do her good."

He raised his open hand. Sam was suddenly sure that he was really going to hit her. She flinched a little, then made herself stand her ground. She measured the distance for a kick and smiled at him.

"Hell, I think she likes it." His hand moved back a fraction, preparing to swing.

To Sam's annoyance, Tom moved between them, blocking Don Antonio from her. Don Antonio grinned. Tom seemed very frail before him.

A horrible, strangled moan distracted them. They turned away from Don Antonio, looking for the source: Miggie, on the couch. She stirred and groaned again, from deep inside. Her body shook beneath the blanket and the moan became choked, "Aaaaaaargh—" as her mouth opened and she vomited slowly onto the newspaper.

"Old Faithful." Disgusted, Don Antonio pressed a button on his wristwatch.

A second later, Sotto reappeared, already holding a towel.

"Get that mess out of here," Don Antonio ordered. Sotto nodded, apparently having caught the lip movement, and impassively began wiping Miggie's face.

"I guess we'd better get to bed," Sam said. "It's been a long day."

Tom nodded. Too quickly. For an instant she was ashamed for him. Then she saw Don Antonio, well pleased with his work, grinning at her. She put her arm around Tom's waist, realizing too late that there was something odd about this gesture, and urged him away. "Good night. Thank you for a lovely evening."

"Yeah. See you kids. We'll have some real fun in the morning."

"Good night."

As they passed out of the living room and turned toward the stairs, Sam looked back. Sotto was bending to lift Miggie from the couch, still wrapped in her blanket. Don Antonio stood, hands on his hips, like a ringmaster, as though wondering which of them to kick.

On the stairs, Tom moved ahead of her slightly so that her arm fell from his waist. Quite right, she thought. I'm sorry. But neither of them said anything until they had opened the door and entered the room.

"Do you think—?" Tom asked.

"Wait a minute." The room felt strange. She realized that her handbag was nowhere in sight, and the bedspread was not rumpled the way they had left it. In fact, the bed, which was on the right-hand side of the room, should have been on the left. "This is the wrong room."

Back into the hall. Their room was the next down the row;

this time when they opened the door, the odor of stale sweet smoke greeted them. Home.

Sam kicked off her sandals and stretched out on the bed.

"Do you think he was really going to hit you?" Tom asked.

"Who knows?" She saw that he was troubled. "Yes, I do. Isn't that dumb?"

"I think so, too."

"What would you have done?"

"Like I told him, I don't know."

"You shouldn't have worried about me. I was going to kick him."

"Good old Sam." He laughed. "Always direct action. That's because you have a clear conscience."

"Because I've got strong legs and pointed sandals." She stretched her right leg in the air, admiring the muscles. "Isn't your conscience clear?"

"Usually. But these people——"

"Why did you want to come out here?"

"Don't you see? I couldn't stay away."

"I don't understand."

"Sam, they're the people in my book."

It was true. Don Antonio: the father—dissolute, authoritarian, talentless, constantly demanding attention, helplessly obsessed with sex, creating a ridiculous tiny hurricane around himself wherever he went. Miggie: the mother—bloated on what she had drained from others, apparently subservient to her husband, yet triumphing over him in a thousand little ways every day, creating such a perfect cocoon for herself that finally there was nothing to do but withdraw inside in a stupor. What about Sotto? Sam tried to cast him in Tom's book. Perhaps the taciturn undercover narcotics agent who befriended the heroine; a somewhat mysterious figure, never fully explained · who helped the girl instead of turning her in, an action that could only have been caused by a concealed, pure passion for her that Sam had always considered a bit corny. But hadn't the agent been a Greek, and rather small at that?

59

"What does that make us?" she asked suddenly.

Tom shrugged, grinning.

"Well, it's your book," she said, a little crossly. "It may all be some kind of intellectual puzzle to you, but I wish I knew what was going to happen next. He's dangerous."

"Yes."

"Why did he want us here?"

"I'm not sure. Maybe he wants your pliable young body."

"No. It has something to do with the book. The accident."

"Did you notice, on the show? How he started attacking me after I mentioned that?"

"But it doesn't have anything to do with him."

"He thinks it does. He's an obvious paranoid. Maybe he bumped someone with his car."

"Bumped off, you mean. Like the deer. Did you hear it scream?"

"No. I don't think deer make any noise."

"This one did."

"Maybe so."

He didn't believe it. Annoyed, Sam unstrung the sandal and swung it on her big toe. "She likes you. Miggie. Did you notice that?"

"I was afraid I was flattering myself."

"Hah."

"Would you mind if I balled her?"

"I don't think so."

Liar! But as she was saying this, she could almost believe it. And she wouldn't mind too much, if she could always know that he would come back to her. But she couldn't say that.

"Do you want to?"

"Not any more. But she's kind of bouncy looking, isn't she? For an old woman."

And I'm too skinny.

"Tom, let's get out of here. I can say I'm sick."

"What's the hurry?"

"Something bad is going to happen."

"What could happen?"

"I don't know."

"We can go any time. But look, this is a fantastic opportunity."

"Why?"

"Don Antonio is an important man. He could really help us, if he wants to. Think of the people we can get to know through him."

"We haven't met anyone yet."

"I thought there were going to be other people here. But it's quite a compliment, actually. His inviting us by ourselves for the weekend."

Balls, thought Sam, balls. She recalled from her biology course that the embryonic folds of skin that develop into the labia majora of the female grow together in the male to form the scrotum, which contains the balls. Which do not, contrary to popular opinion, necessarily make him anything special.

"All right," she said. Irritably, she rubbed her eyes, which felt scratchy from the dope. Which reminded her: "Want another hit?"

"Not now." He lay on the bed beside her, leaning on his elbow, watching her, very relaxed, very sexy. "Oh, I forgot!"

"What?"

"You haven't seen the bathroom."

"No."

"Wow! Come on." She bounded off the bed and led Tom by the hand to see the bathroom, opening the door with a magician's flourish. "See?"

But somehow the room wasn't as grand as she had remembered.

"Out of sight, it's a bathroom. I think I'll brush my teeth." He turned on an overhead light, and the room became quite ordinary looking. There were two toothbrushes hanging by the sink, as Don Antonio had promised.

"You have no romance."

Tom took the pink toothbrush and ran a neat bead of toothpaste onto the bristles. "Not about bathrooms."

Sam took the blue toothbrush. The toothpaste was light

61

green, fluoridated, mint-flavored, very foamy. The presence in her mouth made her think of Miggie's vomiting. She spit out the foam and quickly rinsed her mouth. Miggie had probably been slender and hopeful once.

When I get old, I'll take my pleasures where I find them. But not like that. I'll find a loving young man who looks like Tom and live on a hill in a castle full of dope. And drink sweet tea and eat baklava. And have a bathroom finer than this.

Tom had flushed the toilet and was unbuttoning his shirt as he left the bathroom. He kissed her neck. "If you hear me snoring in a minute, it'll be because I'm asleep. Jesus, I'm tired."

All right, Tom.

A few seconds later, the bed sighed and the bedroom light went out. She turned off the overhead light in the bathroom. The mirrors sparkled softly in the dim blue that remained.

As if she were underwater.

The gold filigree was on the surface of the mirrors; she was beneath.

Behind the walls of the bathroom, on each side, there were other rooms. She was in all of them.

She turned on the water in the giant bathtub, adjusting it until it was quite warm. The water seemed to come from the faucet with great force.

She tossed her clothes out into the bedroom and closed the connecting door. This door also was covered with mirror tile, and it bounced her back into the bathroom as it closed.

Breasts a little too large for modeling, body too thin for anything else. But in the right angle, to a camera, or in a dark mirror, it looked all right.

Glass eyes.

Glass body.

Glass, glass, glass: the word had lost its meaning. The pattern of a million devilish splinters already there, waiting to be born, each different.

The water was ankle-deep. She sat, legs outstretched, aware

62

of the five images. No, six: one within the mirror in each wall, one in the ceiling, and the one sitting in the water. She felt a quiet fellowship with the others.

When she lay on her back, the water did not quite reach the corners of her mouth. She breathed through her nose. But the pressure of the water against her ribs was frighteningly strong.

And the images in the walls had disappeared.

She sat up quickly.

Leaning back on her hands, she edged beneath the stream of water from the huge faucet, letting it cascade over her torso.

Like a lover's fists.

The water struck her head, pinning her hair to her face and neck like wild tentacles of seaweed.

She could not see.

The water was up to her belly. When she moved violently away from the faucet, she made a massive wave that broke against one wall.

The water wanted to get inside her.

Of course, if it gets too deep, I can just stand up.

She clasped her knees with her hands as the water crept over her breasts.

The image in the wall facing her was starting to drown.

There seemed to be small, jellylike creatures with hard, stinging arms in the darkest parts of the water, near the wall. Advancing toward her, then scurrying back. Cerulean blue and poisonous red, like crabs. But almost colorless in the darkness.

Dope dream.

Stop it!

She stood resolutely, water streaming off the images as they rose with her, and punched the knob to turn off the faucet. The water was above her knees, an odd feeling, swirling around the tops of her legs as she stepped to take the soap from its crevice in the tile wall.

When she soaped her hair, the images turned to gray-haired old women. She ignored this.

The soaping was a ritual, driving away thought.

Something seemed to be crawling around her toes.

Stop it!

She lifted each leg high out of the water to wash. The soap washed off each as she placed it back in the water.

She had to get the soap off the rest of her.

She flung herself into the warm black water, forcing her head and body under, holding her breath as she frantically combed her fingers through her hair, wiped them over her body, getting off the soap. It was over in a moment. She got to her feet, finding the steps, and ran up them, away from the water.

The towel was wonderfully thick and dry. The water in the tub was like ink, shimmering on the surface. She stared as she dried her hair, wondering how she had had the courage to go in there. Finding the drain lever, she pulled it up. A shock seemed to go through the water; it drained so quickly that the final sucking gurgle came as she finished toweling herself. The bottom of the tub was clean and shining.

She turned off the night-light and found her way to the bed in darkness. Tom grumbled comfortably as she slipped under the covers. She hugged him from behind, cupping herself to him.

It was a good thing that Tom was already asleep, or she might have told him about the bathtub. He would have laughed at her and then looked at her very closely. She didn't want him to do that. When the freaky fears overtook her, she took herself away from Tom: she would stay in bed with the pillow over her head, sleeping, or take walks at night in the filthiest and most dangerous parts of the city, or read thoughtless books in a corner of the apartment, a fixed smile on her face, until she could recompose the Sam that pleased him——

She began to fall asleep as the coolness of skin on skin became warmth.

3

The best sleep is the sleep that you don't remember.

She pushed her nose into the pillow like a rooting pig.

She reached out greedily for Tom, but he was not there.

The sheets were thin and slick, the mattress was too soft. The light in the room was all wrong.

Irritably, she pushed the clinging sheets from around her head. Unwanted images scrabbled through her mind. Her eyes were scratchy, her lungs raw. A faint line of light showed beneath the heavy green draperies.

No Tom.

She went to the window and pulled back a corner of the drape. The bright sunlight seared her face; shying away like a mole, she let the cloth fall back.

Perhaps he was in the bathroom.

Sam pushed the door open almost belligerently and turned on the overhead light. No one was there.

This morning, the appliances seemed garish, offensive. Her body looked clumsy, the skin flaccid, like a boiled egg, in the mirrors. She tried not to look at herself as she retreated to search for her toothbrush in her bag. Her hand brushed the little bundle of foil and the tiny pipe, paused for a moment, then went on. She touched the toothbrush in the bottom of the bag, recognizing it by the nasty, shiny feel of the plastic. Anyway, better mine than his.

She got her own toothpaste, too. Returning to the bathroom, she concentrated on the faucet, on the rosy-pink sink bowl, spreading the toothpaste on the brush. But as she was scrubbing her back teeth, she forgot and looked at herself. The black hair hanging straight, the eyes slightly pink and cross-looking, the small nose, and foamy mouth.

I am going to be an old woman not very long from now.

Spitting out the toothpaste in disgust, she took handfuls of cold water and scrubbed her face, then rubbed it fiercely with a towel. And stared at herself: The skin glowed pink, but her hair was straggly from having been washed, and the eyes were petulant. She pulled her brush viciously through the hair. God help me if Tom saw me now.

She dressed quickly, scornful of the clothes, and got out of the room.

The hall was empty, the house silent. She tried to walk without noise, thinking she might keep to herself, scout out the territory. But at the bottom of the stairs a huge shadow detached itself from a pillar: Sotto, smiling happily.

Despite herself, she smiled back. From the fog in her mind she dredged out the signals: index and middle finger extended, the pinky held upward: HI!

Delighted, Sotto returned the greeting. He nodded toward a door off the hall. Sam held up her hand, meaning, Wait. She took the alphabet card from her skirt pocket and studied the letters.

BREAKFAST? She raised her eyebrows inquiringly.

Sotto looked puzzled for a moment, then took the card and pointed toward the K, making it with his hand. She repeated. He shook his head and gently moved her thumb to the right position. Satisfied, he opened the door for her.

In contrast with the living room, the dining room was austere. The ceiling was fifteen feet high, stark white over white walls, with dark, hand-hewn beams that looked out of place.

66

A modernistic chandelier, seemingly made of pewter, with bold curves concealing the light bulbs, hung low over the long, narrow table.

In the center of each long wall, facing each other, two abstract canvases summoned conflicting emotions. The styles were identical; there was no doubt they were by the same artist, but one was saucy and carefree, with a joyous wildness of color, while the other was a fugue of browns and blacks, instantly depressing.

The table, shining like wet black silk, was tightly surrounded by a dozen black wood chairs with broad straps of red velvet for backs, like directors' chairs. In the center of the table, a vase of a dozen gigantic plastic yellow roses. At the far end, Miggie, cheerfully waving a piece of toast smeared with strawberry jam.

"Good morning, dear, sit at this end."

Obediently Sam walked the length of the room and waited for Sotto to pull out a chair around the corner of the table from Miggie. The seat was hard, and the sagging back made her sit round-shouldered.

Sotto placed a printed menu and a pencil in front of her.

"I wouldn't try the omelette, dear, his omelettes are abominable."

Oblivious, Sotto tapped the line on the menu that said "French-Style Omelette," and made a lip-smacking noise. Sam shook her head, pantomiming a yawn. She circled "Grapefruit Juice," "Toast," and "Coffee." Sotto nodded understandingly and took the menu to the kitchen.

"You look ravishing this morning, you know," Miggie said. Her own eyes were bloodshot but cheerful. "By the way, I've forgotten your name."

Sam found that her right hand, resting on the place mat, was trying to spell SAM. She made herself speak: "Sam."

"Oh, yes. I'm Miggie."

"I know."

"I have the most awful time with women's names. Isn't

67

that funny? Because I can always remember a man's name. Your friend's is Tommy, isn't it?"

"Tom."

"He's very cute."

Sotto reappeared, carrying a tiny crystal glass of grape juice. Sam glanced at the alphabet card, holding it in her lap surreptitiously, and spelled out FRUIT. Sotto nodded agreement happily as his fingers repeated the word with lightning speed. He went back to the kitchen.

"Are you married?" Miggie asked diffidently. "I mean, to each other? I didn't quite catch that."

"Actually, not."

"I think that's a mistake, if you like him. Of course, perhaps he doesn't have much money."

"He's just made a lot of money." Sam tried the grape juice. Not bad at all. She hadn't had grape juice in years. "By the way, have you seen him this morning?"

"I saw he and Donnie talking on the terrace." Miggie stressed the *he* slightly, as though correcting Sam's grammar.

"Money isn't very important to us," Sam said, realizing she had left this out.

Sotto returned with her toast and coffee, carrying the plates between the thumbs and the knuckles of his forefingers. Sam tried to spell out THANKS but forgot the K again, and failed to get his attention anyway.

"You can't spend all your time in bed."

This irritated Sam immensely. "I didn't mean that at all. There are a lot of other things that don't cost money."

Miggie held up a hand. "To a woman, dear, the most important thing is security. And there's only one kind of security that means anything, and that's money. What would all the things you think are important now mean if you found yourself out on the street without a cent?"

"I've been alone before."

Miggie ignored this. "A woman has to think of the future. A pretty boy is one thing when you're young and pretty yourself, but it means an awful lot more when you're starting to lose your looks. Tommy is a nice boy, but you're making a fatal mistake if you simply plan to drift along with him."

"I'm not drifting along." Am I?

"What'll happen when he gets tired of you?"

"I might get tired of him first."

"No. Ninety-nine times out of a hundred, it's the man who gets restless. You have to get them in the first moments, when they think they're in love. Then they're vulnerable."

"That's cold-blooded."

"It's important for a girl to understand. Frankly, I pissed away a dozen chances to marry wealthy men, and it was only when the wrinkles started to come that I realized what I'd done. I didn't have more than one good year left when I met Donnie, and I made sure of him. Marry, that's the key. Marry early, and often, if necessary."

"Marriage is a trap."

"Oh, dear, I'm afraid you've been listening to those feminine liberation people. Really! Of course it's a trap. But the important thing is to be the trapper, not the one who's trapped. If it doesn't work out, you can always get a divorce, you know, and you're bound to be better off than before, if you take care whom you marry. But you *must* marry."

"All the married people I know are miserable."

"Perhaps, but I doubt they're any more unhappy than they would be if they were single. The ones who are unhappy are the ones who have unrealistic expectations, the ones who insist on absolute fidelity and so on."

"I don't sleep with anyone but Tom." This sounded stiff and silly to Sam even as she said it.

"Oh, how sad! You see, if you were married you wouldn't have to worry about that. You'd sleep with other men naturally, as a matter of course. Everybody does. It's expected. And the men are expected to have other women. Once they understand that, most of them are quite happy to be married. But the marriage contract gives a stability to everything, and that's important to a woman. If this young man has money, I advise you to marry him at once. Face it, darling, there's only one thing a man wants from a woman that he can't get from other men, and once you've given him that, what else is there?"

"Doesn't a woman want the same thing from a man, then?"

"Oh, yes. But you see, she has to get it by subtlety. It's simply anatomy. A woman can't really rape a man, you know. Not unless he wants to be raped."

"I guess that's true." Sam was confused.

"Of course. You haven't eaten your toast, dear. Would you like something else?"

"I don't think so. I'm not really hungry."

"I'm not either." Miggie waved her toast and licked off some of the jam. "But I'm on this fantastic diet, and the doctor says I should eat a good breakfast." Some of the jam had gotten on her lower lip; she pushed it daintily into her mouth with her little finger. "Anyway, the important thing to remember is that there are literally hundreds of attractive men, perhaps thousands, in New York alone. Do you think Donnie is attractive?" She asked this with a sudden sharpness.

"Oh, yes." This sounded unconvincing. "I'm sure he is."

"Good. Do you want to sleep with him?"

"Oh. No, I don't think I would."

"He's a wonderful lover. Really. His equipment is marvelous."

Sam suddenly remembered. "In the car, before we picked you up, he was saying something about your being sick. That you couldn't have sex."

Miggie burst into laughter. "Oh, the dear! Isn't that precious? Did he really?"

"Yes. He said you had cancer."

"Oh, Lord! Isn't that something?" She laughed till tears came to her eyes, and she began to choke on a bite of toast. "Isn't that the end?"

"It's not true?"

70

"Oh, that's *too* funny! He had you believing that?"

"Yes, I guess so."

Miggie let loose another peal of laughter; then, suddenly, she became serious. "Donnie is a lamb. But he's a little mischievous, and he doesn't always tell the truth. You must remember that."

"All right." There was a pause. Sam looked at the toast, but she really wasn't hungry.

Miggie licked her finger and ran it over her plate, picking up crumbs. "If there's anything else you'd like to do, you don't have to sit here with me, you know. It must be boring."

"No, not at all."

"I think I'll have some more toast. Are you sure there's nothing you'd like?"

"I usually have just a cup of coffee in the morning."

"You ought to try the jellied eel."

"Actually, I think I'll look around for Tom."

"Whatever you like. The swimming pool's in back, down the hill. You can change there."

"Thank you." Sam was up and backing away from the table.

"If you need anything, ask Sotto or Donnie. They'll be eager to help, I'm sure." Miggie waved Sam away. "Run along. If you like a drink, the bar's in the living room."

Sam retreated around the table and opened the door by which she had entered.

"Ha-ha, *cancer!* That's too much!"

Sam waved weakly and closed the door behind her. I really do feel ill, she thought. That's no lie. I ought to get away from here. No, damn it, they got me out here, and they can damn well put me up for the weekend.

But where's Tom?

The huge entrance hall, lit by a skylight, looked almost drab today, which pleased her. She mounted the stairs firmly, marched down the hall as if she owned the place. But as she was opening the door to their room, she thought she saw something dark move at the end of the hall. She looked again, saw nothing, and went on into the room.

At first she thought she had come into the wrong room again because the bed was neatly made, the curtains open, and everything in its place. But her handbag stood at the foot of the bed. She searched it hurriedly and found the foil-wrapped chunk of hash. But who had made the bed? Sotto? Of course, they have other servants, a maid or something. She went to the window.

The room must have faced east, because the sun streamed into her face, causing her eyes to flinch away. Dopey. Outside, the world was very bright, very much alive.

Probably there were ants darting everywhere through the greensward, in instant, vibrant communication through super-sensitive antennae, picking up crumbs, juice, meat; pursued on all quarters by voles, moles, shrews, mice, flickers; darting up and down the grass-blades, green like plant blood, forever expectant.

Sam liked the idea of the ants. She made up a story about them:

Once a famous ant found a crumb of chocolate icing. He brought it to the nest, and the queen decreed that everyone should have a taste. She ordered the vicar to cut the crumb into equal portions for everyone. But there were so many ants that each portion was a single atom of chocolate icing, and the icing entirely lost its flavor when divided into such small particles, leaving on the ant palate only a tantalizing phantom of the true flavor, like the ping of a stone striking the bottom of a bottomless well. And each ant, on tasting this ghostly ecstasy, rushed up into the world to seek the reality. To seek endlessly. The finder ant was given a velvet couch near the queen's, on which he lay sighing languidly and sipping the nectar that was brought to him. He became quite potbellied. When a favored cousin was permitted to approach the couch to ask "What was it really like?" a faraway light would come into his eyes, his belly would expand a few nanometers as he inspired, rolling his liquid eyes toward the earthen dome of the throne room, and he would exhale a cosmic groan, an almost sexual wail. Then the petitioner would back and scrape away, his antennae trailing the floor, his own eyes downcast in thought, until he passed from the room, when he would streak for the entrance of the nest, perhaps bowling over one of the guards in his frenzy to return to the quest for the icing. The guards would jeer at the pilgrim, making coarse jokes to each other, but deep inside they felt the same longing and emptiness. As for the queen, she was pleased with the state of affairs, for it kept her minions ceaselessly on the forage, and she felt no such fond cravings herself, for her taste buds had been dulled by decades of mind-less screwing——

Dissatisfied and irritated by the story, Sam rubbed her eyes. I could go back to bed, she thought. Damn it.

She blinked.

Well, there was even a bloody *bluebird* singing on a limb of the maple tree outside the window. That's the last straw, Sam thought, and smiled. Probably just caught an ant.

Her lethargy dissipated as she tried to imitate the bird's song. After all, Mr. and Mrs. Don Antonio are probably perfectly nice people. They don't have anything to do with Tom's book; that's *his* hangup. Chirp, chirp. Even if Don Antonio was in some kind of hit-and-run accident, it has nothing to do with us. The bluebird eyed her, and flew away. Even if they're all complete lunatics, which seems likely, there's no reason not to enjoy the weekend.

The view from the window was magnificent, in a way. It reminded Sam of a well-kept golf course. The grass receded from the house in carefully coifed waves, giving her the giddy sensation of sitting on someone's head. Clusters of trees and clumps of shrubbery were set about with a carefully planned randomness, which, however, over the large view Sam commanded, reminded her of a wallpaper pattern about to yield its secret of repetition.

A couple of hundred feet down the hill, an impossible oak tree, a giant bonsai ninety feet high, twisted its black trunk into obviously artificial angles, culminating in a frowning brow that might have been the product of some Sunday painter's diseased imagination. Absurd. Furthermore, no roots could be seen at the base. The oak rose cleanly from a carpet of lime-green grass growing right up to its trunk, unmarred by a single fallen leaf or acorn. There was less litter in the great expanse of grounds than in Sam's apartment in New York.

No, wait! There, over the swelling of the hill, the landscaper had left one primitive tangle of brush, a dark, curly, equilateral triangle apparently masking a natural gully. But the effect was weakened by the precision of the boundaries forced on the area, giving it a false, theatrical quality like a bearded lady's leer. It seemed unlikely that any wild creatures could live in such a small area.

Oh, well, thought Sam, turning away from the window, it's his fantasy.

She decided to go swimming.

It was a puzzle whether to carry the whole handbag to the pool or just take the things from it that she would need. Awful bother to forget something and have to come all the way back here. On the other hand, the bag was heavy, and she would look a bit strange lugging it down to the pool, especially since Don Antonio had seen her stuffing it with the peanut butter and the other junk.

I don't care what he thinks.

Or it might be easier to change into the bathing suit here *and* take the bag. But she would feel funny walking through the house in a bikini.

Oh, the hell with them.

Sam picked up the handbag and walked into the hall, almost slamming the door. And stood there, wondering if there were a back door, some way to get outside without going through the entrance hall.

She became aware of Sotto standing in the shadow at the

rear end of the hall, smiling. Her friend. She looked for the **P** on the alphabet card and then quickly spelled out POOL?

Sotto nodded suavely and made a swift series of motions with his fingers, losing her immediately. He laughed silently, like a friendly dog, at her bewildered expression and repeated: FOLLOW ME. He beckoned with a finger like an Italian sausage. Sam nodded violently. His meaty shoulders presented themselves to her as he moved toward the rear of the hall with small, neat steps.

To her surprise, when they reached the end of the hall, he led her up the staircase instead of down. Surely the swimming pool can't be on the roof, she thought. Miggie said it was out back. He must have misunderstood.

She wanted to say something, to attract his attention somehow, but he mounted the steps implacably. These stairs were narrow; his body, turned slightly sideways, still filled the space between railing and wall, and Sam had to bump her handbag along ahead of her.

The distance seemed unnaturally long, as though the staircase had skipped a floor, but finally it made a sharp angle, rose four more steps, and debouched into a tiny, bare hall with only one door beneath a peaked skylight. Sotto produced a large key ring from his pocket.

He glanced at her. POOL? she spelled again. He shook his head and put his finger to his lips in warning.

All right.

The door was small, built for some attic gnome. Sotto flung it open and stood aside to allow her to enter; the hall was so small that she had to brush against him, though he shrank politely against the wall, and her elbow ricocheted off his abdomen as off a boulder. Sotto followed her into the room and shut the door softly behind them.

The room was in proportion with the door and hall; a bed, bureau, and desk, Sotto, and she completely filled it. She was reminded of a room in a college dormitory. Sotto opened another small door, revealing a tiny bathroom with a shower instead of a tub. Sam shook her head politely, and then, realizing he was showing off his living quarters, nodded appreciatively. He shut the door.

Three of the walls had large windows, giving the room a broad view of the estate. On the other wall were crossed pennants saying NY Giants, a gun rack with two rifles, a panel with buttons and lights, apparently for signaling, and the stuffed head of a raccoon, smiling mischievous thoughts. The bed was neatly made, with no spread but a red-and-black-striped blanket and a naked pillow.

Absent-mindedly, Sam began to say something complimentary. Sotto quickly held up his hand. He took a pad of paper from the desk and wrote with a ball-point pen, then handed the pad to her: I THINK ROOM IS BUGGED.

YOUR ROOM?

YES.

VERY NICE.

THANK YOU.

She sat on the bed. After an awkward pause, Sotto sat next to her. She took the pad and wrote: WHO BUGS YOUR ROOM?

DA.

WHY?

MENTAL.

OH.

ALL ROOMS BUGGED, YOURS TOO—EVEN OUTDOORS, IN BUSHES.

Who cares? Sam thought. It's his place. She wrote: THANKS.

Sotto took the pad and paused, studying her. The conversation had nearly filled the top sheet of paper. He turned the pad sideways and wrote along one edge: YOU ARE IN DANGER.

Sam, unconvinced, made no reply. Sotto neatly circled the initials he had written earlier: DA.

WHY?

I DON'T KNOW.

76

DOESN'T MAKE SENSE. She underlined this.

The sheet of paper was full; Sotto ripped it off and crumpled it into a large ashtray.

On the fresh sheet Sam wrote: WHAT CAN HE DO? KILL YOU.

Sotto's handwriting was large and girlishly curlicued; he even dotted his *i*'s with little circles. The words looked absurd, so bald on the white paper. She would have giggled if she hadn't remembered that the room was bugged.

She wrote: YOU WOULD STOP HIM.

MIGHT NOT BE ABLE TO.

WHY?

TICKLISH SITUATION.

On impulse, she wrote: HOW DID HEADLIGHT GET BROKEN?

His face became impassive. BETTER NOT TO ASK.

ALL RIGHT.

After a moment, she added: DON'T WORRY—TOM WILL LOOK OUT FOR ME.

TOM IS HUSBAND?

NOT HUSBAND, FRIEND. She wrote this firmly.

It seemed to bother Sotto. He asked: TRUSTWORTHY?

And gave her a fresh sheet of paper, again crumpling the used one into the ashtray.

She replied in large letters: YES.

Sotto took the pad, studied her answer, and shrugged doubtfully. He restored the pad to his desk, dismissing the topic, and began spelling something with his finger. Sam missed the first few letters and shook her head. He repeated: SWIMMING POOL.

Sam nodded. Sotto stood. She stood. He pointed.

Down the hill, in the second fold of lawn behind the house, the swimming pool sparkled an impossible powder blue. It was shaped like a boomerang, set in a flagstone oval; in the interior angle of stone lay Tom on his back, wearing either a borrowed pair of white trunks or his underwear, one elbow crooked over

77

his eyes to keep off the sun, the other cushioning his head. The white shorts made his body seem as vulnerable as a baby's. She felt a rush of joy as she realized how much she had been missing him this morning, how foolishly she had been afraid, without admitting it to herself, that something had happened to him, how glorious it was going to be to see him, to talk to him, to touch him.

Sotto was thrusting the pad into her hand with a question: YOU LOVE HIM?

Sam shrugged, almost indignant, but her neck felt hot and she knew she was blushing. Sotto wrote: SEEMS TO BE NICE YOUNG MAN—TELL HIM TO BE CAREFUL.

THANK YOU.

IF YOU NEED ME CALL.

YES, THANK YOU.

WATER IS NICE.

I'M GOING SWIMMING NOW.

Sotto nodded, tearing the sheet of paper off the pad. She realized he must burn them in the ashtray. He opened the door and stood politely waiting for her to leave.

GOODBYE, she spelled with clumsy fingers, holding her bag in her left hand. Sotto repeated this swiftly, nodding. She noticed a large bald spot at the top of his head, around which his black hair curled in tiny, oily breakers. "Thank you," she said aloud, forgetting his warning, but he did not seem to notice that she had spoken. She left, feeling oddly unfulfilled by the silent conversation, and the door shut noiselessly behind her.

The heavy bag was awkward as she went down the narrow stairs; she had to watch her feet to keep from tripping. She hurried ahead, thinking of Tom and the cool water.

At the landing, she wondered which way to go. Surely the back stairs would be quicker—she glanced down the hall and saw Don Antonio standing by the door to their room, smiling sardonically. Startled, she stood as he approached without haste.

"Get lost?"

"No. Yes, I guess I was. I was going to go swimming."

"Thought the pool was upstairs? Ha-ha."

"I wanted to look around the house. It's interesting."

"There's nothing up those stairs but Sotto's room."

"I know. He sent me down again."

"I bet he told you some of his crazy stories while you were up there."

Don Antonio was standing peculiarly close to her. She edged away. "Oh, no."

He leaned closer. "He's completely off, you know. Same head wound that made him a dummy."

"He seems very nice."

Don Antonio smelled of stale liquor, but also sweaty and male. The bastard. His hand touched her neck and lingered there. Sam bent away, but the hand remained.

"A pretty kid like you would be just his type."

"I thought you said he was impotent."

"Oh, sure. I don't mean he'd hurt you. But he has fantasies. You can't believe anything he says."

"I wouldn't know, since he can't talk."

The hand squeezed her neck slightly. "Yeah, that's right."

"I was just going to go swimming." Her body ached with the effort of restraint from flight.

"No hurry. We could talk for a while." But now he leered in a completely artificial way, ludicrously, and the threat was gone, if there had been any. Despite herself, she felt sorry for him. She patted his hand and removed it from her neck.

"I really think I ought to go. I saw Tom at the pool."

"From the window upstairs?"

"Yes, of course. Sotto showed me his room."

"Miggie might be at the pool, too," he said, almost to himself. "You didn't see her?"

"No. Is there a back way out?"

"Sure. Down the stairs and through the kitchen."

"Thank you." Sam started down the stairs.

"See you later, kid."

Glancing back, she saw that his face, half turned from her,

seemed to be full of sardonic triumph, as though he had successfully manipulated her again. She almost turned back, infuriated, to ask him what the hell he was so pleased about. But no, that was what he was trying to do, make her curious. It was just another fraud, like that silly joke of his. Geeks. I'd like to see a pack of women's liberationists get him cornered——

The stairs ended in a tiny blank hall with steel swinging doors to the left, like those in a cheap restaurant, and doors of carved wood on the right, which she knew led to the dining room. The hall was a cage; she pushed her way quickly to the left, into the kitchen.

Now this room, thought Sam, is impressive.

For one thing, it had two refrigerators, something she had never seen before, plus a chest freezer. And three ovens. A huge chopping block, ten feet long and three inches thick, ran along one wall beneath a hanging row of large cleavers, carving knives, butcher knives, carving forks, and a sharpening stone. All the appliances, sinks, light fixtures, everything metal, had a brushed stainless-steel finish, giving the whole room the appearance of an operating room. The lights were long fluorescent tubes—cold, dazzling white, drowning the sunlight that entered through a tinted picture window over the sinks. The cabinets and woodwork were painted glossy black, the walls brutal white. There was not a spot or blemish on anything. Not a dish, fork, pot, or pan was in sight, nor a scrap of food. A faint, sickly odor that Sam identified as that of disinfectant hung in the air.

She couldn't imagine a meal being prepared in this room; quite possible, on the other hand, to imagine a television commercial being filmed here, or a murder being committed. She checked the sinks and confirmed that there was a large, powerful disposal unit. Very funny.

Intrigued by the huge, square refrigerators she opened the door of one to find an enormous joint of meat, the hindquarter

80

of some animal, wrapped in plastic, flanked by smaller packages bound in butcher paper.

Surely we can't be expected to eat all this.

She picked out one of the small packages and unwrapped it: crimson hamburger, with the soft, mealy appearance of expensive meat. Remembering the dogs, she rolled the meat back in the paper and pushed it into her bag. Absolutely never be missed. Anyway, they probably feed those poor dogs cornflakes; that's why they're so bad-tempered.

Pleased at having asserted herself, she turned toward the door, thinking happily of joining Tom poolside, but stopped short, seeing her hostess through the glass.

Miggie was waddling energetically in the direction of the pool. She wore a pink bathing suit made of some strong material like canvas; not a bikini, for the top and bottom strips were too wide, the bottom being in fact about the proportions of a huge diaper, with matching pink laces tied in a bow at the navel. Her belly pouched over the front of the suit; rolls of fat trembled at the sides. Below, the flesh of her legs quivered as her feet delivered powerful blows to the turf, propelling her forward. The top of the suit, rigid because of the stiffness of the material, rode up and down over her ribcage with the weight of her breasts. It was as though a hard, wiry person was moving inside the pneumatic body, which followed its directions reluctantly. Her blonde hair slopped over her face and ears, but Sam glimpsed in her face an iron determination, a fixation on some distant idea.

When she was out of sight below the rim of the hill, Sam stepped out the door, once again indecisive. She wanted to swim, to see Tom. But not with Miggie.

The dog snarled almost in her ear. Sam whirled toward the noise, terror-stricken.

The animal was crouched back, preparing to spring. The huge, boxlike jaws gaped at her, slaver dripping from the corners of the mouth, the eyes glittering viciously in the naked black head.

He leaped.

At the last moment, his body turned, so that the fence, which she had not seen because her attention had been so strongly compelled by the dog, caught him in the shoulder and flung him back to the ground.

He landed on his feet, eyeing Sam, who was sagging away from him, her body limp from the shock that hadn't come. His tongue dangled over the side of his jaw, one eye rolled at her in amusement. She realized that the son of a bitch was laughing at her. The other two dogs were lying at the other end of the pen, watching the sport.

"Rowf-rowf!" Sam said, with contempt.

The dog jumped toward her, landing with his head between his forepaws outstretched on the ground, and hindquarters rearing foolishly in the air. He flung himself up and backward, away from her, and rushed toward the other end of the pen, barking furiously, leaping over the other two, circling inches from the fence at top speed, landing again in the same position in front of her.

"Rowf-rowf!" she repeated, more loudly, getting into the spirit of the game.

He leaped back, nearly flipping over, and raced away on a circuit of the pen. As he approached her again, Sam yelled "Rowf!"; away he sped, even more wildly, so that he was back in an instant.

"Rowf!"

Away he went. More wild barking, scrabbling of toenails, higher leaps.

"Wait a minute," she said reasonably, as the dog approached in a cloud of dust. He skidded to a halt in front of her and sat attentively, panting from the fun. "I've got a present for you."

Making sure no one was in sight, she got the package of hamburger from her bag. The dog cocked his head to one side, with intelligent interest.

"You're really a pretty nice dog. About the nicest thing in this whole place."

She tore off a lump of meat the size of a golf ball and poked it through the fence. The dog approached, sniffing the meat and her fingers carefully, and backed away a few inches.

"Oh, don't be paranoid."

He sat, looking alternately at her face and the meat in her hand. Impasse. In the background, the other two were studying the situation alertly. Sam felt as though she were losing face again. She wished she knew their names, or even what kind of dogs they were. They were built like Great Danes, but larger and heavier, with close black hair like a bear's.

"Dammit."

The dog's ears twitched forward a fraction, as though waiting for a familiar command. Inspired, Sam ordered, "Beg!"

He balanced on his haunches, paws held out and downward with a rather pansyish air. She flipped the ball of meat off her

84

fingernails and through the mesh; his mouth opened for an instant, showing teeth like enameled nails, and snapped shut resonantly.

The other two now rose and strolled forward diffidently, eyes on Sam. What a sense of power! They ranked themselves on either side of the first dog, awaiting her fancy. A dog will always love you if you feed him.

She felt a rush of affection for them. If anything happens, she thought, not knowing what might happen, you'll take care of me, won't you?

"Want a hit?" she asked.

Her listeners observed her with polite attention, not understanding.

"I'll show you."

Once more Sam made sure no one was watching. She took the foil-covered package from her bag and carved three lumps of hashish the size of peas, taking care to get them the same size, to be fair. She divided the rest of the hamburger into equal portions and pressed a lump of dope into the center of each.

The balls of meat were too fat to go through the fence, so she rolled them into long cylinders.

"Beg!" she ordered.

The three big, black bodies rose solemnly, perfectly intent.

"This is really good stuff," Sam advised them proudly. In quick succession she thrust the treats through the fence. Whump! Whump! Whump! The jaws snapped shut, the dogs relaxed on their haunches again, as if asking, "Is that all?"

"You won't feel anything for about an hour," she told them. "Then just ride with it. I think the dose is about right."

She giggled suddenly at the absurdity of it and thought about having a hit herself. But it was too early; she hadn't even seen Tom yet, and she didn't want him to think she was a hopeless dope addict.

Sam wiggled her fingers at the dogs, her fellow conspirators, and picked up the handbag. "Bye-bye. I'll come see how you're doing later." The nice surprise in store for the dogs made her feel warm and kindly; she turned to look at them once more, and they were in the same solemn row. Dumb, in the sense that Sotto was; but she had the nonsensical feeling that once they had been through the dope experience, they would be able and eager to talk to her. Unreal. To be inside a dog's head.

The turf was both unnaturally hard and springy underfoot, as though it were an artificial surface covering rolling hills of asphalt. Passing a rather gawky, theatrical shrub, apparently a lilac, Sam noticed that the grass seemed to grow right up to its trunk, like the grass around the oak tree she had seen from her window. Suspiciously, she knelt and crushed a few of the meaty blades between her thumb and forefinger, but the blood stained her fingertips green, and the odor was quite authentic. So much for that fancy.

And yet she could not dispel the fear that this whole landscape, house, dogs, and all, was some sort of stage-set established solely for this weekend, for the benefit of Don Antonio's fantasies and plans, whatever they were. She felt continually that she had seen it all before, somewhere. That head-high, perfectly clipped hedge, for instance, was exactly where she had known it would be——

Oh, come on! I saw that from the window in Sotto's room. And as I step around the edge of the hedge, down the slope twenty yards or so is the swimming pool, where Tom is lying, with the bathhouse on the right——

He wasn't there.

The pool was deserted.

Damn, damn, damn! It's my own fault, fooling around with those crazy dogs.

But she had the feeling that someone had been at the pool a moment before. As she walked closer, hesitantly, she noticed that the surface of the water was disturbed by conflicting ripples that ran the length of the pool, turned on themselves, and skittered back again. Drying footprints led from the chrome

86

ladder at the inward bend of the pool, off the flagstones, and became lost in the grass.

Two sets of prints; one large and flat-footed like a bear's, which must be Tom's because his feet had no arches at all; the other tiny, with distinct outlines of heel, front pad, and toes: Miggie. Miggie had been on her way down here.

The footprints, where they left the flagstones, were heading in the general direction of the bathhouse. Of course, they're dressing. They must be through swimming already. I'm late as usual. But he could have waited for me.

Now that, she told herself, is a dumb, girlish attitude. The water looked inviting, she wanted to go for a swim, so she would go for a swim. She didn't need Tom to tell her what a great woman she was and hold her hand.

The bathhouse was a low, modern little building, with sides of offset vertical boards stained to resemble redwood. The center portion, she found, was a single overhead shower, screened from front and rear but open to the sides. To the right was a door labeled Guys, to the left one that said Dolls.

How about one called Freaks?

She pushed open Dolls, expecting to see Miggie, but the room was empty. She left the handbag inside and went to knock on Guys.

"Tom?"

No response. She opened the door a few inches, a guilty schoolgirl, and saw his clothes hung neatly on one of a row of gigantic nails. He was always neat. Where could they have gone? She closed the door silently.

As she went back to Dolls, the absolute quiet of the place struck her. No noise of wind in the trees, no voices, no sound of birds—As if in retort, she heard a bird's long, low, musical phrase. She slammed the Dolls door behind her, and the bird abruptly was silent.

Her loneliness rattled off the walls of the dressing room. It was fetid, gloomy; little light squeezed through the vertical

87

slats, but she did not turn on the overhead light. She had caught sight of herself in a full-length mirror: lemon blouse, white skirt, gleaming little fraud; limp black hair, dark face like a stone. Her features were too small, insignificant bumps of flesh. How little of her showed on the outside!

She felt the beginnings of panic. Careful! Damn fool. But she could not shake the feeling: as though someone were impersonating you, that was the way Tom had put it in his book. So where was he, with his delicate perceptions?

Pressing her face against one of the slats, she could glimpse a sliver of the sun bright on the grass outside. Silent outside, damp and empty inside. It would be an awfully good place to have a hit.

She put only a small pellet in the pipe, and it was gone in two puffs. Because, after all, she was not feeling completely at ease, and it would be better to stay somewhat in control. Just enough to take the edge off, which it was doing already.

She knocked the little ash carelessly onto the floor and replaced her tools in her bag. She sat with her elbows on her knees, holding her face. Now what to do?

I can't go outside wearing the same things I wore when I came in here because this is a dressing room. I came in to get dressed. Undressed.

Facing carefully away from the mirror, she unbuttoned her blouse, slipped it off, let it drop—slop—to the floor, brushing her with an unwanted caress. The elastic of the skirt and panties pulled at her legs, she tugged them off, hating the sight and feel of her own skin. She moved faster, pulling at the mass in the handbag, found the bikini, yanked it out, had it on in seconds, stuffed the other things back in the bag, pulled on the door, found it stuck, pulled with both hands, opened it with a bang, burst into the outdoors, stood, stupefied, unable to see in the brightness, looked in every direction, saw no one. Her heart began to thump less frantically.

She made her legs lift, one after the other, carry her to the

88

flagstones as she carried the bag. No one was watching her, no one at all; it was all right.

She sat on the hot stones, crossing her legs. Tom had been here, right here. He would be back.

Sun flickered off the water. A bird repeated an abstract phrase. The sun baked a thick smell off the grass and the flagstones; an insect chirruped hurriedly in the heat.

She had just the slightest pain, headache, a stitch in her head, a thin red line along her right temple. Quite common, when you were tense.

Where was Tom?

Any sort of relaxation would drive the headache away. A warm body on hers, to stretch against, to let the muscles relax, coil, and burst.

She lowered her shoulders against the stones, letting them sear her skin; stretched out her arms, keeping the flesh just above the hot surface for a few moments so it would cool enough to be bearable; spread her legs, resting their weight on the heels, then slowly relaxing them against the stone, a delicious pain, burning on the top and bottom, trembling with cold along the edges.

Where the bathing suit covered her, the heat seemed even more intense, drawing perspiration, baking her beneath the cloth. Her behind shifted against the stones, against the sun; the sweat held her to the stones, the sun was a weight like a lover above her, a yellow mask over her tightly closed eyes.

The stitch in her temple grew suddenly acute, then burst and vanished.

A long time ago, somewhere. Lake—Something, what was its name? High school. The same sun beating on her, the same utter calm knowledge of waiting, of the slightly incredible, frightening, marvelous thing that was going to happen.

Drawing strength from the sun. Being completely open, without panic. Gathering heat to be released somehow in a personal explosion.

89

And that funny boy. Donald. No, Dennis.

Lily pads and dark brown water. The slats of the raft, on empty oil drums, painted battleship gray.

Eyes closed, who cares what the whole world around you is doing? But somewhere near, you can sense him watching with the shy, ravenous eyes, not knowing that you're waiting for him. You are the center, pinned by the sun. Very patiently waiting.

With so much power gathering inside you, you can wait. No matter when it comes.

The nerve ends slumber, dazed by the heat.

A splash somewhere, it seems very far off. If you opened your eyes, you could see the circle of ripples on the brown water, the lake fringed by trees that all seem to lean inward, shimmering in the heat.

Strange little blood vessels throbbing in your belly.

Perhaps just to sleep for a little while, and wake lazy with the same strength——

Sun like someone sitting on your face, drugging you——

Heat.

Thoughts, images, all fading. The mind curling up——

Something soft and warm was moving across her belly, slowly, caressing her, manipulating the skin in delicious hot little circles, surrounded by coolness.

Lips, it must be Tom's lips, mouth, surrounded by the cool shadow of his bent head.

Jesus, how lovely!

As if in colors, a ring of burning red, tan, circled by pale skin.

Her hips twitched in reflex, her legs bent helplessly and moved a little farther apart, her arms stretched above her head along the hot stones, her fists half-clenched in a shudder that sent waves from her fingertips wracking through her neck, collarbone, breasts, ribs, belly, to the exquisite heat between her thighs that was demanding the soft, sucking mouth.

No one could be watching; he was shy about that.

90

The mouth slipped down her belly, a hand pulled at the bottom of the bathing suit, almost brutally. She raised her hips to allow the hand between her legs, and as the thick, sensual tongue dug into her navel and two thick fingers thrust along the length of her clitoris, thrusting her overpoweringly, blindingly to the edge of the chasm, as every muscle coiled unbearably, preparing for the release, as the red storm gathered in her mind, a split second away from bursting, she realized that something was horribly wrong, and forcing her eyes to twist open, into warped slits, she saw Don Antonio's lumpish body bent over her like a goblin feasting on carrion, on his knees, his torso covered by obscene black hair, the flesh hanging slackly from his belly and chest in flaccid, old-man's breasts——

"No!"

The gathered power in her muscles, her tensed legs, acted instantaneously in revulsion, flinging her body up from the stones, bowling over Don Antonio as one knee struck his chest and hurled him past the edge of the stones into the pool with a gigantic splash.

The spray struck Sam as she was halfway to her feet, frantically pulling the bathing suit up around her; the moment seemed frozen, the fragments of water hanging in the air, the depression in the water where Don Antonio's weight had pulled it down like a blue-and-white china bowl, his hairy body in the depression like that of a fat rat, the blue-and-white bowl of the sky overhanging, the sun a white-hot ulcer. The gently rolling slope, quite still, the turf and neatly clipped shrubbery, except for the echo of her cry and the sound of the splash which permeated all but faded as Don Antonio's head rose from the waters, roaring and sputtering, one hand wiping the water from his eyes, the other batting the surface to keep him afloat.

Her limbs seemed as unwieldy, as thin and fragile, as curtain-rods. She pulled her feet away from the edge of the pool, finding the handle of her handbag, dragging this as though it were the most important part of her, but weak with terror of the beast in the water, which was now yelling at her as she reached the grass and scuttled away. "Bitch! You dirty bitch! You *liked* it!"

At the corner of the shrubbery by the bathhouse, she saw behind her that his paw had grasped the side of the pool. His head reappeared over the lip of the stones, roaring. "Bitch!"

She stumbled around the shrubs, which hid her from the pool, and then could go no farther. Her strength left her, she sank to the grass, leaning against the handbag, and waited for him to come.

Her legs shook uncontrollably, she could not raise her arms. Her belly seemed hollow, her head light and substanceless except for a fierce pain in the empty place above the back of her neck. Waiting for him to come, waiting for the yellow teeth to meet in her flesh.

The pain above her neck throbbed and grew.

Had there been a splashing, dripping, as he got out of the pool? There was no sound now except for a cricket in the shrubs behind her.

Would she be able to hear his footsteps in the grass? She did not care.

Her head lolled on her neck, defenseless. Her eyes wanted to close.

She realized that a part of her wanted him to come after her, to pin her here like an insect and burn out this terrible tension. Her legs were still trembling. At the memory of his mouth on her, her shoulders drew together, shivering. And she was revolted by her own need.

Bzzzz. A bee coursed by her feet, looking vainly for clover among the fat grass-blades. The bee hovered petulantly, then vanished.

She and Tom had no sexual restrictions on each other. If one of them wanted to ball some *third party,* there would be no questions asked; the subject might or might not be mentioned casually. It had been one of the first things they had discussed seriously. She had brought it up herself, after the first night, afraid he might try to set some sort of limits on her. Oh, no, he agreed completely, absurd to try to dictate rules for anyone else. That way led to hypocrisy and jealousy hangups. They dismissed the subject and went on to other things. And since the freedom was there, they had felt no need to test it. She hadn't, anyway, and she was sure Tom hadn't, either. They were free.

Then why feel self-disgust because the ugly man had made her shiver? *Bitch.* She spelled the word idly with her fingers.

She felt an irritable need to do something, she didn't know what. Pushing herself to her feet, she stood listening, but there were no human noises, no splashing from the pool, no voices except the low insect murmur all around.

She stepped around the corner of the shrubbery, looking toward the pool, but no one was there. The water that had splashed onto the flagstones had almost evaporated.

Nowhere on the perfect lawn could she see a sign of life; at the top of the hill, the ugly house brooded like a mausoleum, its upthrusting chimney looking pitifully slight against the perfect sky, its windows blank and introspective. She did not want to go back to the house.

She studied the sterile expanse of lawn, shrubs, and trees down the hill. The corner of a small building, perhaps a summerhouse, was now noticeable in a depression shrouded by dank green shrubbery. She had no desire to investigate this; the sight of it made her cold.

She lifted the handbag and started back toward the main house.

The sun was quite high. It must be after noon, she thought, and realized that the nagging pain in her gut was probably more from hunger than anything else.

This cheered her up. After all, no one is at her best on an empty stomach. She increased her pace, thinking of the two refrigerators full of food.

Which reminded her of her friends the dogs. They must be feeling pretty good by now. In many ways, the high you got from eating the stuff was nicer than the one you got from smoking; it lasted much longer, sometimes hours, so you didn't have to go through a series of ups and downs. You had time to explore your new perceptions in a relaxed way because you could forget about the straight-you for a while; the high-you became the real personality.

She was a little worried about whether or not the dogs would appreciate this. Anyway, the experience would be good for them because they obviously had been supernervous. Their attitude couldn't help but be improved.

People talked a lot about whether pot or hashish changed your personality—that is, people who had never used it. Anyone who had smoked dope knew it did. The more you smoked, the larger share of your time was occupied by the high-you, and the less by the straight-you. It was simply a matter of how far you wanted to swing toward the high end of the pendulum. And most people needed a good push in that direction. Don Antonio, for example, might be wonderfully improved by getting out once or twice. Might really be a sort of interesting person to know, if you could get behind the walls of nastiness and vanity——

5

"Yoo-hoo!"

Sam, who had been drifting toward the dog pen, paused and looked toward the house. Miggie stood on the edge of a terrace at the rear, waving her hand stiffly, like a little pennant on the end of a stick. She now wore a short terrycloth robe, apparently over her bathing suit, which made her look like a pink porcupine. Sam doubted whether Miggie would profit by the dope experience.

"Yoo-hoo! Luncheon is ready."

Reluctantly, Sam gave up on visiting the dogs and bent herself toward the terrace. But luncheon, that sounded all right; she hoped they would have hamburgers, huge steaming platters of hamburgers on soft buns, with pickles and ketchup applied in the kitchen so the juices would have soaked into the buns, and those good, mealy French fries, greasy golden and slightly crisp on the outside. If she ever had someone to cook for her, she would order that for lunch every day.

The terrace was partly sheltered by the two wings of the house, which was why she hadn't noticed it before. The floor was the same carefully shaped flagstones as around the pool, with even joints of half an inch of concrete between them. A large, obviously plastic palm tree sloped out of a redwood box in one corner. Sam wondered how it would look in the snow.

She looked at the three people seated at the table.

"Hi." Tom, oddly subdued, seemed to look at her with curiosity. She wondered if he could have seen her and Don Antonio at the pool. No, but she felt estranged from him and looked at the stones beneath her feet.

"Hi." And then looked up. But he was playing with his fork.

Don Antonio sat at the head of the table, which was wrought iron and covered by a lace cloth. He stared straight ahead, ignoring Sam. On his left sat Miggie, a tiny smile curled in her cheek as she watched. There was an empty chair on Don Antonio's right, between him and Tom, for Sam. She took it. The chair also was wrought iron, with iron slats for a seat.

"What are we having?" she asked, thinking of hamburgers.

Miggie seemed about to answer, but a clinking of glasses interrupted them. Sotto was stepping through the door from the house, a napkin over his arm, carrying a green wine bottle and four glasses like tiny bubbles in his enormous hands.

White wine, Sam thought. She didn't think you would have white wine with hamburgers. The strain of sitting at the hostile table was making her intensely hungry. Hamburgers and French fries, and a vanilla milk shake.

But here was Sotto, her only friend—except Tom, of course —setting delicate glasses that would ring like bells if you tapped, in front of each of them, and each looked away as if to deny his existence. The last glass he placed before Don Antonio, holding its stem between thumb and forefinger. He rotated the label of the bottle back and forth beneath the master's nose, synchronizing its motion with the oscillations of the eyeballs as if checking off cue cards, until Don Antonio nodded curtly.

Sam saw the label as Sotto turned the bottle: a California brand that she had bought herself once or twice because it wasn't too expensive.

Sotto produced a silver capsule with a long needle; he

96

slipped the needle through the cork, pushed the top of the capsule, and the cork slid out with the faintest of pops. The labor-saving device was absurd in his powerful hands. Sotto gently dripped a quarter-inch of the golden wine into Don Antonio's glass; Don Antonio made circles with his hand, swirling the liquid as if he were warming brandy, and drank the portion all at once, licking his lips. He nodded ponderously, indicating his approval, and the rest of them, even Sam, relaxed as the ritual was ended. Sotto refilled Don Antonio's glass, moved next to Miggie's, then circled the table to attend to the guests.

From the other side of the house came a weird howl, starting low and mournful, then rising to a joyful peak and degenerating into a humorous, lazy yapping.

"What was that?" Miggie asked.

"I believe it must be your dogs," Sam said calmly.

For the first time since she had sat down, Don Antonio looked at her. "Yeah, you said it, there. The dogs. That's right. Smart."

"But Donnie, they've never made a noise like that before. What's wrong with them?"

"Mia must be coming in heat again."

"But she just finished being in heat two weeks ago."

"Well, how the hell should I know? Crazy dames!"

Sotto, oblivious to all this, had left the wine to warm on a silver stand next to Don Antonio and was disappearing through the door to the kitchen. Miggie made a face at Don Antonio, which he did not see, and then looked mischievously at Tom. Tom's ears turned slightly pink. Where had they been all morning?

Sam dismissed the thought quickly, she didn't want to know. He couldn't have, not with this wrecked old woman. And I don't care, anyway. Like Tom said, what good would it do for me to try to stop him? And he couldn't have.

The yapping came again, very slowly, very much like a laugh. Don Antonio pointedly ignored it. "I had a guy on the show once that used to hunt tigers with a baseball bat."

"Really?" Sam was interested.

"Jaguars," Miggie said.

"Yeah, one of these sportsmen. Every summer he'd go down to Nicaragua or someplace, out in the jungle with one guide and a Louisville Slugger. He said he used to hunt with a gun, but after a while it got boring: bang, and the jaguar was dead. So he got the idea of going after them with nothing but a bat."

"He killed them with the bat?" Tom asked.

"Uh-huh. He was a big guy, like Sotto. He said if you got them just right, across the forehead, you could smash the skull. The trick was to get the jaguar to charge you at just the right moment, in a clearing or someplace, where you'd have room for a good backswing. The first time they went out, he said, he was scared to death. See, you have to follow the jaguar until it gets angry, maybe a couple of days. Then it gets on your back trail and comes up behind you. Then it charges, and you smash it."

"Wasn't that very dangerous?"

Just like a dumb dame, Don Antonio's expression said. "No, he said it really was easier than getting them with a gun. He did it four or five years, until he got tired of it. Also he used to give the stuffed animals for Christmas presents, and the bat ruined the hides."

"Oh."

"Did he go back to hunting them with a gun?" Tom asked.

"How the hell would I know?" Don Antonio said morosely. "He was only on the show one time. I don't know what he wanted to go out in the jungle for anyway. He was one of those guys who inherited his money and didn't know what to do with himself." Don Antonio spread his napkin in his lap and looked around belligerently for Sotto. "What the hell are we having for lunch?"

Sotto eased through the door carrying four soup bowls on a silver platter raised above his head with one hand, like a waiter in a crowded restaurant. He set the bowls before them and returned to the kitchen. Don Antonio looked sourly at Miggie.

"Why doesn't he put the bowls on the table before we sit down?"

"Because this is the way it's done." She turned to Sam. "Sotto used to work in a restaurant, you know. He gets very upset if things aren't done just right."

"Oh. I didn't know."

Sotto returned with a silver tureen on his platter. He lowered the tureen to Miggie's left; she ladled a pastel green liquid into her bowl, murmuring "Thank you" like a polite mistress.

Gravely, Sotto presented the tureen to Sam, who poured a small amount into her bowl, thinking of hamburgers. The soup was cold, the green, bilious against the white bowl; the odor, that of some chalky vegetable overlaid by the metallic smell of the can it had come in.

As Tom was leaning backward to take his soup from the tureen, he dripped a bit on his bare chest. Across the table, Miggie's tongue appeared piggishly in the corner of her mouth, away from Don Antonio: a joke, meaning, I'll lick it off.

As Tom's ears turned red again, and Sam controlled an impulse to crack her soup bowl upside down over Miggie's head, picturing the sensational color combination of pallid soup and bleached hair, Don Antonio said loudly, "What the hell *is* this?"

Miggie started, but her husband wasn't looking at her. He was staring down into the tureen with disgust.

"It's asparagus, darling. You like it."

"I like this?" Dramatically, Don Antonio filled his bowl, clanking the ladle against the china. Miggie raised her spoon, smiling appreciatively at her soup, preparing to give the signal for all to begin. Not noticing, Don Antonio quickly ate a mouthful of his and grimaced. "Asparagus? Bird-drop is more like it. Hey, that's pretty good, bird-drop soup. Ancient Chinee dish."

Miggie, testing her soup with aristocratically pursed lips, ignored him. Tom, heavily embarrassed, diddled a bit of his own into his mouth, eyes down. This left Don Antonio with only Sam as an audience; he grinned and winked at her before he remembered that he was angry at her.

Sam, who was tasting her soup and not liking it, smiled back recklessly. "My favorite meal is hamburgers."

"Hey, yeah, mine, too." Don Antonio laid his spoon on the tablecloth, spreading a green blotch. "You can't get anything better to eat than a really good hamburger. And I'm not talking about one of those joints in New York where they charge you two bucks for one burger and then fuck it up with mayonnaise."

"Donnie! Not at the dinner table!"

"Yeah, some dinner table. You can't eat the food; you can't talk. What good is it?" He returned his attention to Sam. "I'm talking about a place like McDonald's. Now the guy who started that place knew what he was doing. He got a formula; he got a hamburger that was the essence of hamburger: meat, bun, a little ketchup, and a couple of slices of pickle. Simplicity, that's what genius is."

"McDonald's is good."

"You bet it is. You know why? Because he didn't gimmick up his food so you couldn't tell what the hell you were eating."

Sotto had returned; he held his open palm at Don Antonio's right, inquiring whether the master had finished with the soup. Don Antonio jerked his thumb like an umpire ordering the soup out of the game. Sotto hurried around the table, stacking the bowls and saucers in one hand, as though to remove the offender from Don Antonio's sight. Sam had taken only a couple of mouthfuls of hers, hoping the next course might be more substantial, and when Sotto dumped the other bowls on top of hers, soup oozed onto the saucer.

"It's the same thing with books; you can't tell what the hell they're about any more." Don Antonio's withdrawn mood, which had never been very convincing, was totally gone now as he began talking to Tom. "Hell, they've got meanings within meanings. If you get through with a book and say you enjoyed it, people think you're a dope."

"Well, I don't think because a book has something to say, that means you can't——"

"You know what I used to like? Spy books. James Bond. But the goddamned intellectuals have fucked those up, too. I tried to read a spy book by one of those new British guys a couple of years ago. I gave up after the first two chapters. I couldn't tell what was going on. I'm going to read your book because I've got a kind of personal interest in it. But I hope something *happens* in it."

"Oh, yes——"

"The last book I read where anything happened was by Jack London. A paperback. It's too bad the guy's dead, or I'd get him on the show. I wish I knew how that guy thought up his stories."

"A writer doesn't just think up a story and write it down."

"Well, how does he do it?"

"He creates his characters, first, and maybe a basic situation. Then he has his theme, which is really nothing more than his own perceptions about the characters and the situation, his feelings and understandings about them."

One of the dogs howled again, briefly. No one but Sam seemed to pay any attention.

"That sounds like a lot of malarkey," Don Antonio said. "What about the action? The plot?"

"I'm getting to that. But the thing that makes a book good, or even important, is the perception of human relationships by the writer."

Sotto reappeared with a large platter, which he offered to Miggie. It held a milky-red oblong on a bed of lettuce, surrounded by fluted chips of cucumber and topped by a creamy gob, apparently mayonnaise. Tom paused in his speech to look at this. Miggie cut off a slice and deposited it on her plate, then carefully overlapped three slices of cucumber next to it, smiling at Sam. But as Sotto passed to Don Antonio, she shrank away, awaiting his outburst.

Don Antonio did his part nicely, Sam thought. As Sotto pre

sented the platter to him, he pretended at first not to notice. Then did a double take, not too exaggerated. His lip curled. "What is this supposed to be?"

"It's a tomato surprise, Donnie."

"It looks like a tomato disaster. Take it away." He waved Sotto on.

Miggie took a bite of hers, as though cajoling a child, and smiled delightedly. "It's delicious."

"Is it too much to ask to have something to *eat* on the table?"

"This is very good. I got the recipe from a magazine. I'm sure Sotto spent hours working on it."

"What's for *lunch?*"

"An average serving, like I took, has only seventy-five calories."

Sam helped herself to a slightly smaller than average serving.

"Jesus Christ, am I on a diet? I don't think so." He turned to Sam. "Are you on a diet?"

"No, I'm too skinny. But whenever I eat anything, I just get more top-heavy."

"That's all right, kid, it looks good on you, believe me." He turned to Tom. "Are you on a diet?"

"No." Tom was tasting his tomato surprise. "But this is pretty good. Not too bad."

Sam ate a little bite of hers. It was very cold, with a surprising consistency, like a hard, oily slush, and tasted of tomatoes and mayonnaise.

Taking a small object like a transistor radio from his pocket, Don Antonio pressed a button. Sotto, who had been returning to the kitchen, wheeled around sharply and came to the master's side. Don Antonio snapped his fingers and made a writing gesture; Sotto handed him a small pad of paper and a pencil. "No reason we should all starve just because Piggie's got too much lard on her tail. Who's for hamburgers?"

"I'll have one as long as you're going to," Sam said quickly.

Tom nodded. "I've really got an appetite today."

I'll bet you do, Sam thought.

"Three hamburgers." Don Antonio wrote on the pad. "Big, juicy ones. Pickles and ketchup, right?"

"Right."

"Right."

"And sesame-seed buns. Toasted lightly, with a little butter, how's that?" They nodded. "Some people think the butter makes the hamburger too rich, but just a little brings out all the flavor, wouldn't you say?"

"Stop it!" Miggie shrieked. "All right. Four hamburgers." She waved four fingers at Sotto and pointed at herself, nodding emphatically.

Don Antonio shook his head. "I don't think you ought to. You're supposed to be on a diet."

"You lousy sadist!"

"I'm just worrying about you. The extra weight's not good for your heart. And you want to keep yourself attractive to men, don't you?" As he said this, his eyes flicked briefly toward Tom, and Sam suddenly felt sympathetic toward him.

"That's one thing I don't have to worry about." Miggie was defiant. "I've never had any shortage of men."

"All right." Don Antonio made another note and handed the pad back to Sotto, who departed for the kitchen with his silent, flat-footed gait. "We'll have lunch in a minute." He turned to Tom. "So what were you saying?"

"I don't remember."

"Talking about the plot."

"Oh, yes, in a novel. I was saying that the plot, if by that you mean the exterior action, is incidental."

"I don't buy that. If you don't have action, all you've got is a bunch of people sitting around talking, or some kind of psychological crap."

"Well, incidental is the wrong word. Secondary, that's what

I mean. A good writer doesn't start with a plot; he starts with people in a situation, and the action follows naturally. It's inevitable, like in a Greek tragedy."

"If that was true, everybody would know what was going to happen. Nobody would have to read the book."

"But your perceptions and opinions are different than mine; that's the whole point. What you think somebody might do, or what he's feeling, in a certain situation, is different from what I think he might do. When you read a book someone else has written, you're tuning in on him. And if he's a good author, you can learn something."

"You really should read Tom's book."

Don Antonio frowned at Sam, as though admonishing her that women had no place in such a high-level conversation.

"Also, even though I may have a complete concept of each of the characters when I start, I can't communicate this to you all at once. It's impossible. I'd have to write a forty-page essay on each one, from the top of his head to his toenails, and who would read it?"

"No one."

"But in a novel, every development reveals a little more about the people. Sometimes the things they do are unexpected, even shocking. But if the writer is good, you feel a kind of recognition; you say, 'Yes, that's the kind of person he is, or she is.' The people in the book should remind you of people you know, give you insights about real people."

"If I read a book, I want to be entertained, not lectured to."

From the kitchen came the noise of a small, groaning machine. An electric meat grinder, Sam thought, and suddenly remembered the hamburger she had given to the dogs. Lord, I fed them my own lunch. I hope they're getting some fun out of it.

"There's no law says you can't be entertaining at the same time. The best humor is when something happens that's totally unexpected, yet you recognize it as absolutely true to life. That's what breaks you up, the recognition."

"Yeah, okay," Don Antonio said glumly, "but how can I enjoy a book when I'm thinking about all that other stuff?"

"You don't think about it when you're reading. In fact, I hardly thought about it when I was writing the book. But when I got finished, I saw what the process was. Like a judge making a decision in a court case. He doesn't start from *A* and follow a chain of logical reasoning to arrive at his conclusion. He makes his decision on an emotional basis and then goes back and looks for precedents and reasons to prove he's right. I'm sure a mathematician or any kind of scientist does the same thing: he discovers intuitively and then goes back to see why."

"But what about something that's a complete accident?" Don Antonio finished his glass of wine and reached for the bottle. He topped off Tom's glass and then refilled his and Miggie's. "Don't you drink?" he asked Sam accusingly.

She realized that she hadn't touched hers. "I'm sorry, I forgot." She tried a sip. It wasn't bad: yeasty, like fresh bread. "It's good."

Don Antonio didn't hear her. He was watching Tom intently.

"How do you mean, an accident?" Tom asked.

"I'm thinking now of the actual accident in your book."

"Oh, the hit-and-run. That wasn't a pure accident."

"You claim the guy did it on purpose?" He was incredulous.

"No, no. But I would think of a pure accident as being something like a meteorite hitting you on the head, that you had absolutely no control over. This man was an alcoholic; he was driving drunk, or he wouldn't have hit the little girl. He became an alcoholic because his career was washed out; he didn't have the strength to face that. So the accident resulted from his own character, his alcoholism."

"Just because a guy takes a few drinks doesn't mean he's an alcoholic."

105

"DA, I wrote the book, and you haven't even read it yet. Take my word, he's an alcoholic."

Don Antonio chuckled; a little falsely, Sam thought. "Yeah, I guess it's your book. But some people are pretty free with that term."

"Anyway, whether he's a true alcoholic isn't the point. The accident is caused by his drinking, and his drinking is a sign of his corruptness."

Don Antonio seemed about to reply angrily, but was interrupted by a fascinated sigh from Miggie. They all looked around.

Sotto had emerged from the kitchen, carrying a platter of hamburgers that might have been lifted in every detail from Sam's fantasy. He set the platter in the center of the table, as if it were beneath him to pass around something so common.

Sam counted quickly: seven burgers. This struck her as very odd, a number deliberately calculated to create dissension. She saw Miggie also sizing up the situation. The forgotten tomato surprise on their plates had melted and drawn into globs.

"Well," said Miggie, "we might as well pitch in."

Quick as a striking snake, her hand speared a hamburger and presented it to her mouth. Three more left the platter in different directions.

There was no question of conversation; each ate with his eyes on the others, trying to avoid the appearance of gluttony without losing his chance at a second burger. But Miggie was far ahead of them at this game; her technique was flawless. Without seeming to rush, she took a bite of the hamburger; it didn't appear to be a very big bite, but a fourth of the hamburger was gone. She seemed to chew only once or twice before the mass slid evenly down her throat, at the same moment as her mouth was biting off another fourth. As she took in the last quarter of the burger, pinky delicately extended, her left hand was reaching for a second. The others were only half finished.

Miggie had made her second hamburger disappear, chewing the last bite now with exaggerated thoroughness, as the others

106

were finishing their first. Don Antonio glared at the dainty motions of her jaws. There were two hamburgers left on the platter, four people at the table. *Zugzwang.*

"I don't believe I want another," Miggie said sweetly, around her mouthful. "I really am watching my weight. Unless nobody wants a second."

Two hamburgers for three people. Don Antonio lifted the platter, presenting it to Sam. "Go ahead." Sam shook her head. "It was your idea," he insisted, "you should have an extra."

"Well——" That really seemed fair. He twitched the platter in the rhythm of a bullfighter tempting a bull. Suddenly feeling mean toward both the men, she put the bigger of the two remaining hamburgers on her plate.

Around the corner of the house, one of the dogs howled happily, interpolating notes like a musician flying high. Don Antonio set the platter halfway between Tom and himself. "I wonder what's wrong with those black bastards," he said crossly, not seeming to watch whether Tom took the remaining hamburger.

Tom's hand moved indecisively toward the platter, then stopped. Miggie observed the play alertly, her eyes shifting from Tom to the hamburger to Don Antonio. Oh, no, Sam thought, she's not going to get three.

"Back to your book," Don Antonio said. "The star——"

"You mean the old man?"

"Yeah, I guess so. Aren't you pretty hard on him? I thought the author had to be in sympathy with his characters."

"Oh, I'm sorry for him, all right. His values are false, his life-style is silly, and that's what gets him into trouble. I don't make any judgment on him as a human being."

"I don't see how the hell you can separate those things. If you say what a man does, the way he lives, is no good, then the man's no good either. Why couldn't you have the accident happen to the kid instead?"

"Because it wasn't really an accident. The plot grows out of the possibilities inherent in the characters, or it should."

107

Tom was engrossed in his subject again, though it seemed to Sam that he was repeating himself. Don Antonio nodded and absent-mindedly plucked the last hamburger from the serving platter. Miggie grimaced. Tom didn't notice.

"But the exterior plot isn't crucial."

"Not crucial," Don Antonio repeated, chewing and nodding.

"When I talk about an exterior plot, I'm implying the existence of an interior plot, which is the interaction between the personalities and feelings of the characters, especially the parts that are normally hidden. That's the center of the book: what's going on inside them, the conflicts of their desires."

"But how is that any different from life?" Sam asked.

Tom looked at her in surprise. "The difference is that the author can intensify it, can show you the interior conflicts more sharply, and that you have more time to contemplate them than you do if they're actually happening to you. Also, you can really share someone else's feelings—the author's—which you can never do to that extent in life." He glanced at the empty serving platter and frowned slightly. "Anyway, that's what I think the author should be trying to do."

"What's for dessert?" Don Antonio asked.

"Cantaloupe."

He grimaced. "Don't we have any ice cream?"

"Well, no. I don't think so."

"I bought a quart of butter crunch last weekend."

"Yes, but I think actually that's all gone."

"Actually, the whole progression of the novel should come from the interior plot." Something nudged Sam's leg sharply under the table; she looked at Miggie, wondering if this was some kind of signal, but Miggie was looking at Tom. "The action can be minor, even trivial, as long as the emotional content has force."

Sam lifted the edge of the lace tablecloth and saw Miggie's pudgy bare foot inching up her leg. She reached down and pinched the instep, where the skin was soft.

"Owww!"

108

"Sorry, I dropped my napkin." Sam spoke politely, but she knew her face must be ugly.

Sotto was clearing the table.

If it had been Tom's leg, what would he have done? Gone on mumbling something about "interior plot"? No, that was unfair. Probably he feels sorry for her. It's not his fault that she's annoying him.

Sotto served the melon, a thin slice for each. The silence at the table was crippled, echoing his.

What do I care? Sam dug into her cantaloupe savagely, then noticed that she had beaten her hostess by half a count. What the hell, my manners are certainly up to the level of the hospitality here, where the hostess tries to get your man into the bushes, and your host attacks you poolside—Bitch! Why did he call me that?

It struck her suddenly that what Don Antonio had been doing to her at the pool was rather more interesting than she would have expected. She would have thought his style would have been missionary position, dump the chick helplessly on her back, give her a couple of quick pokes and call her frigid. Perhaps the fact that he was Italian—she studied him as he bent over his melon; the lumpy, troll-like features were as she remembered them, not at all handsome, but with a certain brutal charm.

I can't handle this.

In contrast, Tom's face at this moment reminded her of a flower, petals bent gracefully inward. She admired this while one part of her wanted to claw it away, to rip his skin and seize his hands and shriek into his face: "Look at me! Listen to me!"

She put her hand on Tom's leg. He looked at her, slightly surprised, and smiled readily. His attention returned to his melon. She patted his leg and removed her hand.

As they were finishing the dessert, one of the dogs howled with a strange, hiccoughing percussion. Sam hoped it was not turning into a bad trip.

Don Antonio tossed his spoon onto the table and stood.

"I'm going to see what's wrong with those neurotic bastards. Excuse me."

"Let's go see, Tom."

"All right."

Miggie heaved herself up from the table. "Really! We spend more time worrying about those silly dogs than they do about us, and they're supposed to be watchdogs."

Miggie lingered behind as Don Antonio strode around the corner of the house. Politely, Tom waited for her. Impolitely, Sam adhered to him; she could not stomach turning the corner herself and leaving him with this lard-witted witch, turning the corner and not knowing whether he would follow.

"Really, I don't know why Donnie got those dogs." Miggie spoke from Tom's left, as though talking to Sam. "They've given us nothing but trouble."

"They're very handsome," Sam said.

"They eat twenty pounds of food a day."

"I was looking at them this morning."

"They're really quite tame. Donnie romanticizes everything."

As Tom's diffident pace brought them around the house, they saw Don Antonio standing, hands on hips, in a rage in front of the dog pen. He held a short, stout stick in one hand. "Look at these sons of bitches!"

Two of the dogs were lying on their backs, tongues lolling in the dust, laughing at Don Antonio. The other was apparently trying to sit, but his haunches kept sliding out from under him, and one or the other of his forelegs kept buckling; he looked like a drunk trying to samba sitting down.

Don Antonio crashed his stick against the chain-link fence. "Sit! Sit, Lucifer! Bad dog!"

The dog made a final effort, stretching vertically, nose in the air, trembling with concentration, but did not get the angle quite straight. He toppled sideways like a tower falling, giving a low, strange howl of self-amusement, then an involuntary grunt as he hit, rolled over once, and came to rest with his paws over his nose on the ground, grinning up at his master.

110

"Bad dog!" Don Antonio yelled. "Cocksucker! Get up!"

"Those are interesting dogs," Sam said. "What breed are they?"

Don Antonio glared at her.

"Half Newfoundland and half greyhound," Miggie offered.

"Not greyhound, damn it, Great Dane. Sit, King!" In unison, the two dogs lying on their backs rolled all the way over.

"They certainly seem friendly. I wouldn't have guessed it from the way they were acting last night."

"These dogs are sick. Mentally ill. I don't know what's wrong with them."

"Just because they're being friendly, you think they're insane? That's a strange attitude."

"They're not supposed to behave this way. It's unnatural."

"Maybe they were sick before, and they've just got well."

Lucifer suddenly seemed to recognize Sam. He inched toward her on his belly, his hind legs trailing behind him, tail swiping the dust. His damp nose pushed through the fence, and his eyes rolled up at her.

"Hello yourself." Sam stroked the nose.

"Better watch it," Don Antonio warned. "He might turn vicious any moment."

"I can't believe that. Nice doggie!"

She turned to see if Tom was getting full enjoyment out of the situation and caught him trying to edge away from Miggie, who was surreptitiously squeezing his buttock. He looked so miserable that Sam laughed.

Don Antonio whirled and looked suspiciously at them all. "Someone's playing some pretty funny games around here. And I'm going to get to the bottom of it."

But nobody seemed impressed by this statement, not even Don Antonio himself. Miggie crossed her arms innocently and studied the dog pen. Don Antonio tossed down his stick and walked toward the rear of the house. "I'm going to take a nap."

"Oh, dear," said Miggie, in a slightly louder than natural tone, "he's angry. I'd better go with him." She blinked her eyes several times quickly and smiled at Tom. "You two have a good time. Drinks in the living room at four, or earlier if you want them. We're very informal here. Sotto can get you anything you want."

Her hand waved limply at Sam. Her waddle did not seem to cover much ground, but she was gaining on Don Antonio as they turned the corner.

6

A terrible thing was happening: Tom felt uncomfortable at being alone with her.

He studied the dogs. "What do you think is wrong with them? They looked pretty vicious last night."

"I turned them on, gave them some dope." Sam patted Lucifer's nose. "I don't think they ever had any before."

"You mean they smoked it?"

"Don't be silly. I fed it to them in some hamburger."

He laughed. "They seem to like it."

"Sure. That's a bunch of stuff, about them being fierce watchdogs. Anybody would get mean if you kept him locked up in a cage all day."

"Don Antonio was upset."

"He's a pig."

Tom gave her a look meaning, Be reasonable.

"He tried to get me at the swimming pool," she added.

"Get you?"

"He tried to fuck me."

She didn't know what reaction she had expected, what she had wanted, but when Tom smiled patronizingly, she was ready to kill him.

"Are you sure?" he asked.

"Of course."

"What did you do?"

"I kicked him into the pool."

Tom burst out laughing.

"What's so damn funny? I was scared. He sneaked up on me, and he's strong."

"Hey, listen, I know you don't like him, but that's one thing you don't have to worry about."

"Why?"

"He's impotent."

"Huh. How do you know?"

"Miggie told me. All that stuff about Sotto being impotent, about her dying of cancer and not being able to have sex, you remember that?"

"I asked her about it at breakfast. She laughed."

"Yes. He makes all that up. It's compensation for his not being able to himself."

"That's what she says."

"I don't know why she'd lie about it."

"To make you feel sorry for her. And you do, don't you?"

"I guess so. She's an old woman, she's losing her looks, she's desperate. Don't you think that's sad?"

"If you put it that way." Sam stuck her hand in his. "All right, she's just a pathetic old woman. Hey, I've got an idea."

"What's that?"

"Let's take a nap ourselves."

"Are you tired? I thought you slept late."

She looked at him impishly.

"Oh, *that* kind of nap. Come to think of it, I did get up pretty early." He smiled. "Lead on."

Not wanting to see anyone, wanting to keep Tom for herself, she led the way toward the front of the house. She thought for a moment that she sensed someone watching them; perhaps she could make out Sotto's leaden face hanging at the kitchen window. She pressed Tom's hand tightly: This is all that matters.

Sam hardly noticed the grotesque house, the absurdly mani-

114

cured grass, the low evergreens around the foundation. The sun she was aware of only as warmth; the twittering of the birds seemed to be part of a song in her head. You're the only one, Tom, the only thing that makes me alive. That makes me love, that makes me proud.

As they came into the cold cavern of the entrance hall, she took his arm, feeling the stringy muscles unmasked by fat. She disregarded the icy shadows at the back of the hall; perhaps someone was there watching them, perhaps not. What was the difference? They're like vampires, sucking up all your attention until you forget what you want yourself. Children's ghosts. If you ignore them, they don't exist. We don't need them, don't want their approval, their mousey grins and neurotic laughter, prizes for winning games whose rules they invent themselves. You're the only one, Tom.

Watching him, she stumbled on the stairs, and he smiled down at her.

Stupid place for that step, anyway. Who decided to put it there? When we have a house, if Tom ever wants to have a house with me, there won't be steps to trip you up on the way to bed. The bed will be in the center of the house, so we'll never be more than a few steps away. A round house, like a ball, not some god-awful modernistic castle.

She realized that she had expected some presence in the upstairs hall, but no one was there. Second door on the left? Sam thought she had left the curtains open, but they were drawn now, giving the room an air of tight secrecy.

She slammed the door behind them, indulging herself. Tom looked startled. Well, I've got a *few* surprises left in me. She could not find a lock on the door. It was not important; the hell with them anyway.

"Home, I think not," she said.

"That bed looks good. I really am tired."

"What time did you get up?"

"I don't know. Before dawn. I went walking around the grounds. You know what this place reminds me of?"

"A jail."

"No, a mental institution. The way the grounds are kept. And there's a wall about eight feet high all the way around, with a wire on top. I think it's electric. Big steel gates at the end of the driveway. We must have come through them last night."

"We didn't stop."

"I know, it must be automatic."

"If you're rich enough, I guess you can have your own asylum." She unhooked the top of her bathing suit and tossed it on top of the bag. And shook her chest playfully. But Tom wasn't looking at her; he was stripping off his own bathing suit. He caught it on one toe and tossed it across the room, then sank onto the bed. "This was a nice idea you had." He stretched on his back, hands folded behind his head.

"I know." She dropped the bottom of the bathing suit on the rug and slapped his chest. "Wait a couple of minutes, I've got to go to the bathroom."

"Um." His eyes closed. She looked at his unguarded body, comparing it to the strained posturings and muscle-flexings of Don Antonio's. That was the difference: not the ugliness of the flesh, but the corruption of the spirit, the accumulation of deceptions, like fat, the automatic pretense. If Tom had deceived her, he could not be lying here so free, so open, waiting for her. That's what they don't understand. They talk of loyalty, but we trust.

The blue light was still glowing in the bathroom, the mirrors playing their slick games with each other, but she was not beguiled. How silly, to glorify a bathroom! And then to hedge even on that, because the only place you couldn't see your reflection was when you were sitting on the toilet, she noticed. The chest-high wall, covered with black tile, blocked the mirrors from view.

She was suddenly sick of all these meaningless designer's tricks and made a rude noise, hoping Don Antonio actually had wired the rooms and was listening. See what he'll make of that.

She flushed the toilet.

116

The whole trick of being rich was to surround yourself with a veneer of gadgets, servants, architecture, furs, tweeds, makeup, that gave you a spurious air of mystery. Sam washed her hands; the pink soap shimmered strangely in the blue light, covering her hands with thick suds that smelled like chemical flowers. It was very easy to forget that you were not a manufactured thing yourself, that you did not really smell like flowers. And that as you grow older, you began to smell like rotting meat instead.

For the first time in days, she thought of her parents. She always pictured them sitting side by side in front of the gaudy color television screen, denying each other's existence, exuding decay like a brown, greasy cloud and communicating their loneliness like a disease to the child.

To hell with them and their disappointment.

She dried her hands carefully and pulled the wrinkles from the towel: one more useless thing she had been taught. The important things they had never mentioned to her: how to love someone, how to give without getting something in return, how to leave them. These things she had to learn herself; she was determined to learn.

Sometimes she felt as if the past few years had never been, that she was still the child in her parents' sterile house, willfully misunderstanding their conventional signals. As if she were demonstrating her new life on a stage, acting it out as her parents sat disapproving in the shadowy audience, where she could not quite see them, waiting for the play to be over so she could rejoin them. She had even considered, horrified, that they might approve of Tom now that he was successful. She could hear her father say, "Nice enough young man. Give him a haircut and he'd be perfectly presentable."

She shut the bathroom door quietly.

Tom had half rolled on his side now, his forearm next to his shaggy head, the wrist bent away from him. It was one of his favorite positions for sleeping. His belly sagged, relaxed; his chest moved in and out, in an even rhythm. Tom could fall asleep anywhere.

She was disappointed; she had wanted to make love to him, but it was her own fault for taking so long in the bathroom. She sat cross-legged on the bed, watching him.

Sam liked to look at him asleep. His face was like a baby's, the chin rounded, the full lips petulant. The hair that had grown since he shaved that morning was golden and soft-looking. Even the position of his hand near his face somehow suggested thumb-sucking.

A tiny frown appeared between his eyebrows, and he made a small sound like a moan. But in an instant his face again was untroubled. Some tiny blot on the awesome clarity of his conscience? Some little thing he had perhaps forgotten to tell her? Hard to believe, angel face. She brushed the tip of his nose with her finger and watched the nose wrinkle and snort in irritation. Horsey. Or a unicorn, for purity and phallic symbolism. Horny.

Once a horny princess lived in a chromium castle by the banks of a great highway. Her father was a powerful king, though none knew it. Her mother, the queen, had once been a famous beauty and had many suitors, over whom the king had been able to triumph only by some wonderful but now-forgotten piece of luck. In the place where the castle stood, there had once been a towering forest, but wizards had struck the trees into paper and subdivided the land into rectangular plots separated by invisible lines. These lines prevented the folk who dwelt by the highway from communicating with each other, and this sorely troubled the princess, who had an amiable and loving nature. When she asked her father why things were arranged so, he could spare her time for only a brief growl, for he was busy chasing down the many vandals and subversives who spread unrest in the kingdom. And the queen, who was in demand socially because of her cleverness at various card games, had no time for theoretical speculation. So the princess decided to look things over for herself. She discovered, to her surprise, that she could pass through the invisible boundary lines merely by ignoring them and putting one dainty foot in front of the other. As she passed along the tarry tributaries of the super-

118

highway, she met no one, for all the folk rode in metal cars with rubber wheels and turned their faces away from her when they observed her eccentric mode of travel. But the princess continued putting one foot in front of the other. To her surprise, the roadway became a dirt track, and then a narrow path through an unsubdivided forest. Since no cars could follow this trail, there were no people there. The princess heard unfamiliar songs, which she found were sung by bright-colored beasties who fluttered through the air. At last the path took an abrupt turn downward; the princess missed her footing and slid the last fifty feet on her royal bottom, coming to rest in a grassy clearing by a brook that coursed the folds of the ravine into which she had fallen. As she stood, brushing the debris from her backside, she noticed an unusual beast cropping grass by the edge of the water and observing her with pink eyes. He resembled a horse, with plump muscular haunches and a thick, bowed neck with flowing mane; however, his color was an almost translucent white, his hooves mottled pink, and from his forehead sprang a thick pink horn, though it shimmered so in the crystal air of the clearing that the princess could not be sure it was not a fantasy. He did not move, but she seemed to be able to read his thoughts, which were expressed in a gruff tone: "I suppose you are a virgin." The princess blushed prettily. "Humph. All very traditional, but I suppose you never paused to think it would make more work for me." "I'm dreadfully sorry," the princess replied politely, "I didn't fully expect to meet you at all." "Wandering in the forest for your health, I suppose," the animal retorted crossly. "Never mind, get on board, for I know a better place than this." He knelt on his forelegs so she might more easily mount. As she straddled his sharp back, which was not unpleasant, he sprang to his feet and was off through the forest at a fantastic speed. She shouted at him to slow down, but the wind of their passing snatched the words from her mouth, and soon she was devoting all her energy to clutching his rolling flanks, attempting to keep her seat as the thorns and branches ripped at her face and hair, and tore away her clothes. "Look out for sudden stops," he shouted, but as he turned to grin at her, she noticed that his face had turned into that of a sheep——

No, not really a sheep, she thought, stroking the golden hair on Tom's thigh. He was fully asleep now; he did not stir. Anyway, what kind of animal would I remind him of? Amused, she considered, but could think of none. Unless perhaps a black squirrel, madly storing away things that never would be used, running shyly away from everyone and then chattering nonsensically when it was least important. Peeping nervously out of my den to scold people when they don't come up to my imaginary standards.

I have an idea of Tom and myself that's not necessarily real, silly plans about the way we should behave that no one could live up to. I feel that because things are so good with us, they should be perfect. So every tiny defect becomes magnified. If he wants to study these weird people for one weekend, that's not the end of the world. If he enjoys being on television, being asked about his book in front of all those people, that's natural. He worked hard for it.

Sam wondered suddenly if she were jealous of his success. No, I don't think so. Anyway, he admitted he couldn't have finished the book without the stability I gave him. Not to mention the groceries. Which isn't to say that he owes me anything, but we have a partnership. That is the way it ought to be. No matter what happens, the basic strength between us—the respect, and friendship, and humor—will always be.

Well satisfied, she bent impulsively to kiss the point of his hip, which was raised crookedly in the air.

And smelled, in the instant before her lips touched his skin, the odor of Miggie on him.

Blood, ammonia, the smell of the monkey house.

She recognized it instantly; her head jerked back as though a flame had been thrust in her face.

An attacking rage filled her. Her hands curled into claws even as she turned her head from the relaxed body before her;

she wanted to sink her fingernails into it, to scrape bloody welts in the skin, pull the hair out, scratch the eyes, crush the testicles.

Bastard! Bastard!

Still the tenderness she had felt for him a moment before mingled with the blind, bloody rage, creating a terrible confusion.

If only he'd told me. Why didn't he tell me?

Son of a bitch. To come into our bed——

He slept on peacefully, but again the flicker of a frown passed over his face and disappeared.

Why her, the fat, moronic bitch? If only he'd told me, if he'd told me I wouldn't be angry; he knew that.

A blood vessel pulsed in his neck; she stared, fascinated. She touched it, barely touched it, with her fingernail. He twitched away from her, mumbling a complaint, continued sleeping. Her fingernail left a faint red line of irritated blood beneath the skin.

It's not as if I hadn't had chances.

"If she wanted to go to bed with you, what good would it do me to try to stop her?" Oh, yeah.

And nice men, too, not pigs. That television director. Hugh Maguire. Long, thin legs, chest like a barrel, ass like a couple of soccer balls. Curly black hair, high apple-cheeks like an Indian. Who was it, Sylvia, said she'd give her left whatever it was for a weekend with him. And he asked me. No. Sorry. Thanks. I'd really like to, but I have this thing going—You think that's old-fashioned? No, it would just be too confusing, and I might like you too much.

I could have. I should have. It wouldn't have made any difference. I would have told Tom, and he would have shrugged.

He has no feelings; how can he pretend to write about human beings?

Bastard!

She's probably forty-five, looks older, with all that makeup. If she'd had a child when she was twenty-three, he'd be Tom's age now. Maybe he has a psychological hangup on older women. But I'm only a year older than he is. Or a little more.

A year ago we would have laughed at this house, at these people. We would have been laughing all weekend. Where did the laughter go?

Somehow the book made it disappear. I hate the book. I hate the people in it.

Bitch!

The horrible self-importance of the middle-aged, Tom is starting to develop that. The facility for inventing excuses to do what other people want you to do.

Did they talk about me when they were doing it?

Or simply grunt like pigs?

If he had done it in the beginning, with someone attractive, I wouldn't have worried. But now, with his sheep face and that fake seriousness, to throw it away——

His skin seemed to have taken on a yellowish pallor, an unhealthy tinge. There was a slight gleam of perspiration over his face. The hollows under his eyes were an unnatural, translucent blue. The hair falling over his forehead seemed dry and lusterless.

Perhaps old age is a communicable disease.

What do her breasts look like? Long and fat, slopping onto her belly.

For some reason Sam could not picture the nipples, she thought of Miggie's breasts without them, horribly round and bald, like fat tumors, photographs of goiters from a high-school biology text.

Rolls of fat on her stomach, curdling against each other, hiding her navel, bagging over her thighs as she leaned forward to kiss him.

And he kissed her.

She had thick lips, curly like snails. Was that interesting to him?

Bastard.

Doesn't he realize? He doesn't.

He's so wrapped up in his intellectual puzzles that he doesn't have any emotions. Hungers, but not emotions.

He doesn't realize that sex is meaningless. How important it is——

She was getting more and more confused.

What an important part it is of our relationship. And when he trades himself away to a stranger, without even friendship, it's meaningless. Worse. Simply to stick it into someone, like a spoon into a pot. As if to say that's all it means when we have sex.

Make love.

The words echoed in her empty head.

She got off the bed, reached in the handbag and found her clothes, began to put them on.

I like Tom. I like him a lot. I'm very fond of him.

She tried to button the blouse. Her fingers would not co-ordinate. Like trying to stuff walnuts into the buttonholes. She forced them through.

I don't need him. In a way, I do. I'm used to him, that's all. There are a lot of other men. I can stand on a street corner and smile. Pick my corner. Wall Street for a stockbroker. Eighth Avenue for a garment king. Times Square for a tourist. Macdougal Street for a freak. Third Avenue for AC-DC. All with hangups, wives, girlfriends, boyfriends, jobs, lies.

I like Tom a lot. I'm very fond of him.

But she could not connect her thoughts about Tom with the slack, handsome body on the bed.

Her clothes felt unfamiliar. As though she were putting on layers of deceptions.

I like him a lot. There's some perfectly simple explanation for this. All I have to do is wake him, and he will explain why it doesn't make any difference. I can just believe it for a while, until we get away from here. Later I can forget.

He stirred in his sleep and sighed, rubbing his nose with the back of his hand. Sam backed away from the bed, horrified.

I can't let him find me like this. Like what? Nervous. Upset.

123

Afraid of what he'll say. That he'll tell me, or he won't tell me. And what will I say?

"Oh."

Because actually it's not important. Just surprising that he forgot to mention it. So unimportant, it slipped his mind, and he fell asleep. Relaxed.

Bastard.

But I like him too much.

Running through the rain, she remembered, laughing and making their feet come down in the puddles where they could. Cold, probably autumn, and she had no hat, nor did he; their hair plastered to their ears, laughing like maniacs at the huddled bigots who stared at them uncomprehendingly. But where had they been going; what had started them running; what autumn had it been? The icy drips down her neck had been hilarious, the lights of the cars glistening off the slick black streets fantastic. And they had not been high, except on each other. A long time ago.

Hardly noticing what she was doing, she tucked the pipe and the tiny foil-wrapped package into the pocket of her skirt.

I need a friend to talk to. I don't have any friends, except the friends we have together. His friends.

She looked back at the bed. She had been wrong; his face didn't look innocent when he was asleep. It glittered with disdain, icy imperviousness that made shivers run down her back.

He wouldn't care if he knew she was looking at him now.

He should be a priest.

Or a victim of torture.

To stretch his body on a rack until the sinews were like guitar strings strung on wooden bones, and when the bones were broken with flexible steel rods kept for this purpose, the catastrophic blast of pain would make him free to scream——

I like him too much.

Slightly bent at the waist, with the desire to vomit, Sam sidled into the hall and closed the door on him.

It is unfair to blame him. Many women would not be at all

upset. This is a neurotic reaction caused by overdependence. I'm just making it worse by telling myself how awful it is, how I can't live without him. If I have to, I can go back to living the way I was before; it's not the end of the world. People are always having nervous breakdowns, if it comes to that. Quite fashionable. Sonia disappears for a few weeks and comes back looking absolutely marvelous. Oh, yes, dear, I was at the funny farm again. The doctors are divinely sympathetic, it's unreal.

Bastard.

It's not really cold in here.

She forced herself to stop shivering and stood straight.

No one was in the hall, of course. Why should anyone be there? She wished to hug herself for companionship, but did not.

Looking from end to end of the hall, she noticed that her attention was like a wad of cotton, hanging up on points of interest as her head turned away, leaving strands of itself behind. The light fixtures on the opposite wall, for instance. There were four. Double brass tubes emerging from a plastic disc fastened to the wall with brass screws. The tubes supported lacy metal bases, like those on kerosene lamps, which held frosted glass chimneys. Inside these must be electric light bulbs, since they shone.

Actually, she was trying to decide which way to go, since she must go somewhere, though it was tempting to just stay here. Not toward the back of the house. The thing, the swimming pool, was that way. But already she was walking the other way, and she forgot about the swimming pool.

Purposefully, she walked the length of the hall. At the front of the hall was the staircase. She walked down the stairs. Her knees seemed somewhat stiff, but she walked fast enough, perhaps too fast.

At the front of the house was an automobile, she remembered, or there had been one; she could not remember whether it should still be there.

Her sandals made evenly spaced snapping noises on the tiles of the entrance hall. She did not look at the objects in the hall, reserving her attention for some emergency that might come.

She had not driven a car for what—for several years—since she had left home. I am really, I really was, a very good driver, she remembered fondly. The earlier Sam now seemed to her a carefree and romantic figure. I can go back to being that any time now. Some cosmic relief was just beyond the front door——

The door would not open. She pulled gently at first on the brass ring with its thick shank, hoping to make her exit noiselessly. She twisted the ring one way and then the other, yanking with all her strength, she thought. There was a large iron lock in the door; someone must have locked it.

The frustration became unbearable, but suddenly vanished. She looked at her two hands tight on the ring. Not important. It could not have been important. She let go of the ring.

A fragile calmness arranged itself around her, as though she were vibrating shrilly under a thick glass bell.

Come see the freak.

Be quiet!

Diffidently she turned from the door to stroll back along the entrance hall, examining the plastic greenery. One unlikely vine with ivy-shaped leaves, lit by a red spotlight from below, bore yellow fruit. She lifted one and squeezed. It was unexpectedly light, hollow, like one of the fake lemons in which juice is sold. When she let go of the fruit, it tapped against the wall with a sound of extreme insignificance that made her want to giggle.

Shhh!

She realized that she was trying not to look at the statue in the middle of the hall. Wasn't that silly? The stone satyr was only three steps away; she closed the distance and stared into his face.

The eyes were blank marbles, sightless, yet the water trickling over them made him seem to wink at her, and his beard ruffled as if blowing in the wind. She placed her palm against his tiny chest; to her surprise, the water and the stone were tepid. The water made her flesh run into his in the dim light, pink against marble. She stroked his belly where the shaggy hair of his groin and shanks began. But the water ran down the bottom of her forearm, off her elbow in a tight little arc to the tile below. Urine. She took her hand away and shook it, snapping the fingers so drops of water flew onto the walls and were lost among the plastic leaves. Dew. But dew was cold and clear. And the statue had been of a lovely girl. No, that was outside.

Dissatisfied, she faced the rear of the hall. To the left, up the stairs, was the bedroom where she had slept. To the right, up those stairs, must be the bedroom of the others. Ahead, through the glass doors, she saw the living room. To the left, downstairs, the dining room and kitchen. She had been in all those rooms.

Where did the door on the right lead? She walked to it.

This door had a different character from the others. It seemed to be made simply of vertical boards, stained dark, tied together by horizontal boards at the top and bottom, like a barn door. There was an old-fashioned wrought-iron latch, and the hinges were black iron straps.

The plainness of the door appealed to her. She rubbed one of the boards, feeling the grain.

Sensing some presence behind her, she turned, but it was only the emptiness of the house, a vacuum threatening to suck her up. A clock ticked in the living room with a cheap pocket-watch tone. The fountain-satyr made his inconsequential noises of water, a senseless melody over the funereal rhythm of time. All the people in the house were separated, like eggs in a carton, to protect them from each other's suffering.

She heard a low sound, almost a groan, from the other side of the door. The sound was indefinable; she could not tell whether it was human; only the pain was indisputable, with an eerie, faraway quality. The sound reverberated inside her, as if she had made it herself.

She lifted the iron latch with no more sound than a whisper. The momentum of her hand carried the door open a couple of inches. She pressed her face against the opening, trying to see inside.

The room was gloomy; she could see a heavy green drape pulled across a tall window. The sun was on this side of the house now; a thin bar of yellow struck the green carpet; but the room was still cool and heavy air bathed her face at the door. It carried a sickroom odor, slightly sweet, as of an animal that had been too long alone.

The sound was repeated. She recognized it as one of grief: the way she felt.

The door moved all the way open, though she was not aware of having pushed it again.

Don Antonio sat with his back to her, at a broad wooden desk. His elbows rested on the desk, his head on his palms, which were clutching his temples, fingers in his shaggy hair. Scraps of paper were scattered on the desk; Sam thought they were newspaper clippings.

He looked very small in the chair. The room, obviously supposed to be his study or den, dwarfed him. Oak beams were mounted on the ceiling, impossibly large and close together, giving an impression of imminent collapse instead of strength. The furniture—a leather reclining chair, an overstuffed couch, dark bookcases to the ceiling along one wall, a television screen the size of an elephant's forehead—was all out of proportion to the figure crushed in the luxurious swivel chair, the broad, bowed, peasant's neck. The television set was not on: another lie.

His hand moved aimlessly on the desk, finding a clipping, picked it up, and after a moment let it flutter back.

He's acting, she thought. Even for himself, he fakes it.

But then he sighed; and, painfully, in the middle it became a sob. Another, and suddenly he was weeping.

Again, the sound echoed in herself, she felt the gates about to burst before her own sorrow. She turned and softly shut

130

the door to the hall behind her, but it moved too easily, and the latch clicked down.

Don Antonio's face whirled toward her. Tears were running down either side of his nose, eroding the lines there, gathering in the corners of his mouth. His hand moved over the clippings to sweep them away; faltering, it came to rest and turned over weakly, fingers curled toward the ceiling as if imploring pity.

As she approached, his tongue reached thickly to draw the tears into his mouth. Without thinking, she placed her hand on his neck and stroked it. The muscles tensed beneath her touch and then relaxed. She glanced at the clippings on the desk:

PROSECUTOR'S
DAUGHTER DIES
IN HIT-AND-RUN

GIRL STRUCK BY CAR, KILLED; DRIVER FLEES

HIT-RUN FATAL
TO DAUGHTER,
17, OF OFFICIAL

SERVICES TODAY FOR ACCIDENT VICTIM

HUNT DRIVER OF DEATH CAR

DEATH TOLL ON PARKWAY: 8 THIS YEAR

FATHER WEEPS AT VICTIM'S FUNERAL

FEW CLUES IN GIRL'S DEATH
—ACCIDENT INQUIRY STYMIED

Don Antonio was studying Sam's face. She pushed a clipping aside to uncover a picture of the girl in a *Daily News* story. The photograph was grainy and blurred, like a high-school yearbook picture greatly enlarged, or an amateur shot of a wild animal. The face was rather long and sharp, but pretty, the big dark eyes downcast with ruminant self-awareness, perhaps amusement at being discovered. There was a smear at one side of the mouth, lipstick clumsily applied. The edges of the clipping were yellowed; Sam wondered how long ago these things had happened.

Don Antonio was looking at her with startled recognition. "You're her."

Sam shook her head kindly.

"Yes." He was intense. "The hair, the face, everything."

"No." She massaged his neck. "I'm myself. She was someone else."

"You're the right age," he argued.

Sam shook her head again. Holding her wrist, he pulled himself to his feet. The tears were still on his face, but it was radiant. "Yes, yes."

He leaned closer. She could smell liquor on his breath; perhaps it was only the wine from lunch.

"I'd better go now. I was just going."

He laughed as though she had made a joke and clutched her other wrist. "You're much prettier than the picture."

"I'm sorry I bothered you. It's all right about the girl. I won't tell anybody."

She knew he was going to kiss her. At the last moment she turned her face, so that his lips touched her cheek. They were wet, not unpleasant. He turned her wrists, forcing her arms behind her, and pressed her body to his. The mingled smells of sweat and alcohol, the heat of his body, made her dizzy.

"Really, I——"

The muscles of his arms pressed against her sides. The bristles on his cheek scraped against her face. She tried to move her legs and belly away from his, twisting to the side, but she was too close, and the movement was provocative.

Really, I ought to scream.

For whom? Sotto?

Tom? So he could come and watch?

"I want you."

132

Come *on*. She thought of kicking him. But every moment that she was pressed against him, she became weaker. Against her will, his desire was infecting her. Under the flabbiness, his body was like iron.

Tom could not hear her. Tom had gone to sleep.

Was it important? Tom had shown that it wasn't.

At least this man could cry. She had never seen Tom cry. At most, once or twice, he had lost his poise, or had seemed to, you could never be sure with Tom. Perhaps it had only been another device. Was he really nervous on the television show, or merely behaving the way he thought he ought to, in his role?

The pressure of Don Antonio's body on hers was insistent. She knew she was responding with little, uncontrollable movements. She did not care. Her fingers moved on his neck, through his hair, over the slight hunch on his back.

His hand twisted her hair, yanking her head backward. She caught a glimpse of his face, demonically intent on her, as her mouth opened and his tongue entered her, forcing from her an anticipatory quiver, a foreshock that caused her knees to weaken and swivel, away, then back.

He devoured her mouth with unrepressed fury, repressed fury unleashed. She had never felt anything like it. His body vibrated, a tuning fork, setting her in sympathetic motion.

He forced her head back farther as his lips moved down over her chin, her neck; his fingers fumbled at the buttons of her blouse, parting it, freeing her breasts. His mouth consumed the nipples, which had become stiff without her noticing. She was afraid he was going to bite them off. Her skin was tingling, flushed, her fingers on his clothes, clumsily pulling at them.

How glorious to be wanted, really wanted!

Her fingers stroked his chest, tickling, pulling the curly hair there. She remembered that it was mostly gray, iron, pepper-and-salt. Electricity.

His mouth covered hers again, his tongue entering, violating her repeatedly. His hand slid down her back, in the furrow of her backbone, diving beneath her skirt. The heel of the hand lodged between her sweaty buttocks, forcing them apart as his fingers slid into her, making her gasp as if she had been impaled on a fishhook. Holding her thus, the other hand on her neck, he thrust her onto the couch, pulling off the rest of her clothes as she came to rest there, knees in the air, waiting for him.

He stripped off his pants. She watched through half-closed eyes as the troll's body approached, no longer distasteful but familiar, powerful, no longer ugly.

As he crouched over her, beginning to batter away at her, her hand found him and guided him inside. Her eyes closed. As the powerful, grinding thrusts began, the remembrance of who he was began to fade. The brutal, exquisite collisions of flesh dissolved the mean reality. Her thoughts became disjointed fragments existing in the instants between.

Spaced out.

His mouth on her neck, hoarse breathing in her ear.

Make love.

Arm bulging with muscle against her ribcage.

Agony.

Like a psychopath, a sex criminal, stealing freedom.

Fantastic movement.

Her legs gathering strength, seeking to crush him between.

All the lies.

Thick body like a wrestler's, slamming from side to side.

Beginning to go.

A strange, thin, moan, beginning to stream from her throat.

Afraid.

Thick fingers curling around the fragile neck.

Red fear.

Heavy thigh muscles pounding into her, uncontrolled.

Burning.

Hips jerking back and forth, searing him.

Black.

134

Scream now almost of terror, frantic mouth sucking fire. Exploding.

A last thrust so deep she did not know she went that far, grinding, forcing, curling up her backbone, and a weird, exulting groan whistling between his teeth.

Jesus. Oh, Jesus.

Again. Shuddering from the pit of her belly to her shoulders, shivering, twisting from side to side. Moaning from the cold.

Murder.

She got hold of the thick wrist, pulled the fingers from her throat.

Hurt.

But oh, Jesus, is that what it's all about?

His weight was like a gravestone on her, his breath beat against her neck. He coughed; the noise was unexpectedly loud. Racking, clearing of phlegm in his throat. Old man.

She tried to twist her neck. There was a sharp pain where his fingers had been. Some cord, tendon, was burning.

Murder. Is that what it's really like?

His weight shifted, rose, their skin peeled apart, he pulled out of her abruptly, shrunken flesh, kneeled, stood, turned away, finding his clothes on the floor. She turned on her side, knees together, hip cocked in the air, cradling her head on her hands to watch him. The muscles of his buttock knotted beneath the fat as he lifted his leg to put his foot in the underwear. Boxer shorts; Tom wore the other kind. He snapped the elastic on his belly and pulled on the slacks, navy blue. He looked at her over his shoulder, peering around the hunch, as if about to give her an order.

She smiled. She felt that he could not hurt her as long as she was naked.

"Better get dressed."

"Is that what it's like for you?" Murder?

"Come on, come on."

He picked the skirt and panties from the arm of the couch

135

and tossed them at her. They landed on her chest. Brushing them off, she stood. Her neck ached slightly, but that was nothing. She felt healed, alive. Vindicated. In what?

She strolled to the desk and pushed the clippings around with a finger until she found the one with the photograph.

"Do I really look like her?"

"Who?" He was annoyed. "Oh, yeah, a little. You can see. You better get dressed."

"In a minute. Why are you in such a hurry?"

"My wife might come in."

"Oh—" She didn't believe him. "You're not afraid of her."

"No, of course not."

"She says you're impotent."

"Hah. What do you think?"

"I don't know. Is that the only way you can do it?"

"Is what? Something wrong with that? You liked it."

She had. Murder. She studied the girl's face in the photograph.

"Come on, forget that. Get dressed."

"All right." Sam gathered her clothes. Why did he care so much about clothes? They were inconsequential things, without form until she filled them out, maybe even a little grimy. What was the difference?

He brushed the clippings together like playing cards, held them vertically and tapped them on the desk so they rode together. Carefully he slid them into a brown envelope. He moved as though to put them away, then looked irresolutely at her.

She smiled. "I won't look, if you want to hide them."

"You're crazy. Why the hell would I want to hide them?" But he watched her carefully.

"I don't know. Why do you sit here by yourself, looking at them?"

"This thing happened the same night the headlight got broken on the car. I was drinking that night, but not so much I don't know I didn't hit anything. It's a frame-up."

"So you sit crying over the clippings."

136

"Crying. Hah."

"Why don't you tell the police about it? Tom was right. You'd feel better. You wouldn't have anything to worry about if you did that."

"He's some great author, right? He knows what everybody ought to do, right? Wrong. He doesn't know the first damn thing about people: all he knows is what goes on in his head. He thinks that's real. Shit. I should tell the cops about it, and then I'll feel all right? Nuts. That's a cliché; it's as old as the Catholic church. You've got to live with yourself; nobody can help you."

"Maybe you're right." The idea made Sam suddenly very sad. "Did you hit that girl with your car?"

"Oh, hell." He turned away, dismissing her, disgusted. The humped back seemed to bristle at her.

But as she took a step toward the door, he turned to her for a moment: "I'll tell you one thing."

"What?"

"That guy of yours. Watch him. He doesn't care a damn bit what happens to you."

She might have made some protest, but Don Antonio had already turned away again. She nodded at his back, Thank you, and went out the door, closing it softly behind her. Wait till I tell Tom——

I can't tell him that, or anything else.

She made herself stop thinking about this. If she did not think, she could appreciate her body, which was wonderfully warm and relaxed, as it had not felt for a long time. She perched precariously on the breadth of the present moment, unwilling to peer into the past or future. Whose phrase was that?

Not important, it was probably a misquotation anyway.

"Damn it, I wish you wouldn't do that!"

Taking the motionless Sotto for part of the house, she had begun to walk around him. He beamed apologetically.

Tired of catering to everyone's peculiarities, Sam continued to talk to him. "I swear, anyone would think you were eavesdropping. Padding around like a hippopotamus. How can you walk so softly when you don't know when you're making noise?"

His hand curled into three variations of a fist.

"What? What's that?"

He repeated: TEA?

"Oh. Yes, I'd love some." She nodded.

Sotto opened the dining-room door for her, then led the way to the kitchen.

"You certainly do remind me of someone," she said to his back. "Not exactly someone I know, but someone I've seen in the movies, or in a magazine. The back of your head, as a matter of fact, ought to be in movies. Playing the back of Hamlet's head. No, that's not right. Falstaff? No, too tragic for that." Tom had got her to reading Shakespeare once. "Perhaps it could play Othello's lordly brow." Absolute nonsense, what was the matter with her? But he did remind her of someone, someone she had seen or heard about——

Sotto stepped into the tiny hall to hold open the swinging doors for her.

It wasn't his physical being, but something about his character that was familiar. Her mind had played tricks like this on her before; it would probably turn out to be some minor personage from many years ago, like the milkman when she was a child.

He puttered around, heating water, preparing the teapot by rinsing it out with hot tap water.

I wonder what his voice was like, when he had it? A deep roar, or one of those high, petulant voices that fat men sometimes have? Did he have an accent? *Mamma mia!* If no one could talk, you wouldn't be able to tell if someone was Italian or anything else.

Sotto set the kitchen table with translucent blue china cups, a saucer of shortbread cookies and fig newtons, like a granny. Milk, lemon, and sugar for the tea. He set a blank pad of paper and a pencil between their places, as if a game were about to begin, or an inquisition.

Sam made a doodle, a curlicue that turned into a snail. She wrote below it: I FEEL STRONG.

She crossed this out heavily, making a shiny black rectangle. She extended the rectangle to make a wall across which the snail was crawling. Sotto looked over her shoulder and smiled approvingly. On impulse, Sam wrote: YOU ARE A POLICEMAN.

The kettle began whistling on the stove. Sotto turned away as she tried to see his reaction.

He filled the teapot, brought it to the table, and set it between them. For a few moments he did not look at her. Then he took the pencil, wrote, and turned the pad toward her: FEET FLAT?

Sam laughed: NO—MY DAD'S ONE TOO.

Sotto studied her, then wrote: I WAS N.Y.P.D.— UNDERCOVER.

NARCOTICS? she asked idly.

NO BUT IT'S BAD STUFF.

BETTER THAN BOOZE—LOOK AT MIGGIE.

He shrugged.

Suddenly uncomfortable, Sam changed the subject: DA KILLED GIRL?

I WAS ON ANOTHER CASE—LOOKING FOR MAFIA CONNECTIONS.

She laughed; it seemed absurd. Sotto looked up, aggrieved, as though he had heard her. He had heard the kettle whistling before, too; she was sure of it. Quickly she wrote: YOU'RE NOT DEAF-MUTE.

CAN TALK BUT ONLY 30% HEARING LEFT EAR—BOMB.

SAY SOMETHING.

NOT SAFE.

YOU CAN WHISPER.

NO.

PLEASE.

Doggedly, Sotto shook his head. He lifted the lid of the teapot and inspected the brew; satisfied, he filled their cups. He offered her the milk, lemon, sugar; she took a little milk because she had never had milk in tea before.

She tasted it: not very good, rather chalky.

Sotto took lemon. He removed the top sheet of paper from the pad and drank his tea, as though the discussion was over. He grasped the handle of the cup between thumb and forefinger, little finger slightly extended. And ate a shortbread daintily in one bite.

DA REALLY MAFIA?

Sotto replied reluctantly: DON'T THINK SO—WAS BOASTING IN NIGHTCLUB, INFORMANT OVERHEARD, BUT I FOUND NOTHING.

CHAUFFEUR JOB WAS COVER?

YES.

WHY DON'T YOU GIVE IT UP?

CAN'T GO BACK ON FORCE—SECRET ASSIGN-

MENT FROM INSPECTOR, NO RECORDS. INSPECTOR DIED 18 MOS AGO.

TELL SOMEBODY.

RECORDS SAY I RESIGNED IN GRAFT INVESTIG. IN CASE DA CHECKED.

THAT'S CRAZY.

Sotto winked at her: NOT SO BAD—POLICE SALARY STILL BEING PAID INTO BANK UNDER DIFFERENT NAME—CAN RETIRE IN 5–6 YEARS.

PLEASE SAY SOMETHING.

He shook his head and ate another cookie.

DON'T YOU NEED TO TALK?

NOT ANY MORE—BETTER THIS WAY.

She drank the rest of her tea and milk. How bleak his life must be—waiting to have enough money so he could do nothing. But it was no bleaker than Don Antonio's, or Miggie's. Or Tom's. Or her own. There was no motion in any of them.

Perhaps Tom was awake now, or she could go and wake him. She recalled the smell of Miggie on him, but the memory no longer disgusted her. They would go back to the apartment, and things would be as they had always been. Perhaps better, who could tell? She had been childish, that was all. Tom had simply fallen asleep before he had told her about Miggie; he had meant to——

She could not quite believe this.

Like a voice inside her, Sotto wrote: YOU WERE IN DA'S STUDY.

She shrugged. And wrote: I HAVE TO GO. THANKS FOR TEA.

HE IS STILL DANGEROUS.

SURE.

She backed out of the kitchen, into the little hall. She paused there, watching the swinging door with its hobnailed steel plate as its vibrations became damped, became nothing. Through the little oval window in the door, she observed Sotto. He sat with his head dangling heavily over the rubbish of the tea, half turned away from her. His body blocked from view the dishes she had used; it was as if she had never been in the kitchen.

Even the little cubicle in which she now stood was strange, as if, though being there, she had not perceived it yet. Or as if she perceived it without being there. Perhaps that was the explanation: she was actually somewhere else, and this was a very powerful though meaningless fantasy of pausing in a little steel hall.

But pausing implied that she was about to do something, that she had just done something——

Momentarily she could not recall what had just happened, could not populate the coming minutes with expectations. A morning-after feeling, not knowing what she had done, but feeling a vast chasm of unspecific guilt slide open beneath her feet. A sensation of starting to fall, horrifying, as warnings screamed in her head, and she began to throw mental lifelines like a spider wildly casting its sticky weblines onto anything, anything at all: the bare light bulb in the ceiling, not so far above; the biology teacher, what was his name, she tried desperately to think—"You are a very good student, Samantha, this is an excellent paper"; the taste of crisp vegetables, celery and lettuce; I have some very good friends in New York who would take care of me, although they're all awfully busy; Sonia; Tandy; Bill; a humming type of electrical noise; wave of dizziness; the apartment is of course still there and I'll be back in a minute, Tom will be back; watching television, maybe we should buy a set; lying in bed reading, a long Sunday afternoon, wondering very idly what the weather might be like outside; playing chess, not exactly letting Tom win, but being pleased when he did; letting things slide; friends go; not answering the door; unplugging the phone——

She saw the walls of the little hall suddenly as the muscles of a womb contracting upon her, the red-carpeted stairs as a serrated vagina up which she walked, holding her double-jointed knees at each step from bending the wrong way, not touching

143

the pink stucco walls, rough and chalky like the walls of a cave, which might slow her down. "What are the seven distinguishing characteristics of life, Samantha?" Motion was one.

The carpet of the second-story hall, at eye-level, was quite clean. No dust. No one.

The last few steps were harder; as she stepped onto the surface of the hall, she swayed backward and had to lock her joints to keep from falling. She stalked down the hall—so far, no farther. Stopped in front of the door, listening for any noise within, perhaps the sound of snoring. A house is memory, each room a compartment containing something forgotten. Locking up portions of the raw, wild outside because only in this way can you bear it.

Her hand, moving to the doorknob, reminded her of a monkey's, agile, fragile, pretty, clever, without intelligence. Out of her control. It turned the knob and pushed the door open.

No one was there, of course. The bed had not been made; the sheets were turned back over the thick covers like a turtle's fat white lips. And a long, shallow depression, where someone had lain.

The curtains were open, but the sun must have been low on the other side of the house now; there was not much light. Her bag lay on its side on the floor; she didn't remember leaving it like that. She rummaged for the little pipe, could not find it, remembered that it had been in her pocket all the time. Never mind. She sat on the bed, her legs sinking in like thin sticks. Her fingers were a little clumsy. Whose fingers? She toppled a scrap of hash into the pipe. The determining factor is strength of ego.

A match flame doesn't really exist; it is a process of becoming, of phosphorous becoming light, heat, gas. And very biting on the lungs. The advantage of partitioning yourself into independent parts is that the pain of one, the lung, can be observed at a safe distance by another, for instance, the head. Luckily, the mechanical hookups are still there, to pipe the good stuff to the head. Which will forget. Hard on the lungs, to catch

144

the trash and pass on the fun. But all the parts can love each other. They're all in intimate contact, bound by wire nerves, looped together by liquid cords of blood.

Does the trembling of the fingers, the shaking of the flame, indict the head?

Sheer shit.

As she was lighting the second match, she came back together. Her joints seemed to snap back into place, the unsureness left her fingers, insincerity and pain left her face as though it had been wiped clean by a rag.

She tucked the exterior smoke into herself. The stinging was nothing—present, but incidental. She thought, It's just him and me. All the rest of this, these people, this house, is nothing. Meaningless inventions. Exteriors.

I've hated him for a long time.

She smiled reflexively, her mouth tight. There was a pit of hopeless terror somewhere behind her, but it would always be there; it was only something to look at. Just an empty space.

She took the last drag from the pipe and calmly knocked the tiny ash onto the floor.

I thought he was something else. I made him something else. I made myself into something else. Something I thought he wanted.

She stood.

But I don't have to be that any more.

And how did I know what he wanted?

She left the room and shut the door firmly behind her. She neither slammed it nor tried to shut it quietly.

She walked the corridor toward the stairs, noting every mote in the air with awesome clarity. Each atom in its place. Every step she advanced brought a new and separate view, like frames in a motion picture that had begun at her conception and extended indefinitely into the future. Usually her senses were blurred, the frames ran together to produce minutes, even whole hours that she hardly noticed had passed, but now she could perceive each clearly.

145

9

Time passed, and she found herself at the bottom of the staircase without any clear memory of coming down. She heard a voice murmur in the living room, a formless, conventional noise. Blit blitty blat blat.

She smoothed her skirt. It was quite dirty. Supremely poised, she entered the living room, a wedge in a conversational pause.

The three people there seemed ill at ease. Don Antonio posed with one hand on the bar, probably about to make a speech. Miggie sat on the arm of the couch on which Tom lounged, her two fingers raised in punctuation.

How silly, Sam thought. What bores! I wish there were some loud music. I'll just have to stir them up myself.

"Well, here she is!" Don Antonio smiled, uncomfortable. "We were about to start cocktails without you."

Tom gave her a lizardy grin, with heavy eyelids. Miggie's wattles shook with good fellowship.

And I'm damned tired of your animal imagery, Sam thought. She said, "You needn't have waited. But as long as I'm here, why don't I make the drinks tonight?"

She noted with satisfaction that they all recoiled, drew into themselves with a tiny shock as she began to assert her new character. Miggie's eyes narrowed a little in their pockets of fat, while her smile broadened idiotically. Tom bit the ball of his thumb, a gesture he used when he sat baffled at his typewriter.

"Hey, yeah, that'd be fine. I didn't think you were interested in liquor." Don Antonio lifted the hinged section of the bar for her to enter. Sam patted his belly casually as she brushed by "Careful," he growled softly, and added, more loudly, "You'll find anything you need."

"Well, now, what can I get you?" She found the rag and mopped the bar, imitating Don Antonio. Miggie began to say something. "Never mind, I'll just whip something up. Do you have a blender? Oh, I see, there it is."

Don Antonio leaned over the bar to watch what she was doing. "What are you going to make?"

"It's an old family recipe. In fact, I wish you wouldn't watch. My mother would die if the secret got out."

Have to put liquor in it, of course, or they won't drink it, she thought. She found a row of clear bottles labeled Vodka and chose one with a drawing of a Russian bear.

Don Antonio had folded his arms ostentatiously and was looking the other way. He peeped slyly at the bottle she had chosen, like a comic spy. Sam wagged her finger at him: naughty. Tom observed them blandly, like a scientist.

Dipping into the open shelves at the base of the bar, she found a jar of pineapple chunks. Fruit was supposed to go well with vodka. She dumped the pineapple and twice as much vodka into the blender jar.

Miggie put her hand on Tom's shoulder. Tom shrugged it off. Miggie's lips pressed together petulantly.

Sam chose half a dozen cubes from the ice chest. She dropped these into the blender. Brown, brown was what she needed. She found a bottle of Worcestershire sauce and schlunked it over the ice.

Don Antonio was watching her curiously. She swayed forward, leaning against the inside of the bar, and felt in her pocket for the rest of the hashish. "Is that a bird?" she asked

Don Antonio, pointing across the room toward the fireplace.

"What? Where?"

She dropped the dope into the blender and slid the top onto the jar. "Made you look!"

The blender had a row of yellow, green, and red buttons; she pushed a green one near the middle, holding her left hand over the lid. The jar vibrated against her belly, then began to shudder and clank deafeningly as it consumed the ice cubes.

"Actually, you're not supposed to put in whole ice cubes."

"It's all right," she said gaily. "Won't hurt a thing. My mother had one of these."

To her surprise, the machine shut itself off. She peered at the jar. The color was really disappointing, a washed-out brown with dirty flecks. She pushed the button again. "Not quite ready. You'll love this!"

"What's it called?" he asked loudly, over the noise.

She brushed her hair off her forehead and giggled at Don Antonio from beneath her wrist. "Old family recipe."

"You sure you need it?"

"No. I mean, yes. You'll see."

The motor strained in the thick slush and was silent. She lifted the jar for them to see. "Perfect!" Anyway, the flecks were mostly gone.

"What's that crud?"

"Curdle. All part of the plan. What glasses should I use?"

"How about the old-fashioned glasses?" He pointed them out.

Miggie stroked Tom's wrist. He removed his arm and pretended to scratch his knee. Why the hell doesn't he be nice to her? Sam thought, irritated.

She slopped the slush into the glasses, trying to be scrupulously fair. Although I should have less, since I already had some, but it's my idea and my dope, and also it does me more good than it will these tight-mouths, although you have to try with people. She gave herself a little more than the others.

Don Antonio carried two of the glasses over to Tom and

Miggie and returned to the bar. He lifted his own glass doubtfully. It looked a little bit, Sam thought, like frog's eggs in pond water. "Frogs!" More animals, damn it!

"What?"

"You must really think I'm cuckoo." She came out from behind the bar and sat on the stool next to Don Antonio.

"Well——"

"It's just that I'm not used to drinking."

"You haven't drunk anything yet."

"Just being near it makes me high."

"Yeah." He looked at her, then at his wife, with a guilty expression. Like God, responsible for everything.

"I think we ought to have a toast," Sam suggested.

"A toast!" Miggie echoed. "To youth!" She clinked her glass dramatically against Tom's.

"To old people!" Sam said, knocking glasses with Don Antonio. He didn't seem enthusiastic. Miggie glared over the rim of her glass.

The drink was not too bad, better than whiskey and ginger ale, except for the texture. It wound around Sam's teeth in glutinous strings, slithering down her throat like a tiny frog army, icy cold and anaesthetizing. She smacked her lips. "Good! Huh?"

Miggie had swallowed half of hers. She looked at her glass. "What gives it that unusual taste?"

"Must be the Worcestershire sauce."

"Worcestershire sauce and pineapple." Don Antonio grimaced.

"It's very good for you. Restores your acid imbalance." How marvelous, she could say anything, and they would listen with the same serious expressions! She leaned toward Don Antonio, gazing at him soulfully. She noticed that he tried to move his body away. "Don't worry," she whispered, without moving her lips.

"What?" Miggie said sharply.

"Acid imbalance."

150

Don Antonio drank the rest of his portion hastily. "Pretty good drink. But I think I like mine straight." He circled Sam and went behind the bar, where he poured his glass half full of whiskey.

"You'll ruin the effect," Sam whispered, again like a ventriloquist.

"What?" he said loudly, almost shouting.

"What?" she repeated softly. He glared at her. You have to try with people, she reminded herself.

She looked away from him, admiring the clutter of the living room. A gentle numbness from the drink was overtaking her. On top of the pipe she had smoked, it was going to be a super-high. She hoped the others would catch up with her, keep her company.

Anyway, I gave them the chance.

Once some Arabs hijacked an airliner and threatened to blow it up with the passengers on board unless their captured comrades were freed. She had not seen how anyone could believe they would actually kill all those people. Tom explained their viewpoint: they would light the fuse; if the dynamite exploded, it would be Allah's will because certainly Allah could prevent the dynamite from going off if he wished.

She was merely giving Allah's will an opportunity to manifest itself.

There was an unaccountable silence in the room.

The stone Cupid with the bowl of fruit on his head looked at her with a marvelously blank expression. One of his legs was bent up behind him; it must have been an uncomfortable position. His eyes were like milk. On either side of him, the wrought-iron ibises waited for the fruit to come to life so that they could spear it with their bills.

The people in the room also were waiting.

What the hell, I'm the group leader, Sam thought. "What the hell, I'm the group leader."

Don Antonio stared at her with a very peculiar expression. As if a basic, final pain were flowering inside him. His eyes

151

bulged white at her; his face had broken into a fine perspiration. She was afraid for a moment that the drug might have brought on some physical attack, but as she watched, the muscles of his face relaxed and his gaze became introspective.

"How do you feel?" she asked gently.

"All right." He looked at her again.

She smiled. As if her face was pressing against his, manipulating his flesh, he smiled with her. For a moment, his face was beautiful, beatific as that of an Italian peasant gazing upon his grandchildren. His attention wandered to Miggie and paused there for what seemed like a long time. He seemed to find something delightful there. He loves her, Sam thought. He sees a ghost, from long ago.

A shadow crossed his face, the expression of a small child who has forgotten something worrisome, but it faded quickly.

"I feel fine," he added.

Sam looked at her own lover, trying to evoke some warm emotion in herself. Stop it. You can't push feelings.

Tom winked at her; he knew what she had put into the drinks. Crocodile grin. As if he had just eaten something, or someone, whole. Swallowed a paragraph of experience. He'll belch it up later. As he swallowed me.

Stop it.

"I feel *awfully* strange." Miggie stood. Absent-mindedly she patted Tom's head and smoothed her dress over her plump thighs, as though she had to be off to an important engagement. Instead, she plucked her glass casually from the coffee table and came to the bar. "Muddled. Perhaps another drink would wake me up."

Don Antonio reached for her glass.

"No, no, that's all right, I'll get it myself." She spoke to Sam as though to the furniture. "Donnie always makes them too weak."

She ducked behind the bar and poured Scotch into the glass, leaving just room for two ice cubes. As she came out, she

152

stopped suddenly, shivering and staring accusingly at Sam. "I've seen on television where they put something funny into your drink. LSD." Her eyes were piggish with suspicion.

"Oh, no. Nothing like that."

"Well, it's strange."

Don Antonio stood and put his arm around her waist. He began to say something, with a tender expression, but Miggie broke away. He sat down again.

Miggie sat by Tom, surreptitiously brushing her hand against his leg. Tom didn't notice; he was staring into something on the ceiling.

Don Antonio's gaze was fixed downward in despair, suddenly; Sam divined that he was looking at the back of his hand. She looked at it too.

Veins like dead blue worms beneath the scaly skin.

Knuckles like pigeon's eggs.

False, worried smiles of skin over finger joints.

Yellow nails breaking up into coarse ridges, circled by dead skin.

Dying.

He was making a little noise: "aaaah—" Beginning to get panicky. Eyes like ripe olives preparing to burst from his head.

Sam lifted his hand. It was dry, without weight. She raised it slowly, afraid it might waft away.

His eyes watched the hand fearfully.

She kissed it slowly, warming it with her lips, and replaced it on his thigh. His face became neutral, ready to go either way.

The silence was deadly.

"Don't you have any music?" she asked gently.

"Songs?"

"Yes."

His face grew leaden with concentration. He stood and walked to a cabinet at the side of the bar, in the wall; opening this, he uncovered a tape player. His hands pawed aimlessly through a drawer of casettes.

153

"Find something happy," Sam warned.

He fumbled a casette into the slot. Pushed buttons. A loud hissing, much too loud.

Don Antonio's voice filled the room, crooning, horribly overamplified so it was as if the whole house was singing in its throat:

> When the love that we knew
> Was to always be true
> In our hearts as it grew. . . .

He stood in front of the speaker, head bowed, nodding in time.

Miggie scratched Tom's pants with her fingernail. He moved his leg away irritably.

> And I saw your honey face
> In an unaccustomed place
> With the loneliness of this:
> A stranger's empty kiss. . . .

Don Antonio turned. Hands on hips, he smiled, swaying to the syrupy rhythm. The volume was overwhelming. He said something to Sam; she shook her head, unable to hear.

The song paused for a castanet solo like a rifle fusillade.

"I'm inside of myself," he said wonderingly.

"Me, too." Sam began to laugh, it was uncontrollably funny. Me inside of him too, him inside of me too, me inside of me too.

His voice began again, singing. Not laughing. He was staring at Tom and Miggie.

Miggie whispered into Tom's ear. Tom nodded curtly, not hearing. She swallowed raw whiskey.

The huge, insincere voice massaged Sam in peristaltic rhythm. Da-da do-do-do de doo. Inside and outside, and in my lady's chamber.

There was a strange odor in the room. She peered here and

there into the shadows, seeking the source. The zebra stripes of the draperies trembled, making her think of a lion.

Veldt musk, hot dry grass, and dust kicked into the face of the sun pressing into the earth where insubstantial little animals rustled.

Cape lions with black manes and a black tuft at the tip of the tail, hard cat-balls trembling against the insides of the haunches as they stretched, yawning, preparing for the day's innocent elemental rage of killing, claws to prick forth the steaming blood and mingle its odor with their musk and their breath, colder than the outside air, bearing the stench of yesterday's rotting meat. Broad muzzle like a gigantic dog's, snuffling in great chunks of air, testing for the presence of the prey; the body almost squat, yet immensely powerful, seeming even larger because of the mane, which extended in a mat down the broad chest.

Tom spoke to Miggie. She laughed with artificial brilliance, an actress seeking his favor. He observed her as if she were a mildly interesting but not terribly attractive insect, his pretty lips turned up, nostrils dilated.

The broad neck bowed forward, brown eyes now flashing with fury. The visage seeming to shimmer in the superheated air.

The scene crystallized for a moment, persisted, as the terrible singing became the reality for Sam. Soupy guitar chords expressing some emotion she felt in herself: not love, not anger, not fear—just the tears shed at the ending of a bad, sentimental movie, a form of emotion without content. Pity, and relief that it was over. Stupid sorrow for the end of something that was a sham. That Tom had created.

Look at him now, the perfect image of the young author. Too perfect.

Didn't I feel the same way when I finished his novel—admiring but dissatisfied, as though some clever trick had been played on me, as though I had been cheated? Carried along by the slam-bang ending, entertained, attention distracted from the shallowness of the hero's point of view, and the author's? What a fraud!

A small blood vessel throbbed in the side of Don Antonio's temple. She could smell his rage, taste its drippings like brass on the side of her tongue. She was in perfect tune with him.

The shallowness of the novel was not intellectual; it was well thought out, rational and clever sometimes to the point of obscurity. But there was a callousness, a lack of concern for the characters, as though they were actors hired for the moment, whom one would not speak to a few months later if one passed them on the street. They did what they were supposed to, with appropriate gestures and speeches taught them by the author. But they were unreal, only carrying out their dramatic functions predictably—just as I play a part for him.

What weird dope! Her own intellect was running away with her emotions, not the way it was supposed to be. Perhaps because of the music, it was a defense to keep from becoming mired in the song's greasy sentiment.

Miggie said something to Tom, her eyes sliding coquettishly around the room, tapping him gently on the shoulder with one finger for emphasis.

A stranger's emp-pty kiiiiiisssss. . . .

The song ended in the middle of a phrase, on a precipice.

"Oh, come *on*. Do you think you're in *love?* How old are you, anyway? I can find a hundred women——"

Tom stopped speaking, hearing his voice alone in the room. The contemptuous curl faded from his mouth; he began to look boyishly charming again.

But Don Antonio was standing, advancing on him. "Goddammit, you pay her some respect, you!"

Fists clenched, short legs bowed, face flaming, he approached like the hero in a Western shoot-out.

Sam clapped her hands together once, noiselessly, as if this were the start of an entertainment.

156

Tom's face underwent a swift series of changes: charm, placation, shock, fear, hatred, friendliness, disavowal, defiance. "Then tell her to leave me alone." He inched down the couch, hands on the cushions, ready to fling himself out of the way. "She's been all over me since we got here."

"Ooo, what a liar!" Her indignation was unconvincing. "I was simply showing a hostess's courtesy. To my husband's guest."

"Shaddup!" Don Antonio circled slightly, cutting off Tom's escape route.

"I assure you I have no interest in——"

"Yah, yah, fancy author-boy. You stink, you know that? You *stink*."

Don Antonio feinted with his shoulder; Tom jumped backward, crouching, with his feet on the couch.

"Wait a minute. Just a minute. I don't know what you're thinking, but——"

"The hell you don't."

Don Antonio lunged, grinning, and roared, "Nyaaah!"

Tom vaulted backward, over the couch, and stood with his hands on its back. The hands were shaking; his face was terribly pale.

Sam began to lose her detachment. She thought Tom was beginning to break up.

Don Antonio rushed to one end of the couch, snarling like a badger, as Tom ran to the other, behind Miggie, who looked coyly over her shoulder at him.

They're all absolutely loony.

Don Antonio's body swung back and forth, faking runs to the front or back of the couch. At the other end, Tom moved in rhythm with him. Miggie's head turned from one to the other.

Don Antonio's eyes bulged comically; the foolishness of the scene began to affect Sam. Her face flushed helplessly into a smile. Stop, stop.

Suddenly Don Antonio dashed around the front of the

couch. Tom was around the back just as quickly. They faced each other across the center of the couch.

With a roar of frustration, Don Antonio ran and leaped over the couch at Tom. Tom, twisting out of the way, flung his hands between himself and Don Antonio, throwing the old man to the floor as he pivoted. Don Antonio's head struck the lion-claw foot of a heavy table with a soft, heavy noise. He lay still.

Tom barely glanced at Don Antonio over his shoulder as he hurried toward Sam: "Come on, let's get out of here."

"What about him? He may be hurt."

"Never mind him. He's crazy. He was going to kill me." Tom's face was twitching with panic.

"He might have to go to the hospital."

"The dummy can take him. Come on, before he wakes up."

Sam walked to where Don Antonio lay. He was breathing slowly. She ruffled his hair. Miggie's head stretched over the back of the couch, watching. Don Antonio's body shifted slightly, and he sighed. His hair was oily; Sam wiped her hand on the back of the couch.

"You know, maybe I was wrong."

There was a new, painful self-awareness in Miggie's eyes. That's good, Sam thought. She asked, "About what?"

Miggie shook her head. "What I was telling you this morning—There ought to be something else."

"I think so," Sam agreed gently.

She looked at Sam in surprise at having this perception shared, and then nodded. "I don't know what." She seemed to be begging Sam for something. "Tom is a very strange boy, isn't he?" she whispered.

"Yes."

Miggie looked away from Sam, down at her drink. All at once, Sam felt very old. She stood. "All right, let's go," she told Tom. "He'll be okay."

"Hurry!" Tom was in the hall, heading for the front door.

"I've got to get my bag."

158

"Forget it."

"It's all my things." She went up the stairs. Behind her, in the hall, Tom shifted from one foot to the other, looking at the door, at her, back at the body on the living-room floor.

She paused at the door to their room, strangely hesitant. She opened the door slowly and saw the handbag by the bed. She walked to it, head down, shoulders hunched, and picked it up.

A room is a memory.

Walking out, she felt suddenly like a coward. But what else can I do? she thought. She pulled the door shut.

Tom was huddling pale by the front door.

"The reason I wanted to get the bag is that I've had these things for a long time," she said, almost to herself, as she approached him.

"What?"

"It's all right to go now, if you want to."

"Christ!"

He dragged her toward the door, dropping her hand as he reached for the huge ring on the door.

Sam looked back along the hall; Sotto stood there, watching them. She waved to him; he smiled.

In the living room, she saw Don Antonio sitting on the couch, head in his hands. Miggie stood above him, tasting a new drink.

"It's locked; it won't open!" Tom's body shook as he fought the door.

"Don't worry." She beckoned to Sotto, pantomiming not being able to get the door open. He approached and courteously tapped Tom's shoulder. Tom jumped away. Sotto drew a large iron key from his trousers, unlocked the door, and held it open for them.

Tom was pulling on her, but she held Sotto's hand for a moment, mouthing: Thank you, goodbye. Sotto smiled and nodded.

Tom pulled her through the grotesque courtyard. The tinkling of the song from *Doctor Zhivago* mingled with the tiny noises of the water playing over the statue of the girl, who Sam now thought looked very much like the White Rock nymph, though she had no wings.

The iron gate to the courtyard was not locked. Tom flung it open. Sam freed her hand from his long enough to reclose it carefully.

"What's the matter with you? We've got to get away."

"You should always leave things the way you found them."

He rushed to the car, peering through the window, but the keys were not in it.

"If you'd wait a little while, I'm sure Sotto would drive us."

"No, no."

The moonlight was gleaming on the pebbles of the driveway, as it had been when they arrived. Tom urged her down the drive, which shone and crunched underfoot like ice. The shadows were as black as winter shadows.

As she looked back at the house, she saw a light go on in one of the upstairs rooms. The silhouette of a tall, thin man appeared, hands on his hips, seeming to brood at the window. She realized it must be one of the mechanical effects to frighten intruders.

The light went out.

She was forced to turn away from the house to keep her footing; Tom was running at top speed.

Far down the driveway, a light came on in the middle of a shrub, casting tangled yellow shadows, and she could see that the front gate was closed.

The light went out.

Time stretched ahead of them.

The white driveway seemed endless.

How silly, to be running away from something that's ahead of you.

There was a blinding light in their eyes. Tom skidded to a halt, holding her out of the light. It was a floodlight mounted on a tree trunk. As they stepped away, around the perimeter, the light vanished, sucking the moonlight out of the air with it. They were running again, in darkness. She slipped, almost fell, but he pulled her to her feet.

He stopped.

Her eyes, growing used to the dark again, made out the iron gate.

Behind them, from the house, she heard a confused barking, then the howling of a dog.

Tom pulled on the gate. It didn't move.

The barking grew louder, then stopped, as though the dogs had found their direction.

"Oh, Jesus."

The gate was topped by iron spikes, set too close together to get a foot between. The walls on either side were head-high. Sam pointed. "We might get over that."

A dog howled, closer.

Tom pointed to a tiny wire supported on short posts a foot above the wall. "Electric."

She rummaged in her bag and found the bathing suit. "Hold it with this."

He wrapped the two pieces of the suit around his hand and reached for the wire.

Sam could make out the racing black figures of the dogs. They were running just off the edge of the driveway. She wondered if this was so they wouldn't make noise on the gravel. They were clever animals.

She reached into the bag again and found the jar of peanut butter. It was a new jar, and she had trouble getting the top off.

With one desperate wrench, Tom pulled the electric wire away. The end made minute blue sparks where it touched the wall.

She tried to hand the peanut-butter jar to him. "Here. Can you get this top off?"

"What? No!" He pulled himself onto the wall. "Hurry up, they're right behind you."

He reached back for her. She handed him her bag. Impatiently, he flung it over the far side of the wall. "Quick, quick!"

The rushing feet of the dogs were very close. She stretched her free hand toward Tom. He pulled her onto the wall, scraping her knee against the edge. There was an angry snarl, and jaws snapped shut beneath her.

Sam turned. "Lucifer!" she said sternly.

Instantly the dog sat still at the base of the wall. She could see his eyes in the moonlight, his long teeth, the other two dogs waiting behind him. His tongue was like wet black velvet.

"I love you," she sang to him. He laughed at her.

"Come *on*."

She wrenched at the top of the peanut butter; to her surprise, it came popping off.

"Beg!"

The dog grinned at her, but sat a little straighter. She leaned down so that the jar would not have so far to fall and dropped it to the grass. He leaned forward, sniffing.

"Oh, really, it's just peanut butter."

All the lights in the house came on at once. The windows were packed with ghostly silhouettes, all seeming to peer down the hill at Sam. They milled around aimlessly, excitedly, suddenly disappearing to be replaced by others. A confused babbling, loudly amplified, reached her, punctuated by the shrill, manic laughter of women at an orgy.

Lights began to flash on and off rapidly all over the grounds, in the middle of bushes, along the wall, in the tops of trees. A siren moaned from somewhere near the house but was cut off on the rising pitch. The steel gate that had barred their escape swung open and shut, slowly, open and shut, like dragon's wings. A floodlight near Sam chattered off and on, showing her blinding fragments of reality.

Lucifer was flung twisting against the wall, as though by a giant fist.

She heard the report of the gun.

Mortar and dust were kicked into her face as a tiny eruption appeared in the wall.

She heard the second shot.

A bullet whined past her head.

The boom of the last shot echoed back and forth inside the grounds.

Tom yanked her to the outside of the wall, forcing her to crouch, and then jumped, holding her hand, so that she had to come with him.

Her foot struck the handbag; she picked it up as he pulled her toward the road. On the other side of the wall, flashes of light illuminated the treetops like a thunderstorm.

The lights all went out at once, and the noises from the house ceased. Tom urged her away.

"Wait a minute, he's hurt."

"Who?"

"Lucifer."

"The dog?"

"Yes. He's been shot."

"Jesus, you're crazy. They were shooting at *us*." Tom was stronger; he pulled her to the roadway. There he paused, looking in both directions. "Which way?"

She pointed to the right. "But we can't just leave them like that."

He didn't bother to look at her. "We'll stay on the road, but if we hear a car coming, we'll get into the ditch. We can hitch a ride on the parkway."

"Don't you even care about them?"

"No."

She had to trot to keep pace with him. They held hands like lovers, chained together by the past.

No cars came.

The road was like a silver-black ribbon in the moonlight, bounded by deep, feathery shadows of brush and trees, as they left the end of Don Antonio's wall. Soon they were walking in the center of the road, he on the left side of the white line, she on the right.

Far behind them, a dog howled.

Tears began to come to Sam's eyes, from somewhere inside her, but she did not know where; and when they stopped, she did not know why they had stopped.

She looked at Tom.

He strode purposefully, but his face had a dreamy look that she knew well. He gazed to the right and the left, up at the stars and the moon, down at the rough surface of the road, even occasionally at her, speculatively, transforming them all into images, characters, plot material, literary nuances——

I hate you, she thought, trying to be gay.

I love you.

(In the apartment, cluttered with memories, the television set whispered to itself in false, confident voices.)